I0715391

Use this for metering

18% GRAY CARD

LEICA M10

THE EXPANDED GUIDE

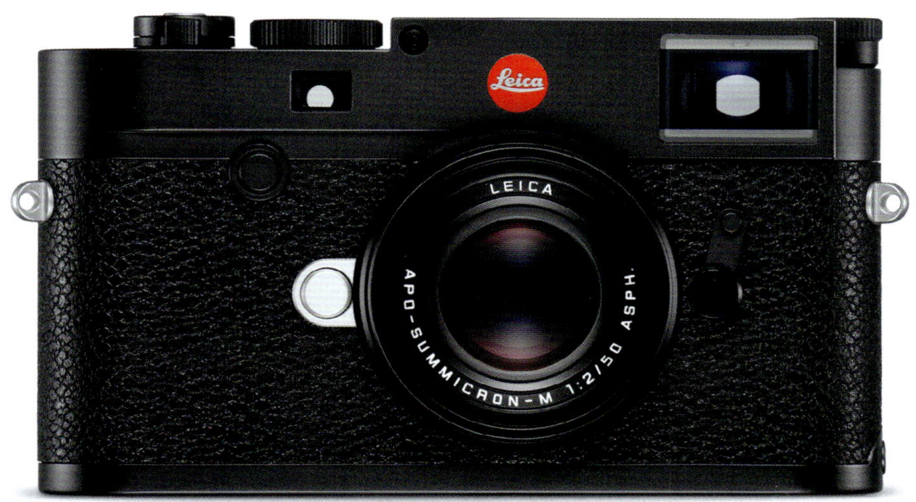

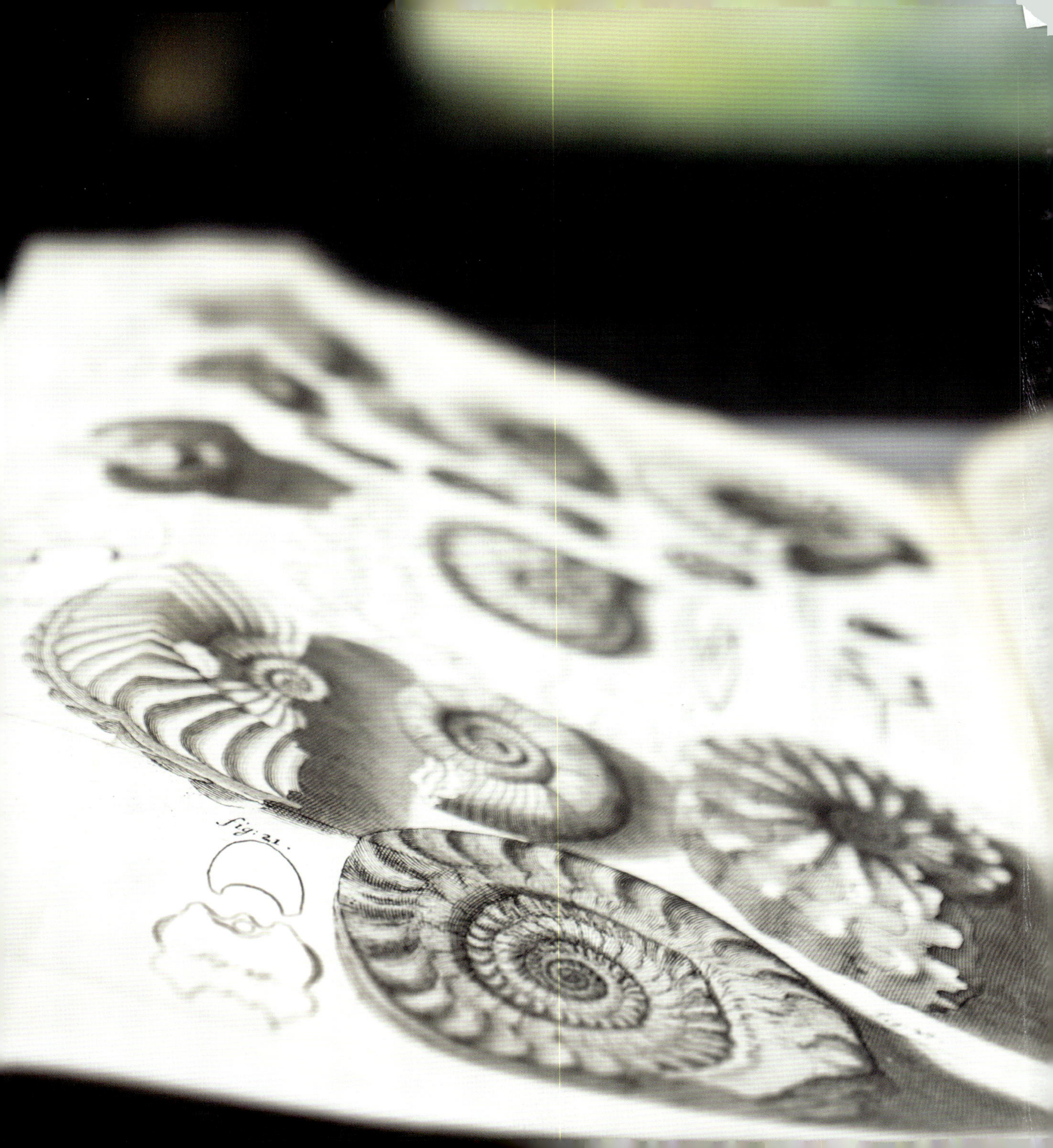

Fig. 21.

LEICA M10

THE EXPANDED GUIDE

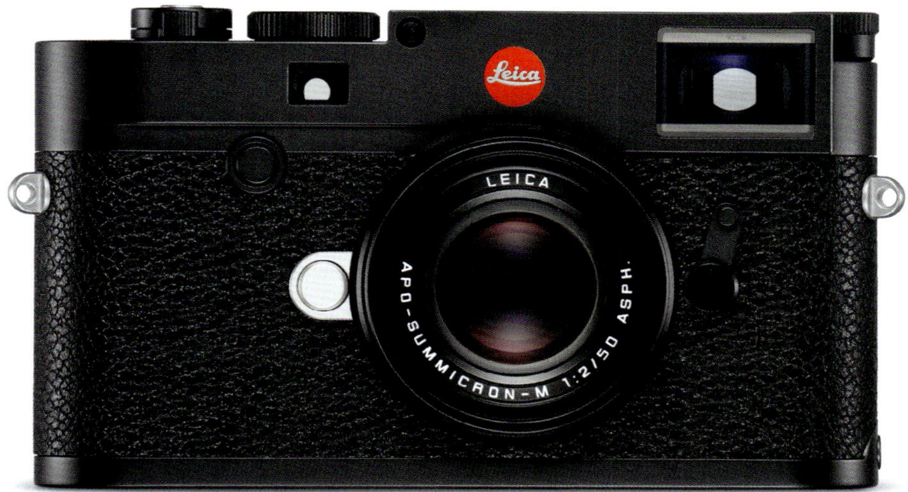

David Taylor

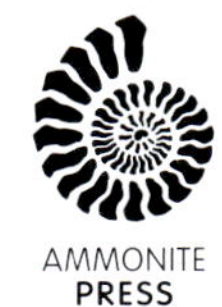

AMMONITE
PRESS

First published 2017 by
Ammonite Press
an imprint of Guild of Master Craftsman Publications Ltd
Castle Place, 166 High Street, Lewes, East Sussex, BN7 1XU, UK

ISBN 978-1-78145-322-3

British Library Cataloging in Publication Data: A catalog record of this book
is available from the British Library.

Publisher: Jason Hook
Art Director: Robin Shields
Editor: Chris Gatcum
Designer: Luke Herriott

Typefaces: Giacomo
Color reproduction by GMC Reprographics
Printed in Turkey

‹‹ PAGE 2
An 18th century book of fossils.

» CONTENTS

CHAPTER 1
OVERVIEW

In keeping with all of Leica's M-series cameras, the Leica M10 is a photographer's camera, so enjoy your journey with it—it is sure to be an exciting one!

Leica is a relatively old company that has successfully made the transition from film to digital without compromising the quality or appeal of its products. The Leica M10 is another chapter in this transition, and although the design may have one foot in the 20th century, the technology inside the camera is as modern as that used in any mass-produced Japanese model.

This guide is an introduction to using Leica M-series cameras in general and the Leica M10 in particular. Within its pages you will find advice about the various functions of Leica's latest offering (and how to make the best use of them); information about Leica M-series lenses and interesting alternatives; and a guide to connecting your Leica to the outside world using the Leica M10's Wi-Fi capability.

›› CREATIVE
The operation of the Leica M10 does not get in the way of shooting, which opens up a more creative approach to photography.

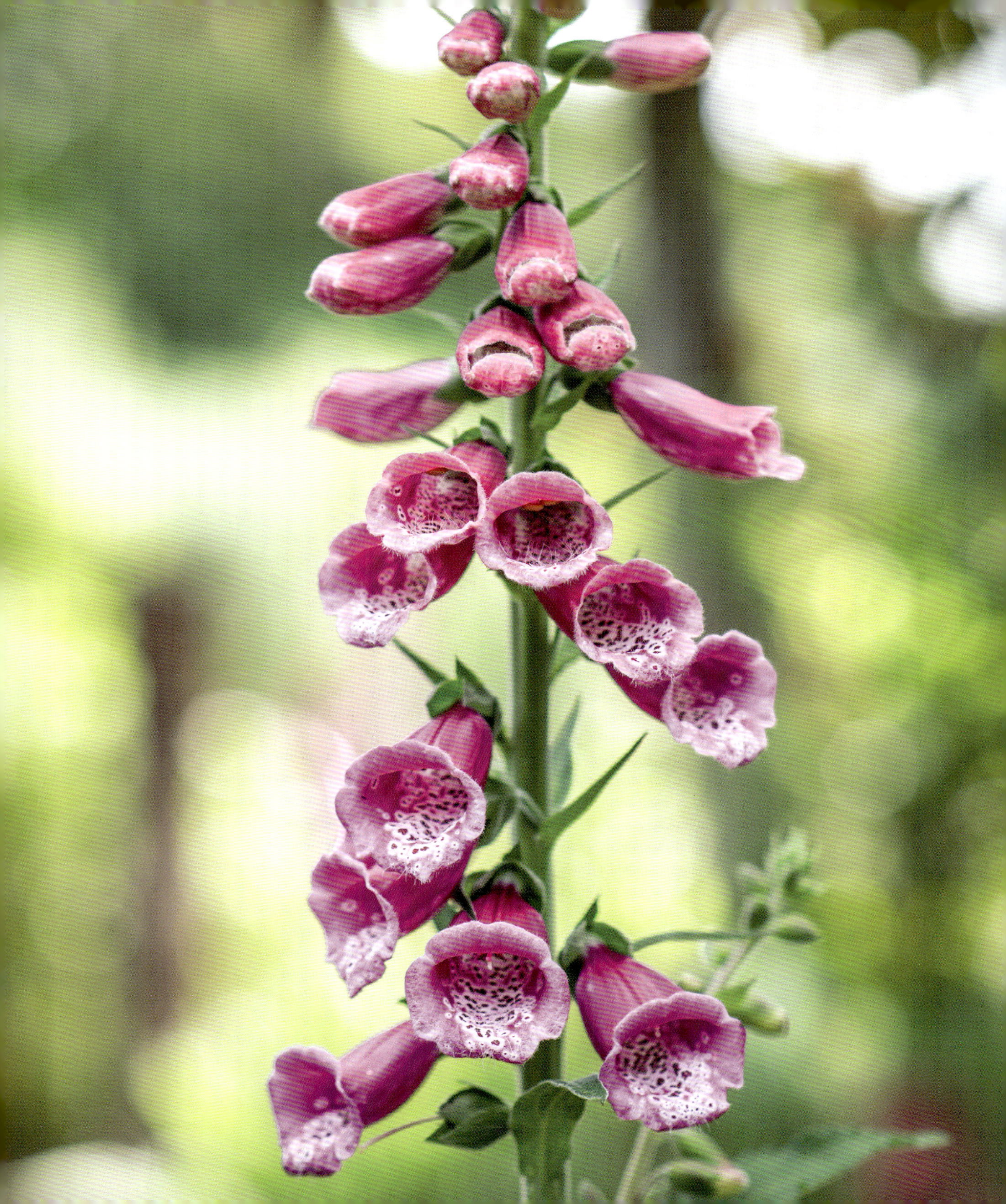

LEICA HISTORY

The Leica M10 is a thoroughly modern digital camera, but its roots stretch back to the early 20th century and a talented technical innovator by the name of Oskar Barnack.

For most of the 19th century photographers used plate cameras loaded with a sheet of glass coated in a light-sensitive chemical emulsion, which made cameras large and cumbersome. In the late 1880s a commercially viable process was developed that married the light-sensitive chemical emulsion to the flexible and light medium of celluloid, the first thermoplastic. This celluloid film allowed the development of early cinema, and the creation of smaller, lighter cameras.

It was the needs of moviemakers that led to the development of perforated 35mm film as a readily available standard. In 1913, Oskar Barnack—an employee at Leitz, a German microscope manufacturer—started experimenting with 35mm film to create a still camera. In 1914, he succeeded in producing his first prototype: the Ur-Leica, which had a negative size of 24 x 36mm.

The First World War delayed progress in putting the Ur-Leica into production, but Barnack—along with his colleague, Dr Max Berek—continued to improve the design. In 1925, at the Leipzig Trade Fair, Leitz was able to introduce the first production Leica (the name being a contraction of Leitz Camera). The company's owner, Ernst Leitz, faced considerable opposition from the board of Leitz and it was ultimately his casting vote that allowed production to commence. Fortunately, the gamble paid off, and by 1932 around 90,000 of the cameras would be in use; by 1961, this had increased to 1,000,000.

The birth of the small-format camera revolutionized photography. It enabled a previously unheard of level of spontaneity, which pushed photojournalism, in particular, to new levels of intimacy and immediacy. It is no coincidence that photography rich magazines such as *Picture Post* in the United Kingdom were launched in the 1930s, shortly after the Leica. For his achievements, Oskar Barnack enjoys a well-justified reputation as the "Father of 35mm Photography."

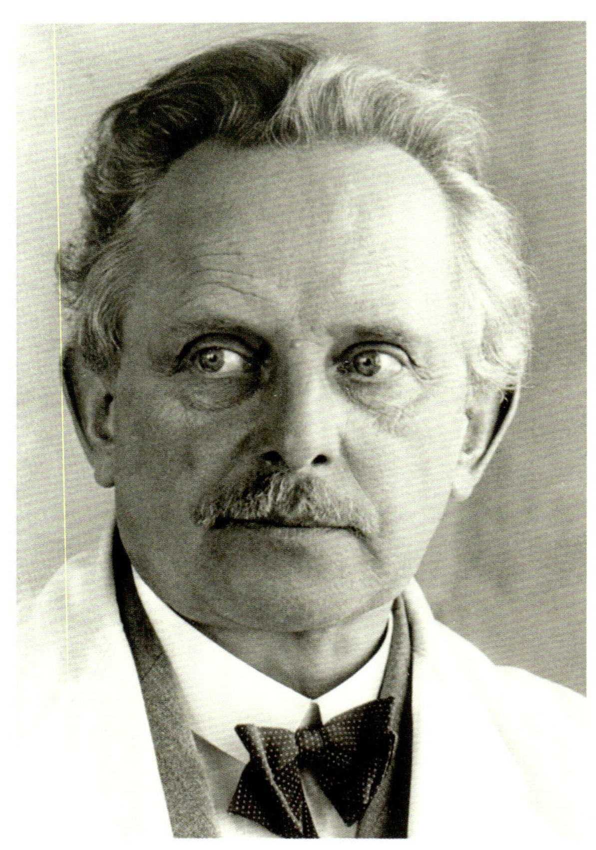

⌃ PIONEER
Oskar Barnack, the "Father of 35mm Photography."
© Leica

› Further developments

In 1930, the Leica I Schraubgewinde was launched. The camera used an interchangeable lens system based on a 39mm diameter screw thread known as the Leica Thread Mount (LTM). In addition to a 50mm standard lens, 35mm wide-angle and 135mm telephoto lenses were also made available.

This was followed in 1932 by the Leica II, which featured a built-in rangefinder coupled to the lens-focusing mechanism, as well as a separate viewfinder. At this point, photographers could choose from a total of seven different lenses using the 39mm screw-thread mounting.

Although Oskar Barnack died in 1936, Leica cameras continued to develop and evolve. From 1933 to 1957, Leica introduced a number of models in the Leica III series, each of which introduced new refinements: the first model added slow shutter speeds down to 1 sec., while the IIIa—the last model for which Oskar Barnack was fully responsible—added a 1/1000 sec. shutter speed.

In 1954, the Leica 250 (another III series camera) was introduced. Nicknamed the "Reporter," the 250 could hold a 33ft (10m) strip of 35mm film, which enabled 250 shots to be taken before the camera needed to be reloaded. This model was also fitted with a spring motor and became the camera of choice in reconnaissance aircraft in the German air force.

⌄ PROTOTYPE
The Ur-Leica of 1914.
© Leica

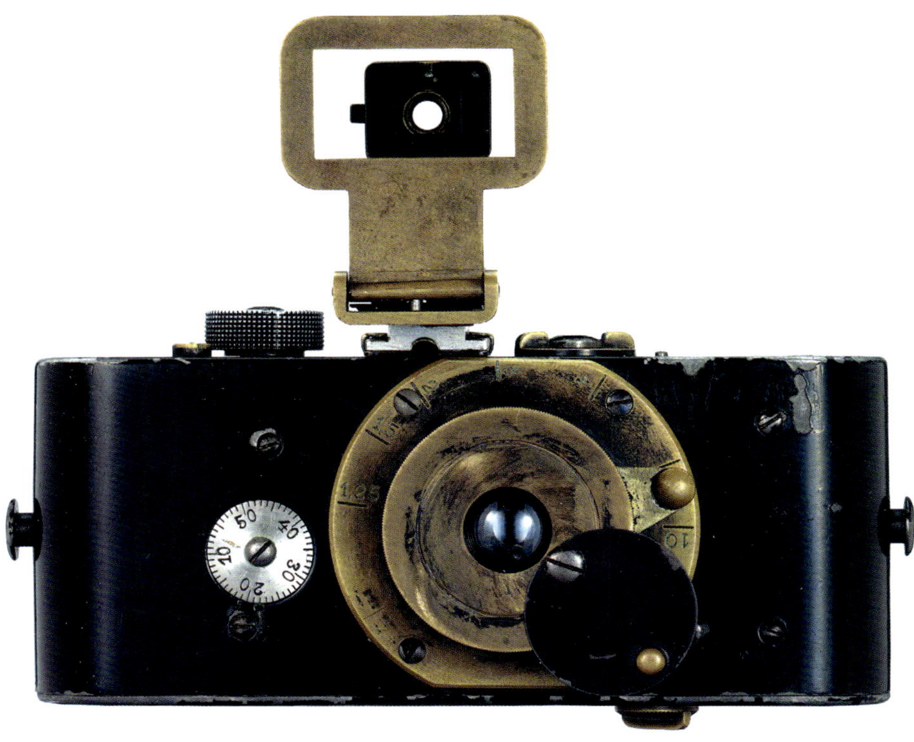

› The M mount

1954 was an important year for Leica and the history of photography. In that year the Leica M3 was introduced at the Photokina show in Germany. The Leica M3 dropped the M39 screw lens mount in favor of a bayonet fitting. This made photographers' lives easier as a bayonet mount enables faster, more secure mounting and removal of a lens. Other innovations included a combined focusing rangefinder and viewfinder in one window and a double stroke film-advance lever.

The M3 was an immediate success. When production ceased in 1966, more than 220,000 units had been made—a record for M-series cameras that still stands today. Its popularity means that it is still a collectible camera, with well looked after examples fetching good prices on the used-camera market.

The M3 was followed by the M1 and the M2 (both simpler and cheaper versions of the M3), with the 35mm Leica M range culminating in the M7 of 2002. Although the basic concept of the M7 differs little from the M3, modern technology such as TTL exposure and Aperture Priority brought the M-series up to date.

⌄ ICONIC
The Leica M3, introduced in 1954.
© Leica

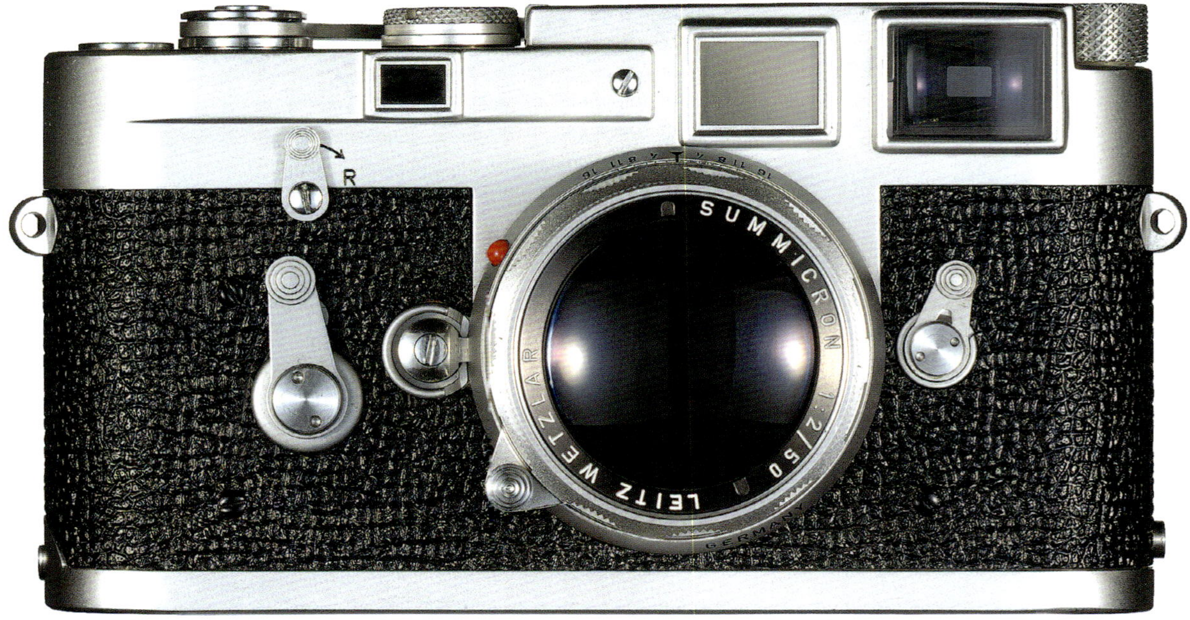

› Leica in the digital age

The first digital Leica M-series camera, the M8, was announced in 2006. This camera used an APS-H 10.3-megapixel Kodak KAF-10500 CCD image sensor. Although there were some issues with the shutter mechanism and LCD, the M8 was well received by photographers looking for a traditional-looking digital camera (and these problems were addressed by the M8.2 in 2008).

At the time that the Leica M8 was released, Leica claimed that fitting a larger sensor into an M-mount body was impossible, which was why it had chosen an APS-sized sensor instead. Fortunately, Leica engineers solved the technical difficulties and, in September 2009 the Leica M9 was announced complete with a full-frame 18.5-megapixel CCD sensor.

Despite its high price tag, the Leica M9 was enthusiastically embraced by Leica owners and quickly gained a sibling in the form of the Leica Monochrom. Unlike most other digital cameras, the Monochrom has a digital sensor that can only record grayscale images, making it an interesting nod to the days when shooting with a Leica camera inevitably meant using black-and-white film.

In April 2013 the Leica M Typ 240 was released. The camera saw Leica shift to a CMOS sensor, which enabled features such as Live View and movie shooting to be added to the specification.

The Leica M10, announced in January 2017, also utilizes a CMOS sensor, but has dropped the movie shooting capabilities. However, it improves on many of the other technological advances of the Leica M Typ 240 to make it a Leica M-series camera for the 21st century.

⌄ DIGITAL BEGINNINGS
The Leica M8, launched in 2006.
© Leica

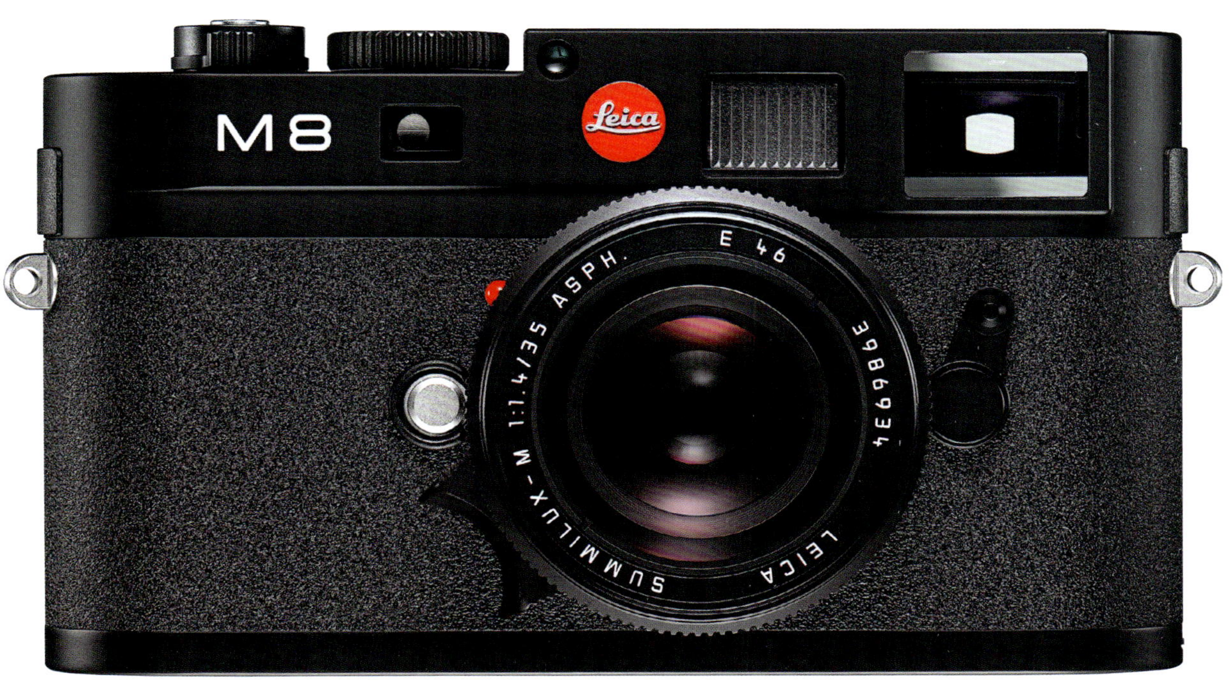

1 » MAIN FEATURES

Body
Dimensions (W x D x H):
5.47 x 1.51 x 3.15in/139 x 38.5 x 80mm
Weight: 23.2oz/65g (with battery)
Body materials: Die-cast magnesium alloy chassis finished
with black synthetic leather coating; top panel and base
plate have solid brass core with silver or black chrome plating
Lens mount: Leica M

Sensor and processor
Type: 24 x 36mm RGB CMOS sensor (full frame)
Aspect ratio: 3:2
Resolution: 24 megapixels
Anti-aliasing filter: No
Image processor: Maestro II

File types and sizes
JPEG resolution (pixels): 5976 x 3992 (24MP),
4256 x 832 (12MP), or 2976 x 1984 (6MP)
Raw resolution (pixels): 5976 x 3992
Raw format: Adobe DNG

Shutter
Type: Microprocessor controlled, metal blade vertical
focal-plane shutter
Shutter speeds: 1/4000 sec.–8 seconds; Bulb/Time
(maximum 125 seconds)
Maximum burst rate: 5 frames per second (fps)

LCD monitor
Type: TFT LCD (color)
Resolution: 1,036,800 pixels
Size: 3in/7.7cm diagonally
Live View: Yes
Brightness: Adjustable

Viewfinder
Type: Optical (rangefinder)
Coverage: 100%
Magnification: 0.73x
Diopter: -0.5 (supplementary correction lenses available
between ±3 diopter)
Support: 28–135mm focal lengths

Focusing
Type: Manual (using distance scale on lens or "split image"
focus confirmation in the viewfinder)

Exposure:
ISO range: 100–50000 in ⅓-stop increments
Metering patterns: Multi; center-weighted; spot
Exposure compensation: ±3 stops in ⅓-stop increments
Automatic exposure bracketing: ±3 stops across 3 or 5
frames at ⅓-, ⅔-, 1-, or 2-stop increments

Flash
Built-in flash: No
Hotshoe: Yes (compatible with Leica M-TTL flashes)
Flash sync speed: 1/180 sec.
Flash exposure compensation: ±3 stops in ⅓-stop increments
Flash modes: Auto slow sync; 1st-curtain sync;
2nd-curtain sync

Memory card & connectivity
Type: Secure Digital (SD, SDHC, SDXC)
Formatting: FAT/FAT 32
Wireless connectivity: Built-in

» CLASSICAL
In black or silver, the design of the Leica M10 feels
"right" in the hand, which cannot be said for all
camera designs.

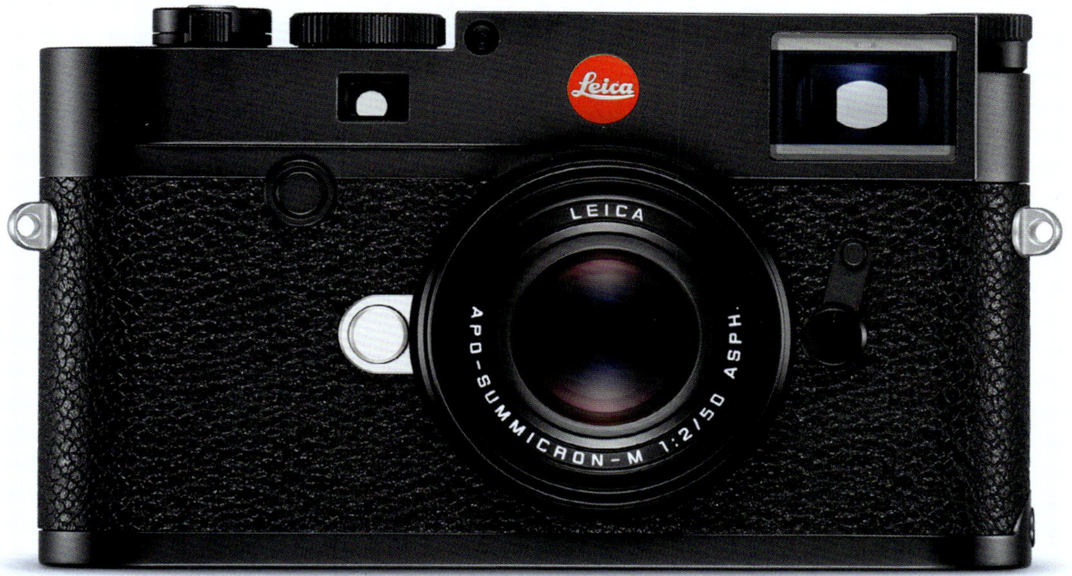

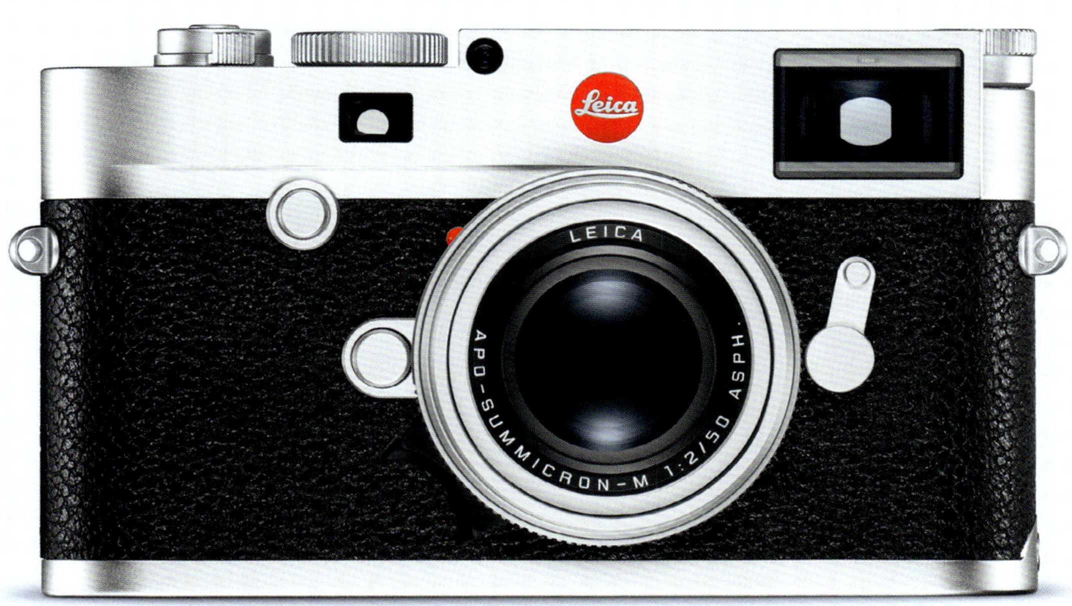

» FULL FEATURES AND CAMERA LAYOUT

FRONT OF CAMERA

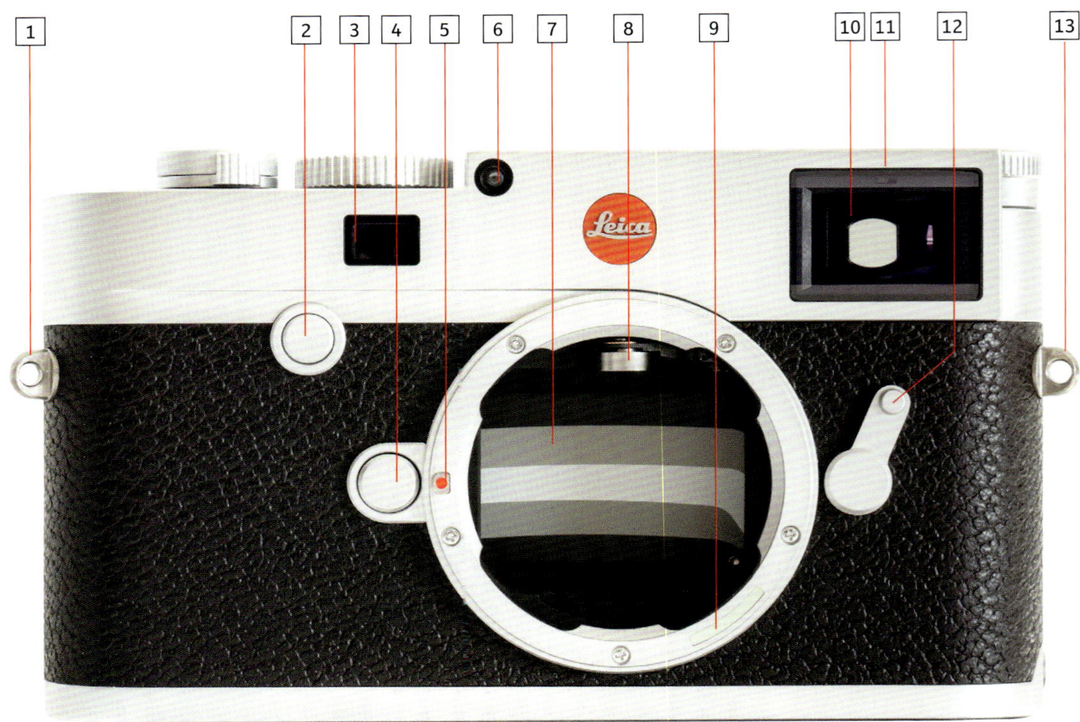

FRONT

1	Carrying strap eyelet	8	Rangefinder coupling arm
2	Focus button	9	Lens identification sensor
3	Rangefinder viewing window	10	Viewfinder window
4	Lens release button	11	Self-timer LED
5	Lens alignment index	12	Viewfinder frame selector
6	Brightness sensor	13	Carrying strap eyelet
7	Shutter blades		

BACK OF CAMERA

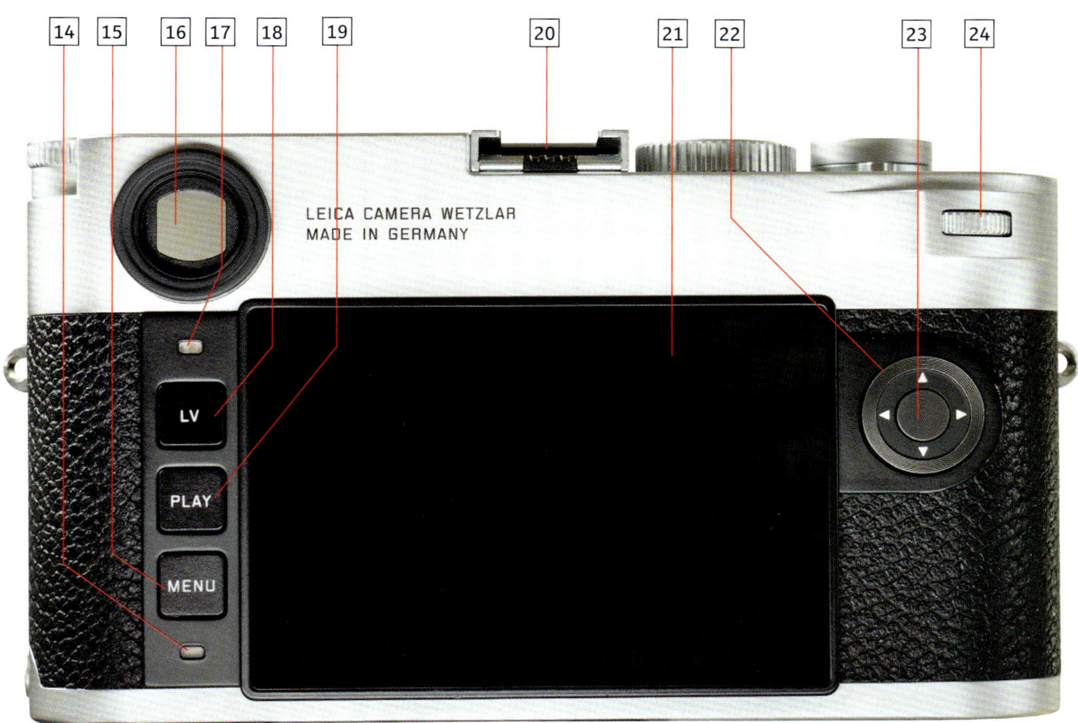

BACK

14	Memory card status LED		21	LCD monitor
15	MENU button		22	Direction pad
16	Viewfinder ocular		23	Selection button
17	LCD brightness sensor		24	Thumbwheel
18	Live View button			
19	PLAY button			
20	EVF/Microphone contacts			

» FULL FEATURES AND CAMERA LAYOUT

TOP OF CAMERA

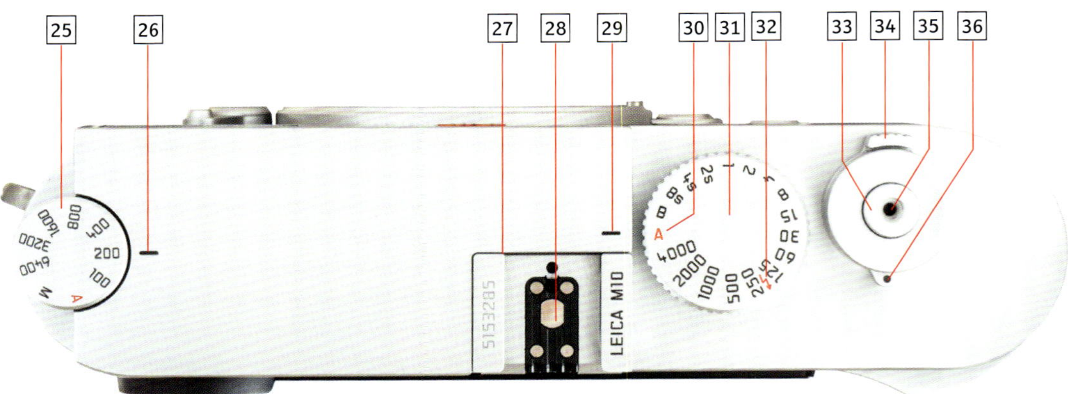

TOP OF CAMERA

25	ISO dial	32	Flash sync speed indicator
26	ISO index mark	33	Shutter-release button
27	Flash hotshoe	34	Power switch
28	Hotshoe electrical contacts	35	Threaded cable release socket
29	Shutter speed dial index mark	36	Power switch indicator
30	Aperture priority indicator		
31	Shutter speed dial		

BOTTOM OF CAMERA

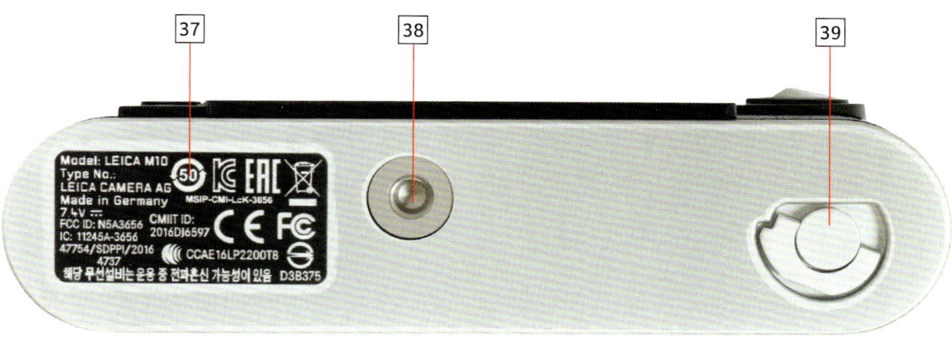

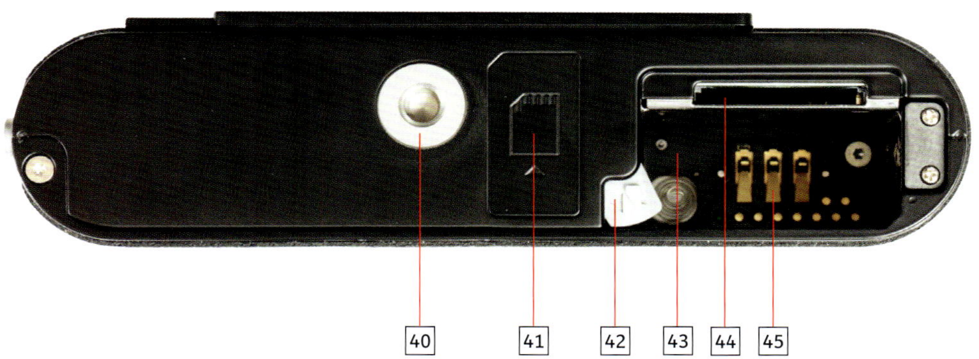

BOTTOM OF CAMERA (with base plate)

37 Information panel

38 Tripod thread

39 Bottom cover release

BOTTOM OF CAMERA (without base plate)

40 Tripod thread

41 Memory card orientation indicator

42 Battery lock lever

43 Battery compartment

44 SD memory card compartment

45 Battery terminals

» SHOOTING INFORMATION SCREEN

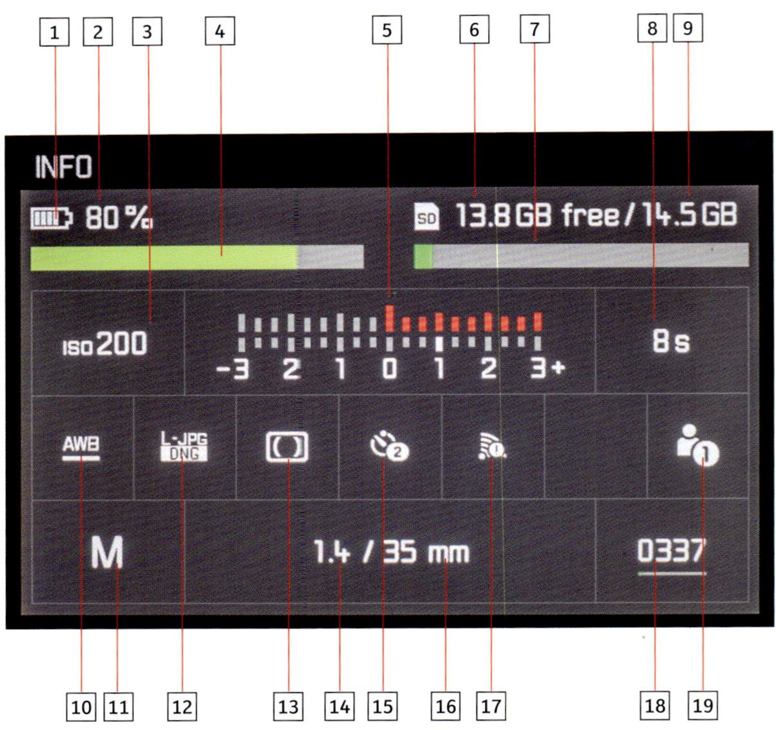

SHOOTING INFORMATION SCREEN

1	Battery status	11	Exposure mode
2	Battery status (percentage)	12	File format
3	ISO speed	13	Metering mode
4	Battery status (proportional bar)	14	Maximum available aperture value
5	Exposure scale	15	Drive mode
6	Memory card space remaining	16	Lens focal length
7	Memory card space remaining (proportional bar)	17	Wi-Fi status
8	Current shutter speed	18	Shots available (number and proportional bar)
9	Memory card size	19	Currently selected user profile
10	White balance setting		

» LIVE VIEW

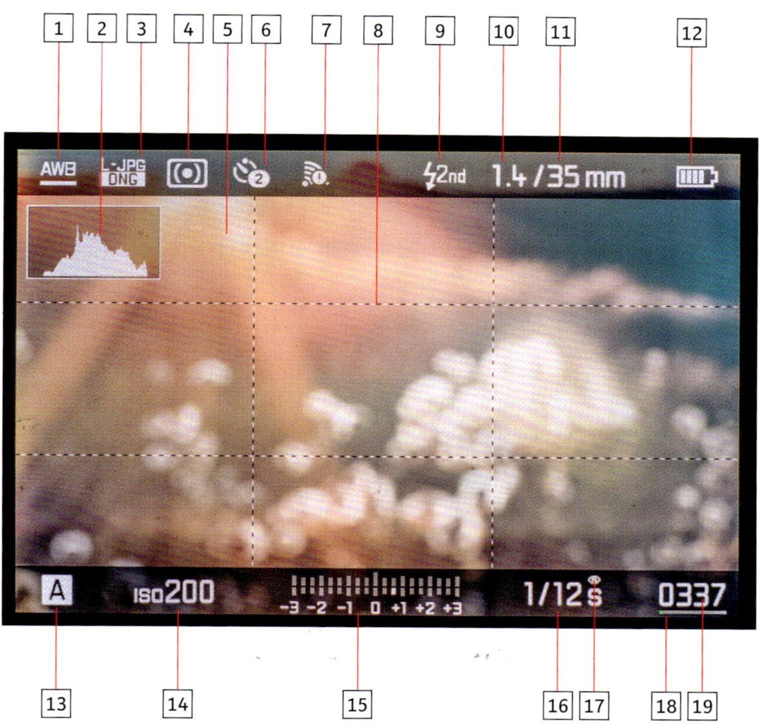

LIVE VIEW

1	White balance setting	11	Lens focal length
2	Live histogram	12	Battery power level
3	File type	13	Exposure mode
4	Metering mode	14	ISO speed
5	Live View image	15	Exposure scale
6	Drive mode	16	Shutter speed
7	Wi-Fi status	17	Exposure simulation indicator
8	Optional grid lines	18	Memory card space remaining (proportional bar)
9	Flash sync mode	19	Number of shots remaining
10	Lens maximum aperture		

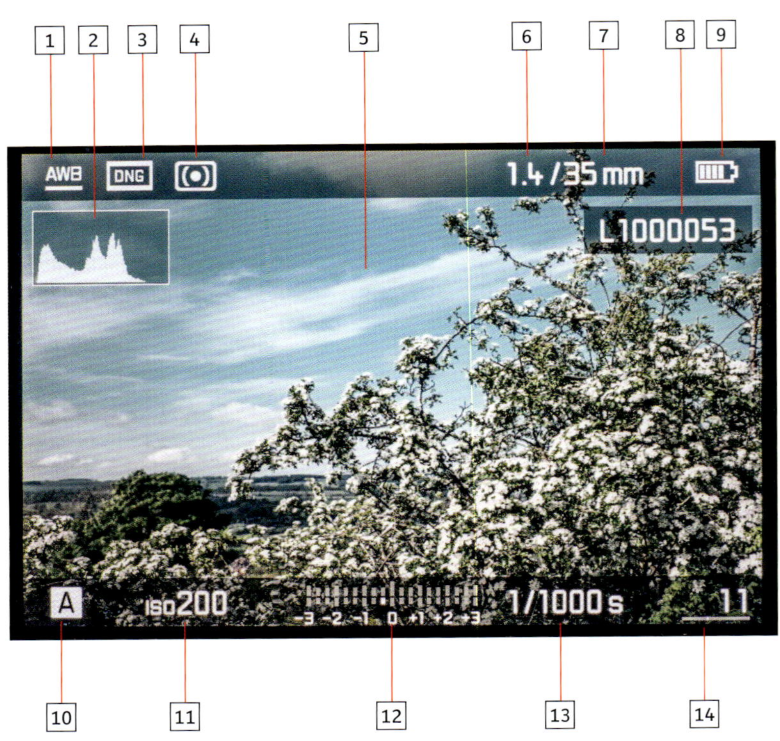

PLAYBACK: INFORMATION DISPLAY

1	White balance setting	8	File number
2	Histogram	9	Battery power level
3	File type	10	Exposure mode
4	Metering mode	11	ISO speed
5	Image	12	Exposure scale
6	Lens maximum aperture	13	Shutter speed
7	Lens focal length	14	Image number

» VIEWFINDER

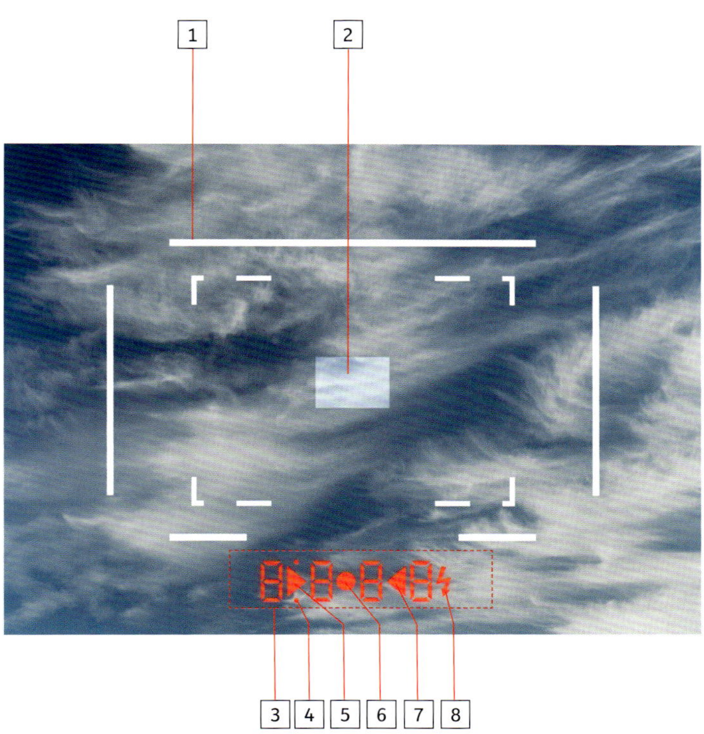

VIEWFINDER

1 Bright line frames (50mm and 75mm shown)	**5** Underexposure warning (manual exposure only)
2 Focus guide	**6** Correct exposure (manual exposure only)
3 Status display (used in different ways depending on the camera setting)	**7** Overexposure warning (manual exposure only)
	8 Flash symbol
4 Information dots: Top (lit): metering lock active Bottom (flashing): exposure compensation activated	

CHAPTER 2
FUNCTIONS

The Leica M10 is the latest in the small—but growing—family of M-series digital rangefinder cameras, which started with the M8 in 2006. Each of these cameras, including the M10, has stayed true to the design heritage initiated by Oskar Barnack.

If you have arrived at the Leica M10 from a DSLR or mirrorless camera you could be forgiven for marveling at the functional simplicity of the M10. This is the secret to the success of the M-series range: they are cameras with irrelevant options stripped away, leaving only those that are necessary to produce pleasing images.

You can pick up and use the Leica M10 purely as a manual camera, where you take complete control of exposure and focus, but it also has automated options that will help to increase your chances of success. Thanks to the addition of Live View you can also use virtually any lens produced for *other* camera systems.

This chapter will guide you through the basics of using your Leica M10 straight from the box. The rest of the book will show you how to make the most of your camera as a creative tool.

❯❯ HOOD ORNAMENT
The Leica M10 encourages a spontaneous approach to photography as you can quickly learn to shoot intuitively with it.

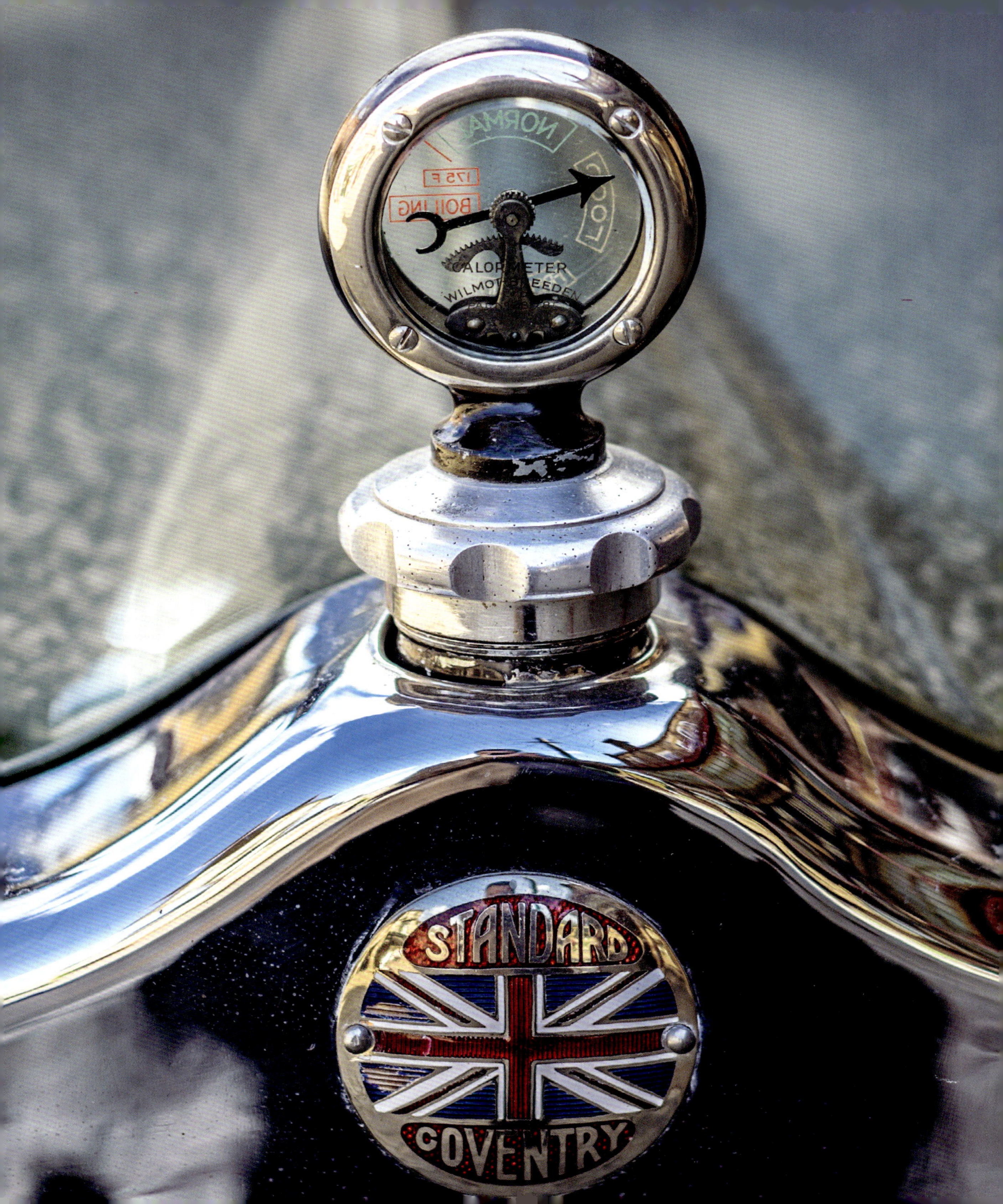

NORMAL
175 F
BOILING
COOL
CALORIMETER
WILMOT BREEDEN
STANDARD
COVENTRY

» CAMERA PREPARATION

› Registering your Leica M

Registering your Leica M10 with Leica means that you will receive offers and support from Leica. You will also be alerted when firmware updates are available. Register your camera at *https://owners.leica-camera.com/en/login*.

› Attaching the strap

Leica supplies a strap that, when fitted to your Leica M10, allows you to wear the camera around your neck for security. The strap can also be wrapped around your wrist if preferred (although this is less secure, your camera will always be ready for use, which is particularly useful when shooting spontaneously).

Leica has simplified the strap attachment process compared to earlier M-series digital cameras. To attach the strap, push the camera's left strap eyelet through the punched hole at one end of the strap, ensuring that the smooth side of the strap faces outward. Thread the end of the metal loop on the strap onto the carrying strap eyelets until the loop is fully attached to the eyelet. Repeat the process with the other end of the strap and the right strap eyelet.

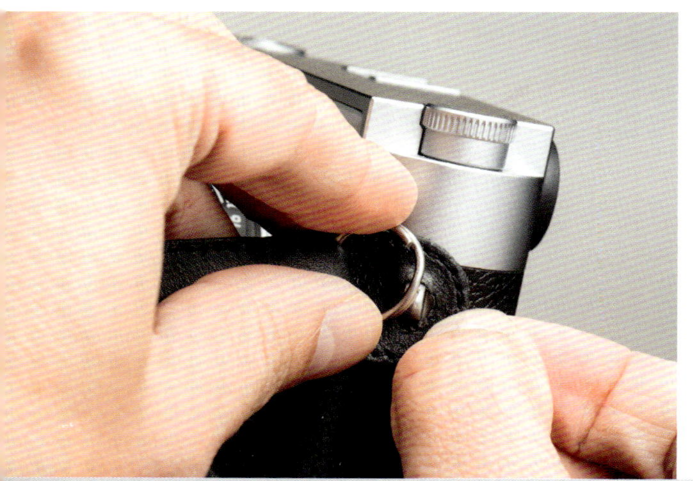

⌄ ATTACHING THE STRAP

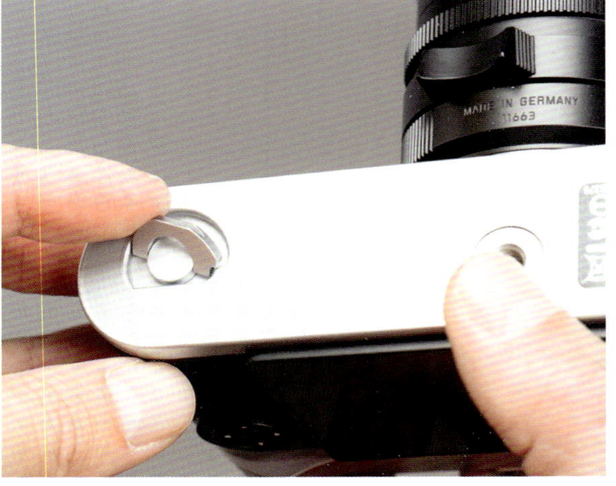

⌃ BASE PLATE
Put the base plate somewhere safe once it is removed from your Leica M10—you really don't want to damage or lose it!

› The base plate

Unlike other digital cameras, the Leica M10 does not have a simple set of doors that cover the battery and memory card compartments. Instead, in a charming nod to the classic 35mm film M-series cameras, you have to remove the camera's brass base plate to access both the battery and memory card.

There are drawbacks to this arrangement, though. For a start, it increases the time taken to add or remove a battery or memory card in comparison to other cameras. It also means that you cannot leave a tripod quick-release plate permanently fitted to the Leica M10; the plate has to come off every time you need to change the battery or access the memory card.

Because of this, it's a good idea to get into the habit of starting each shooting session with a freshly charged battery and empty memory card: this will minimize the need to remove the base plate.

The upside to the base plate (apart from the way it adds to the unique character of using a Leica camera) is that it helps to keep the body of the Leica M10 structurally rigid and imparts a feeling of quality that a plastic spring-loaded door lacks.

Removing and replacing the base plate

Ensure your Leica M10 is switched off, turn the camera upside down, and rest it on something soft but supportive. With the front of the camera facing away from you, pull the bottom release ring up and turn it counterclockwise until there is no resistance. Unhook the base plate from the locking clip and pull it free.

To replace the base plate, hook it back onto the locking clip and lower it down onto the bottom of the camera. Secure it by turning the locking ring clockwise to its original position and then push the ring flat into the base plate.

› Mounting and removing a lens

When you first take your Leica M10 from its box it should have a body cap fitted to the lens mount to protect both the shutter blades and sensor inside the camera from damage and the build-up of dust. Replacing the body cap when your camera is not in use and there is no lens attached is highly recommended.

To remove the body cap, hold the Leica M10 so that the front is facing you. Press the lens release button and turn the body cap counterclockwise until it comes free.

Remove the rear protection cap from your lens. Hold your lens by the fixed ring and align the red index mark on the lens barrel with the lens release button on the Leica M. Push the lens into the lens mount so that the lens and camera connect. Turn the lens gently clockwise until it clicks into place.

To remove the lens, reverse the procedure. Replace the body cap on the Leica M10 and the rear cap on the lens if neither is to be used again immediately.

Warning!

*If you turn your Leica M10 on with the base plate removed **Attention Bottom cover removed** will be displayed on the LCD.*

Notes

- The Leica M10 does not have an automatic sensor dust cleaning system. This means that you will occasionally need to clean the sensor manually. See chapter 3 for information about the procedure.

- Dust invariably finds its way onto camera sensors. Unsurprisingly, this is more likely to happen when you shoot in dusty conditions and regularly change lenses. Locations such as beaches are a particular hazard, especially when if it is windy. An easy way to reduce the risk of dust reaching the sensor is to use your body to shelter your camera as much as possible when changing lenses.

- Dust tends to be more visible in an image when you maximize depth of field by using a small aperture setting.

⋎ MOUNTING AND REMOVING A LENS

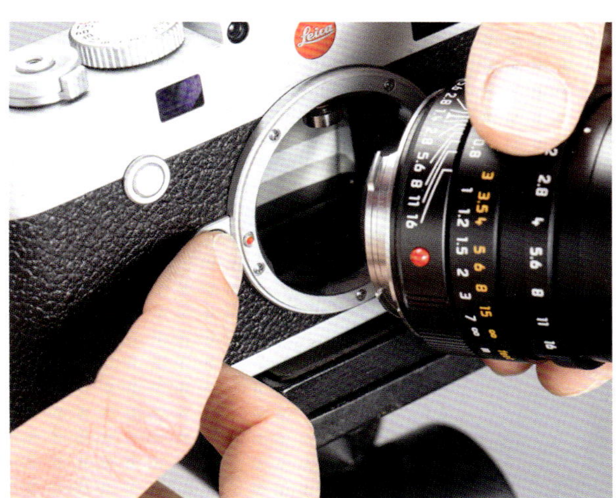

› Battery charging

The Leica M10 is powered by a lithium-ion (li-ion) battery (part number BP-SCL5). This newly developed battery is unique to the Leica M10, so is incompatible with the batteries supplied with previous Leica M-series digital cameras such as the M Typ 240.

Li-ion batteries are used to power digital cameras as they are very efficient for their size and weight. They are also slow to discharge when not in use and don't suffer from "memory" problems. This means that they can be charged without the need to discharge them fully first.

The Leica M10 is supplied with a BC-SCL5 battery charger and an AC power cord designed for the territory in which the camera was bought. To recharge a battery first connect the supplied battery charger to the AC power cord and insert the plug into a wall socket. Slot the battery as far as it will go into the charger with the battery contacts facing into the charger. The battery is shaped so that it can only be fitted into the charger one way. If there is excessive resistance do not force the battery further. Instead, remove the battery and retry.

When charging begins, the green LED next to CHARGE will start to flash. Once the battery has reached 4/5 charge the yellow 80% LED will light up. The battery can be used at this point if necessary. Once the battery reaches 100% charge, the green CHARGE LED will stop flashing and remain lit continuously. Once the battery is charged, turn off the power supply, unplug the charger from the wall socket, and remove the battery by sliding it out from the charger.

Notes
- The battery charger can be used globally (100–240V AC 50/60Hz) with a suitable plug adaptor and does not require a voltage transformer.

- If both charging status LEDs flash together when charging begins this indicates a charging error. Try removing and reinserting the battery. If the problem persists, contact your local Leica dealer.

- The operating temperature of the battery charger is 32–95°F (0–35°C).

- A brand new battery will not be able to hold a full charge unless it has been charged and discharged fully two or three times.

- The battery charger can also be used with a car-charging accessory via the DC 12V socket.

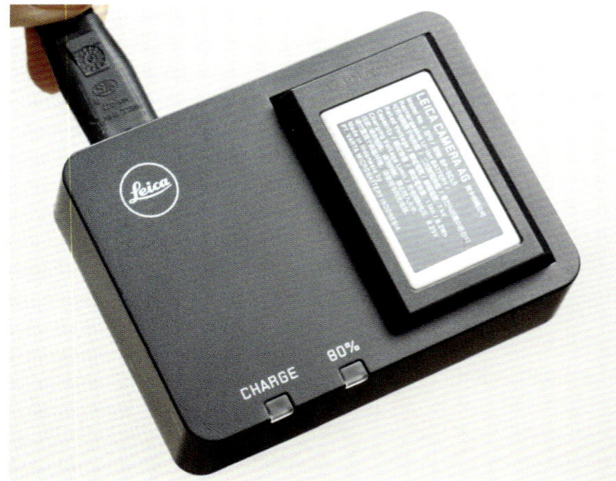

⌄ LEICA BATTERY CHARGER

› Inserting and removing the battery

Always turn off your Leica M10 before inserting or removing the battery. Detach the M base plate as described previously and slot the battery into the battery compartment. The battery terminals should be toward the rear of the camera and you need to push the battery gently against the gray locking lever as you insert it. Push the battery down into the compartment until the lock lever clicks into place and secures the battery.

To remove the battery, push the lock lever to the right (with the camera facing away from you) and pull the battery carefully from the compartment.

› Good power management

The official rating for the BP-SCL5 battery—from fully charged to depleted—is 210 shots, although this can be extended with careful use of the Leica M10:

- Keep your use of the LCD—particularly Live View— to a minimum. Set the menu options you require before a shoot and leave them set.

- Don't check each image as you shoot with a view to editing in the field. A quick check of focus is generally sufficient before moving onto the next shot.

- Follow Leica's recommended routine to keep your battery in top condition. A full discharge of power and then a full recharge every 25 charging cycles will "exercise" the battery and enable it to retain maximum charge.

⌄ INSERTING AND REMOVING THE BATTERY

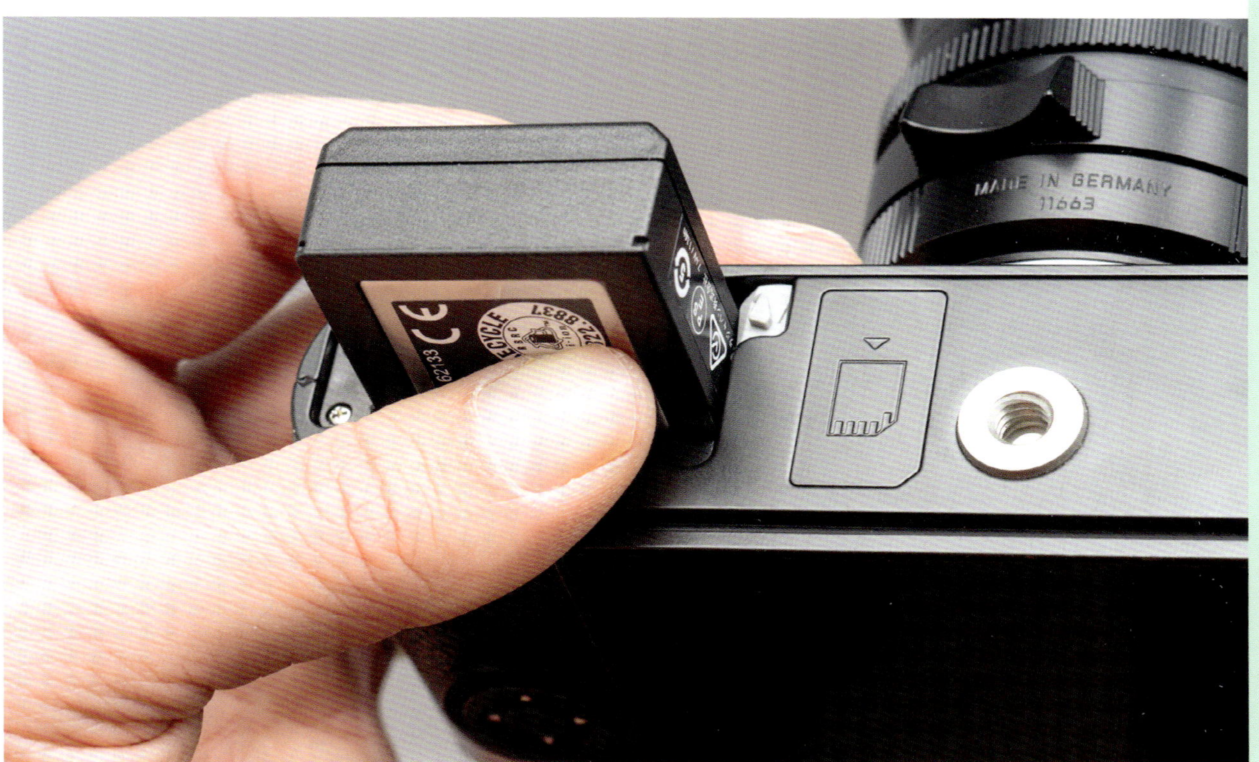

Setting the various shooting and playback options on the Leica M10 involves using a combination of mechanical dials and button controls. The mechanical controls, such as the shutter speed dial, will be covered in more detail later in this chapter.

There are three option buttons arranged vertically to the left of the LCD, which allow you to switch to LV (Live View, see page 36), PLAY previously shot images, or view the various MENU options.

At the right of the LCD is a direction pad that surrounds an unmarked circular selection button. The pad is used to navigate the various menu screens while the selection button selects menu options. Throughout the rest of this book the specific directions you need to press on the pad will be shown as ◀ / ▲ / ▼ / ▶ and the selection button as ●. ✧ will be shown if you are free to press the pad in any of the four directions. The thumbwheel above the direction pad will be shown as **O**.

Any capitalized words refer to the relevant button on the rear of the Leica M; words shown in bold refer to options displayed on the LCD when using the menu or during playback.

› Switching the camera on

The Leica M10's main switch has two settings. When both the red and black marker dots are visible the camera is switched off; move the switch so that the red dot is covered and the Leica M10 is turned on. When the Leica M10 is switched on, the LED at the bottom right of the LCD will flash briefly and after approximately one second the camera will be ready to begin shooting.

Notes
- If left switched on, the Leica M10 will power down after the period of time set on **Auto Power Saving** in the Main Menu (see chapter 3). Press the shutter-release button down lightly to "wake" the camera.

- The first time you switch your Leica M10 on you will need to set the **Language** and **Date & Time** (see chapter 3).

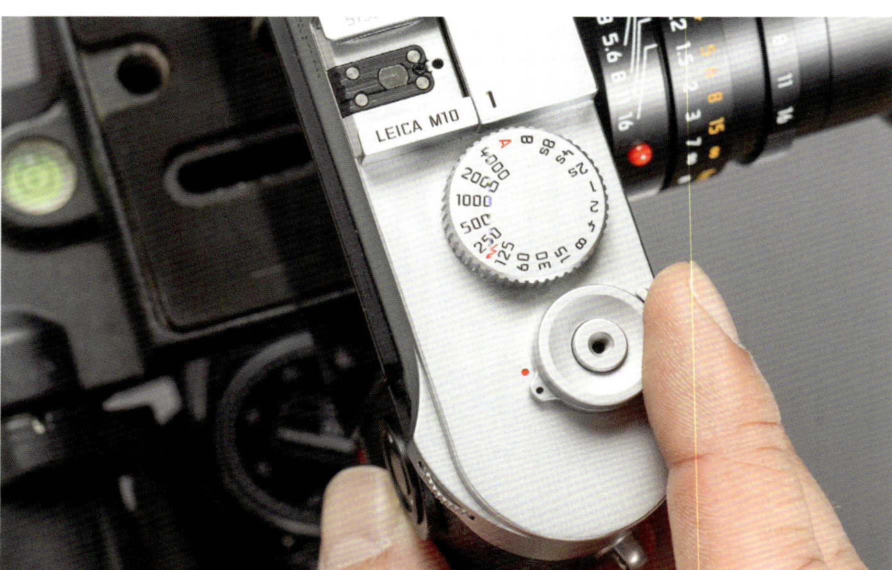

» MEMORY CARDS

› The SD standard

The Leica M10 uses commonly available Secure Digital (SD) memory cards. However, not all memory cards are equal; since its invention, the SD standard has evolved considerably. The Leica M10 is compatible with SD and SDHC memory cards, as well as the latest variant known as SDXC (XC for eXtended Capacity).

Before you start to use a memory card on your Leica M10 it will need to be formatted. The Leica M10 formats memory cards using the FAT/FAT 32 standard, which is recognized by both Windows and Apple Mac computers.

Fitting a memory card

1) Switch off your Leica M10 and remove the base plate as outlined previously.

2) Move the SD memory card's lock switch to the unlock position. When an SD memory card is locked you will no longer be able to save images to it, although you can still view images saved previously to the card.

3) Insert the memory card into the slot on the base of the camera. The metal contacts on the card should face toward the rear of the camera.

4) Slide the card down until it clicks positively into place. To remove the card, push it down slightly until it is released by the locking mechanism and pull it gently out of the slot.

5) Replace the base plate.

Notes
- Pressing ● in shooting mode will display an information screen showing battery power and number of shots remaining, as well as details about shutter speed and attached lens.

- Keep your memory cards away from magnetic sources. Loudspeakers (unless shielded) and microwaves generate magnetic fields. Don't store memory cards in hot places such as a car in summer.

⌄ **FITTING A MEMORY CARD**

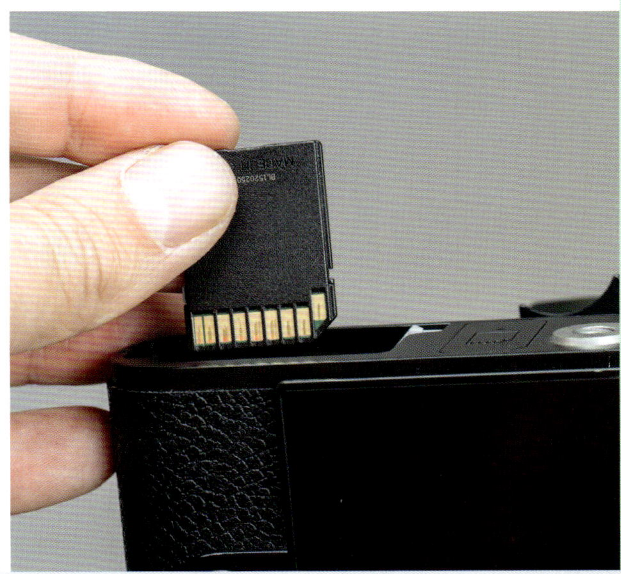

There are two factors that determine the usefulness of a memory card: its capacity and its read/write speed. The former determines how many images can be fitted onto the card (which, as a general rule, is more if you shoot JPEG and fewer if you shoot Raw).

The read/write speed refers to how quickly a memory card can have data read from it or written to it when images are either being viewed or copied to another storage system (such as the hard drive of a PC). Read speed is generally higher than write speed, although both are affected by the device doing the reading or writing.

The Leica M10 is not a particularly fast camera. The maximum frame rate of 5 frames per second is good, but it is not class leading. The camera does not shoot video either, so choosing a faster (and more expensive) memory card over a slower (and cheaper) card will very much be a personal choice rather than a necessity. However, a slow card will make the process of copying images to a PC far more laborious.

The speed of a memory card is often shown as a Class Rating: the higher the Class Rating, the faster the card. A memory card's speed is also sometimes shown as a figure followed by an "x." This figure refers to the speed of the card in comparison to the read/write speed of a standard CD-Rom drive.

Note
- Mb/s stands for Megabits per second and is a measure of the number of bits that can be read from, or written to, a digital device in a second. A bit is the smallest possible unit of digital information. Megabit is shortened to Mb and is easily confused with megabyte, which is usually shortened to MB. A megabyte represents 800% more information than a megabit (a megabyte is the unit used when looking at an image's file size on a computer or on the LCD of your Leica M10).

⌄ **SANDISK 512GB EXTREME PRO**
© SanDisk

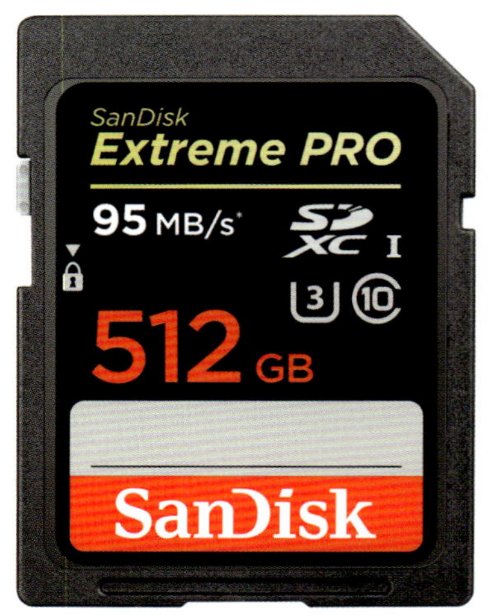

Speed	Read/write speed (Mb/s)	Class Rating
13x	2.0	2
26x	4.0	4
40x	6.0	6
66x	10.0	10

› Formatting

The majority of new memory cards are pre-formatted so they can be used immediately. Even so, it is generally a good idea to format *any* memory card the first time you fit it into your Leica M10. This is particularly true if you have used the card in another camera previously—there may be files saved on the card that relate to the other camera, which the Leica M10 will either ignore or be unable to display and so will not be able to delete.

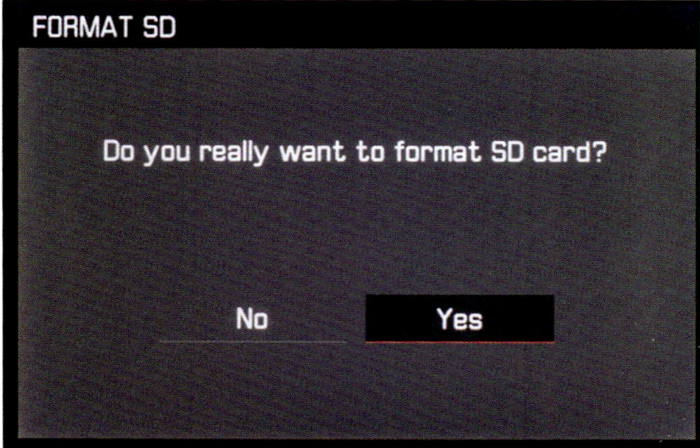

Formatting a memory card

1) Press MENU followed by ▼ until **Main Menu** is highlighted and press ▶ or ●. Press ▼ until you reach the third Main Menu screen.

2) Highlight **Format SD** and press ●.

3) Highlight **Yes** and press ● to begin formatting the card, or highlight **No** and press ● to return to the third page of the Main Menu.

4) Formatting will take longer with slow or high-capacity memory cards. Once formatting is complete the M10 returns to the third page of the Main Menu.

Note
- See chapter 3 for more information about the Leica M10's menu system.

Warning!

Do not remove the memory card if the camera is switched on.

*If there is no memory card in your Leica M10 the following warning message will be displayed on the LCD: **Attention No card available**.*

Do not turn off your Leica M10 during formatting as this may damage both your Leica M10 and the memory card.

» FIRING THE SHUTTER

› The shutter-release button

The Leica M10's shutter-release button has two separate and distinct stages as you press down on it. The first stage occurs when the shutter-release button is pressed down half way. This automatically cancels image playback and wakes the Leica M10 from standby. This first stage also activates the camera metering and viewfinder display, as well as "locking" the required shutter speed when Aperture Priority is selected. Self-timer countdown will be restarted if you previously set self-timer running.

If you remove your finger from the shutter-release button the metering and viewfinder display will remain active for the period set in **Auto Power Saving** (see page 90). If you keep the shutter-release button pressed down

at this first stage the metering and viewfinder display remains active until you release or push down the shutter-release button completely. Exposure compensation can be set using the control dial at this stage.

The second stage is pressing the shutter-release button down completely. This fires the shutter (or begins the self-timer countdown before firing the shutter) to expose the image.

⌄ THE SHUTTER-RELEASE BUTTON

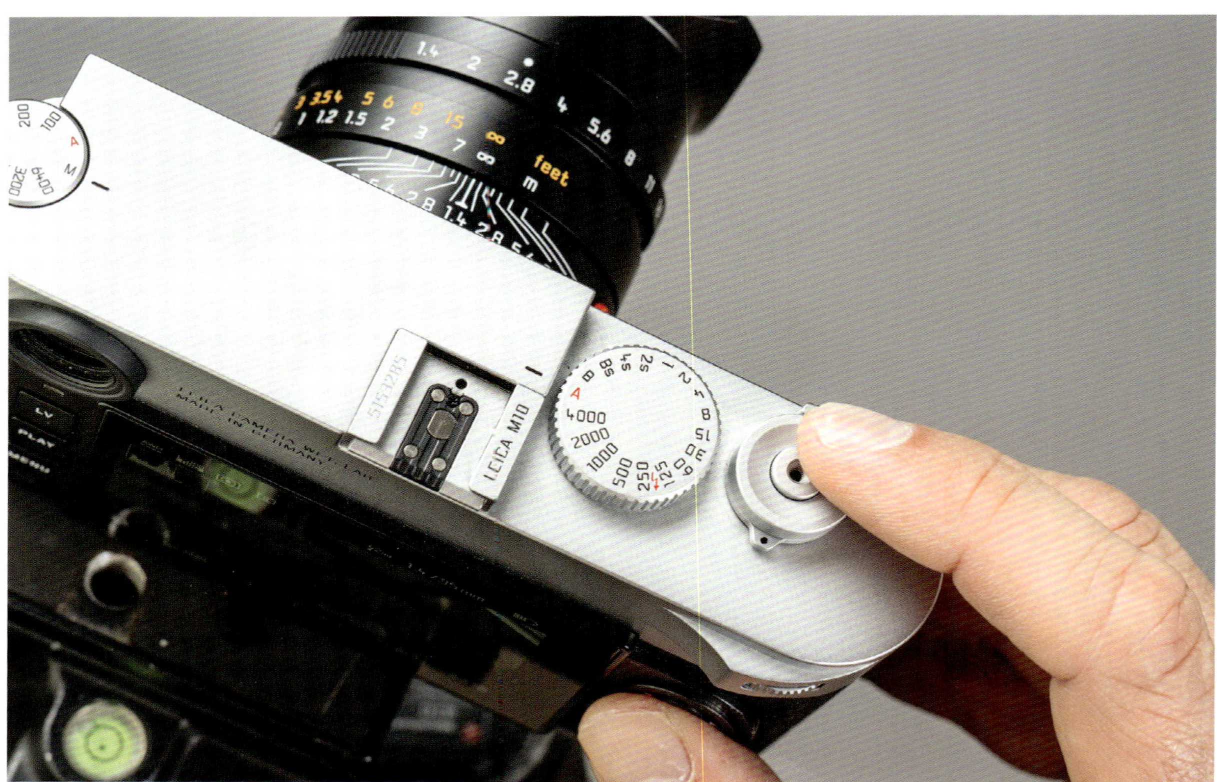

› Cable release

There are two ways to fire the Leica M10's shutter remotely. The old-school method is to use a standard mechanical cable release; a more up-to-date approach is to use the free Leica TL app (iOS only) and control your M10 using an iPhone, iPad, or iPod—see page 178.

A cable release allows you to fire the shutter without touching the camera. This helps to reduce the risk of camera shake, particularly when longer shutter speeds are required. Cable releases are particularly useful when your Leica M10 is mounted on a tripod and the most common user of a cable release in this scenario is the landscape photographer. However, portrait photographers also benefit from using a cable release once an image has been composed and focused. Using a cable release lets the photographer look at and—more importantly— engage with the subject directly, rather than being hidden behind a camera. The shutter can then be fired discreetly at the most appropriate moment.

To fit a cable release, gently screw the end of the release into the shutter-release button thread. Fire the shutter-release button by pushing the plunger down on the cable release.

Most cable releases have a locking collar that allows you to hold open the shutter in B mode (see page 56). The lock is usually a small metal or plastic disk that rotates at the base of the cable release plunger. When the lock is screwed tight, the plunger will move freely back and forth. When the lock is unscrewed the plunger will lock when you push it in. To release the plunger again, press down on the lock. Rotate the lock back so that it feels tight to return to normal usage. To remove the cable release, gently unscrew it from the shutter-release button when the plunger is in the unlocked position.

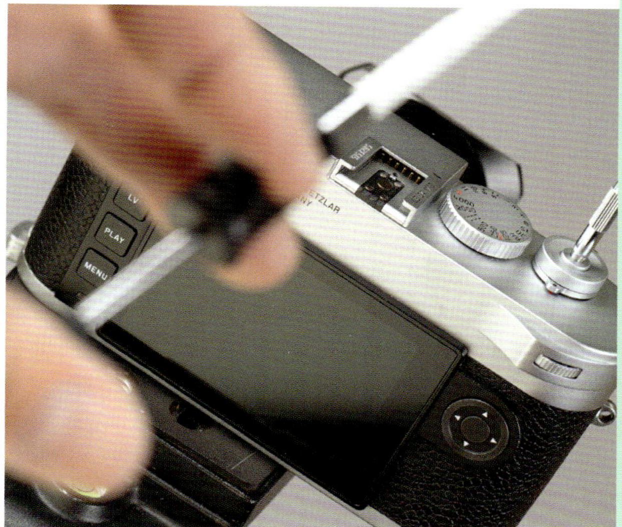

⌃ CABLE RELEASE

> ### Warning!
>
> *When a cable release is attached to your Leica M10 take care not to knock it. Any sideways force could break the cable release or even damage the camera's shutter-release button.*

Note
• The shutter-release button is locked when the buffer or memory card is full; when the memory card is write-protected; when the battery is too old and cannot be effectively recharged or is too hot; the sensor is too hot (typically when Live View has be active for a long period of time); or when the language selection needs setting.

» THE VIEWFINDER

The Leica M10 has a Live View mode that streams a live image from the sensor to the LCD. However, the real appeal of the Leica M10 and its predecessors is the parallax-corrected optical rangefinder. The viewfinder has two main functions: to aid composition and to help focus the lens.

To help you compose your shots the Leica M10 uses bright-line frames visible in the viewfinder. At any time there is one of three pairs of bright-line frames displayed in the viewfinder: 28mm/90mm, 35mm/135mm, or 50mm/75mm. The outer frame shows the scene as it would be captured by the shorter (wider) focal length lens in the pair, while the inner frame shows the angle of view of the longer focal length (see page 107 for an explanation of angle of view and focal length). The combination of bright-line frames alters automatically when lenses with focal lengths of 28mm, 35mm, 50mm, 75mm, and 135mm are fitted.

› Frame selector switch

The frame selector switch on the front of the Leica M10 allows you to manually switch between the three pairs of bright-line frames regardless of the lens fitted to the camera. The main advantage of this is that it can help you decide whether you need to swap lenses to achieve a more pleasing composition.

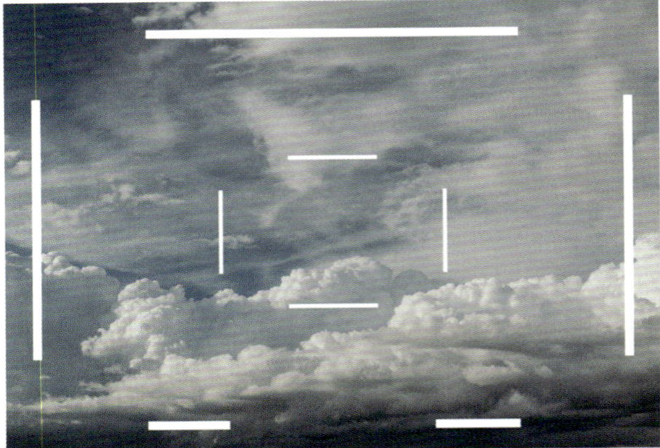

28mm/90mm frames

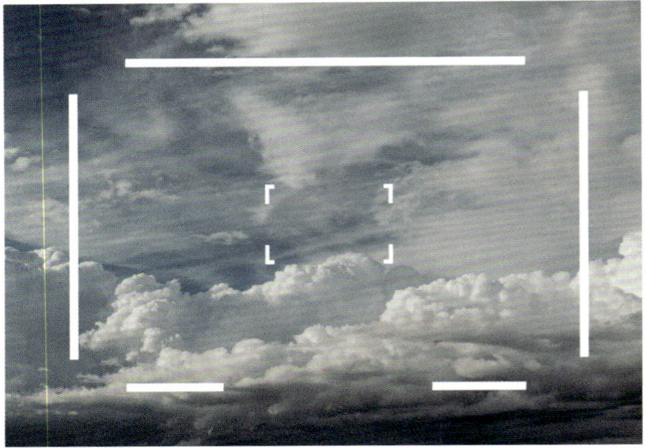

35mm/135mm frames

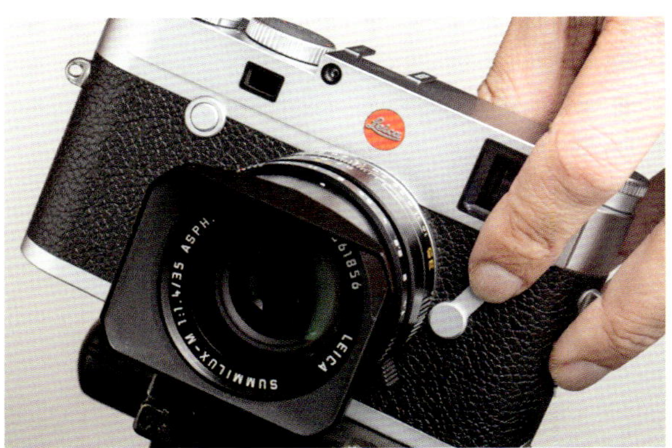

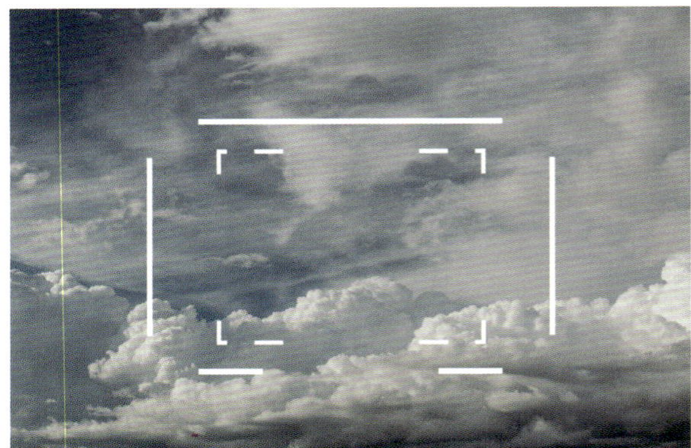

50mm/75mm frames

› Viewfinder: advantages

In a world of fully electronic mirrorless cameras, the basic rangefinder design of the Leica M10 (and its siblings) may seem slightly old fashioned. However, Leica has not abandoned the rangefinder design because it still has a number of advantages over other types of cameras.

For a start, you maintain full view of the scene through the viewfinder as you shoot (there is no blackout at all). This means you can monitor what happens to your subject at all times. This is particularly useful when shooting subjects that move.

A related advantage is that the Leica M10's viewfinder lets you anticipate events more easily. As you see an area greater than the lens' angle of view (except when using wide-angle lenses greater than 28mm) you can see when a moving subject will enter the frame before it actually does.

Another advantage is that rangefinders do not suffer from mirror shock that can occur when shooting with a DSLR. This means that it is often possible to shoot handheld at slower shutter speeds than you could with a DSLR.

Notes
- Parallax is the apparent shift in the position of an object when viewed from two different points in space. To see the effect for yourself, look at an object and then open and close one eye and then the other.

- The viewfinder and lens of the Leica M10 are only separated by a small distance, but without parallax correction even that would be enough to make the viewfinder an unreliable guide in terms of what the lens "sees." Even with parallax correction the viewfinder gets less accurate the closer your subject is to the camera.

- The viewfinder is accurate with lenses between 28mm and 135mm focal length. Wider-angle lenses require the use of a separate viewfinder that clips into the flash hotshoe (see chapter 5).

» BLOCKED
Part of the viewfinder is blocked by the lens/lens hood. This is less of a problem when shooting with long focal length lenses, but it does mean that you have to be careful when composing with wide-angle lenses.

› Viewfinder: disadvantages

Unfortunately, using a rangefinder viewfinder is not all good; there are a number of disadvantages, some of which can catch you out if you are not careful.

A very common mistake when switching to using a rangefinder is leaving the lens cap on. This is easy to do because you may not notice that the lens cap is still fitted to the lens until you shoot and review an image; the viewfinder is not affected by the fitting or removal of a lens cap. A useful clue as to whether a lens cap is fitted is when an unexpectedly long shutter speed is shown in the viewfinder.

Depth of field is harder to judge when looking through a rangefinder viewfinder, particularly when it comes to shallow depth of field. More attention has to be taken of the depth of field scale on the lens to anticipate the extent of depth of field in the resulting image.

Unlike a DSLR or mirrorless camera, there is only one central focus aid in the viewfinder. If you want to focus on a subject that's not central you will need to move the camera to focus before recomposing. This is less of a problem when handholding your Leica M10, but can be inconvenient when it is mounted on a tripod.

It is hard to compose with lenses wider than 28mm and longer than 135mm when looking through the viewfinder. These lenses either require the use of an external viewfinder (either optical or electronic), or a switch to Live View. Even lenses that are suitable for the viewfinder may block the view, particularly when fitted with a lens hood or filter holder. (Many new Leica lens hoods have a notch cut out of the top left corner to improve visibility.)

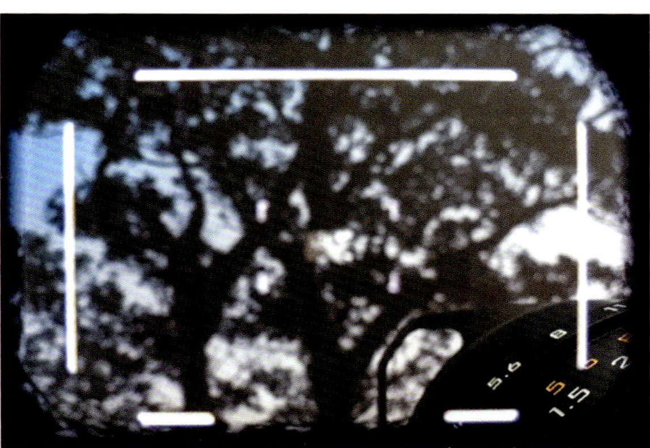

Like its predecessor, the Leica M Typ 240, you can switch the Leica M10 to Live View by pressing the LV button on the rear of the camera. After a short delay the image projected onto the sensor by the lens is streamed to the LCD in real time.

There are two Live View settings. The first shows the entire image without distracting—if useful—shooting information. When composing a shot using Live View this is the preferable setting. The second setting shows shooting information such as the currently selected file type, lens focal length, and exposure settings (with the exception of aperture—as there is no electronic communication between the lens and camera this information cannot be displayed on the LCD). Pressing ● switches between the two Live View options.

> **Note**
> • Although it is not a "traditional" method of shooting with a Leica, there are certain shooting aids that are only available in Live View. These include a histogram, focus peaking, and two grid types to help with composition. The various shooting aids are controlled using the relevant **Capture Assistants** sub-menus on the Main Menu (page 2). See pages 82–84 for more details.

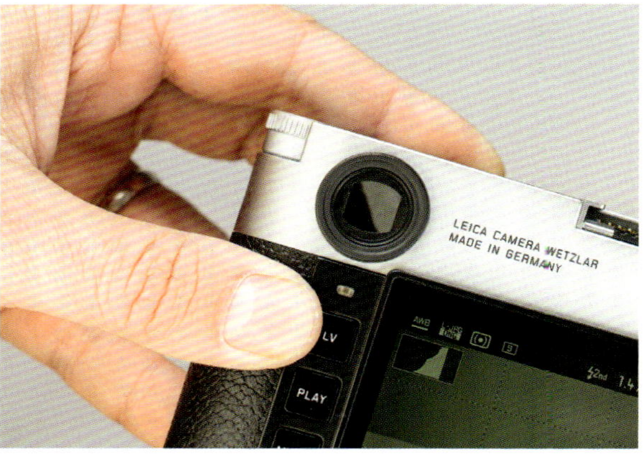

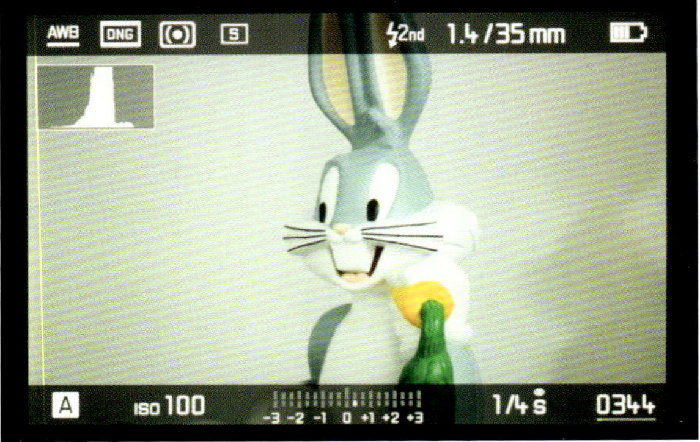

› Live View: advantages and disadvantages

The big advantage Live View has over the viewfinder is that you can more accurately see how an image is composed, particularly when using focal lengths that are not covered by the viewfinder's bright lines. You can also see the change in depth of field as the aperture is adjusted in a way that is impossible when using the viewfinder.

However, using a smaller aperture can have its problems when shooting with Live View. The reduction in light reaching the sensor can make the Live View display appear coarse and grainy, particularly when ambient light levels are low.

Setting a small aperture can also fool you into not focusing correctly. As the depth of field is greater you won't know precisely where the focus point is. Although it is more involved, it is better to set the lens to its maximum aperture and then compose and focus. After that set the required aperture.

Live View also requires the sensor to be active for long periods of time. This is a big drain on the battery, which won't last as long as it would when using the viewfinder only. The sensor will also get hot. In normal conditions this shouldn't be a problem, but use of Live View should be limited when the ambient temperature is high.

Finally, the shutter needs to be closed, opened, closed, and then re-opened whenever a shot is taken in Live View mode. This leads to a slightly more protracted shooting experience than when using the viewfinder. It is not a huge difference, but if you're shooting continuously it will cause the frame rate to drop significantly.

» FOCUSING

All Leica M-series lenses are manual-focus only. To focus a lens you turn the focus ring to the right (when you are behind the camera) to shorten the focus distance and focus on something close to the camera, or to the left to increase the focus distance. If the lens has a finger rest, use that in preference to the focus ring, as it will allow you to control focus more easily and smoothly.

Leica lenses are marked with a distance scale in both feet and meters. The focus distance is read by looking at where the focus index mark on the lens points on the distance scale. All lenses have a minimum and maximum focusing distance, but the minimum distance will depend on the specifications of a particular lens. Due to the effects of parallax, Leica lenses are not designed to focus particularly close. This will be most noticeable if you are used to using lenses designed for DSLR or mirrorless camera systems. The maximum focusing distance is indicated by the symbol ∞ ("infinity") on the distance scale.

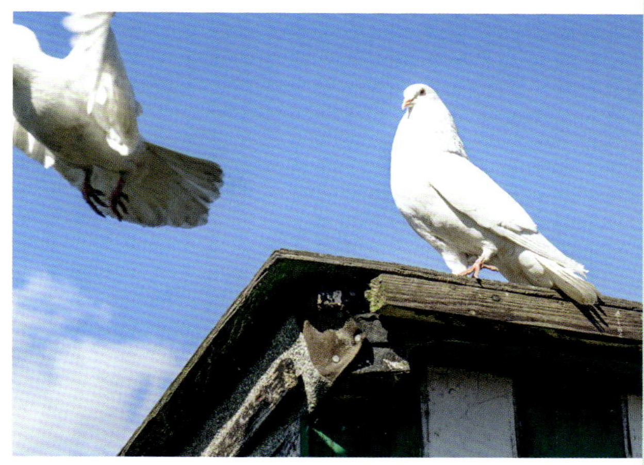

⌃ PREDICTIVE
The movement of animals can, after observation, start to become predictable. These racing pigeons took it in turns to launch themselves off the corner of this shed. By pre-focusing and carefully timing my shots I was able to take a number of successfully sharp frames.

› Pre-focusing

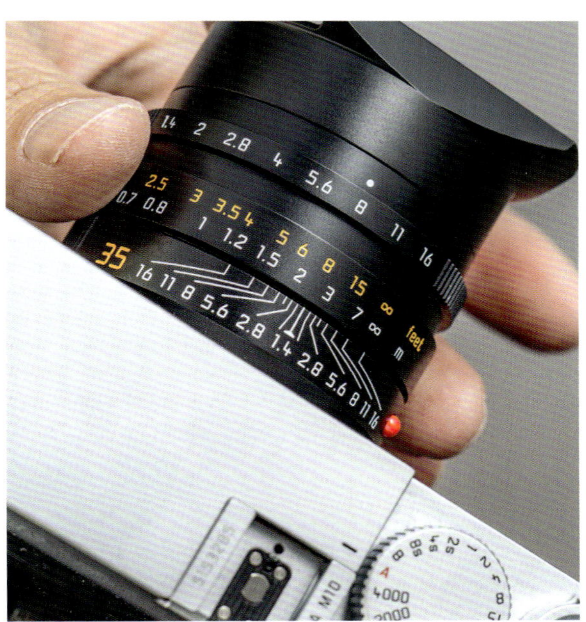

You would think that manual focus would restrict the use of the Leica M10, but many famous photographers—most notably Henri Cartier-Bresson—used Leica film cameras when shooting fast-moving documentary and street scenes. The secret to their success was pre-focusing.

Pre-focusing simply means that the lens is focused at a useful distance before you begin shooting. This should be the distance that you predict your subject will be from the camera when it is in the right position for you to start shooting. This takes practice to achieve consistently, as it requires you to pre-visualize a shot before you press the shutter-release button. It is also easier with subjects that move in a predictable way; erratically moving subjects may not end up where you wish them to be. Using a smaller aperture—such as f/8 or f/11—to increase depth of field will help to mask focusing errors.

› Precise focusing: viewfinder

Ultimately you are more certain of success if you focus precisely. There are essentially three ways to achieve precision focusing on the Leica M10: the first is by using the distance scale on the lens, the second is using the viewfinder, and the third is to use Live View.

If you know the exact distance to your subject (after using a tape measure or other measuring tool) you could focus by turning the focus ring on the lens so that this distance aligns with focus distance index. This is easier to achieve when the focus index mark points to a specific marked distance on the lens barrel. However, there will be times when the focus index mark inconveniently points to a gap in the distance scale. In this instance you will need to use your own judgement about where the lens should be focused.

The second focusing method is to use the focus guide at the center of the viewfinder. This can be used to focus lenses with a focal length of 16–135mm. To focus, aim the camera so your subject is within the focus guide rectangle. The focus guide rectangle will show a double image of the subject. As you turn the focus ring—and the subject comes into focus—the double images will start to converge. Once they align, focus has been achieved. You can check the focus distance on the lens and confirm the viewfinder is accurate, but generally this is not necessary.

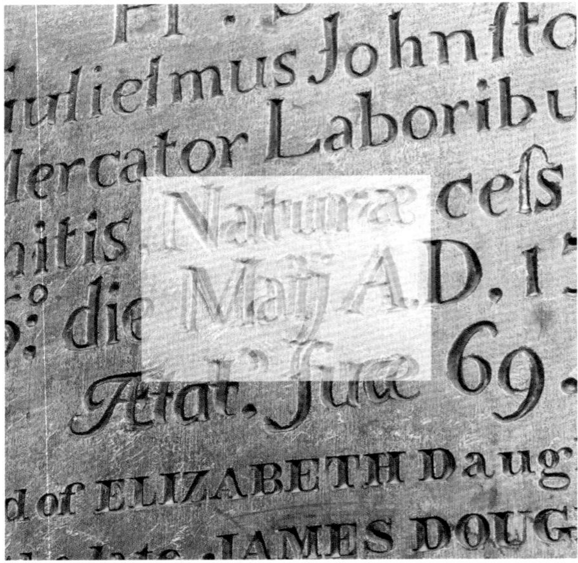

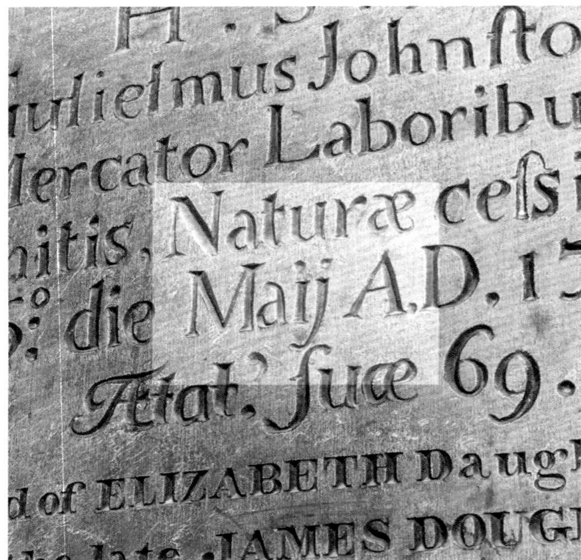

⌃ FOCUSING
The images in the focus indicator rectangle are not aligned (top), so focus for this subject has still not been set. When the images align (above), focus is correct.

› Precise focusing: Live View

Focusing (and composition) is arguably easier in Live View as you see exactly what the camera "sees" through the lens. The only exception to this is in bright sunshine, when it is often far easier to see through the viewfinder than see what is displayed on the LCD in Live View.

Live View offers a number of useful tools to increase focusing accuracy including **LV Zoom** (see page 89), **Focus Peaking** (see page 82), and **Focus Aid** (see page 84). Due to the effects of depth of field, the aperture the lens is set to will play a part in how sharp the image will appear on screen when focusing using Live View. With a small aperture you may not know exactly where the lens is focused, as increased depth of field will mask the focus position. If you want to focus precisely, open up the aperture to its maximum setting, focus, and then close the aperture to the required value.

Note
- Temporarily setting the lens to its maximum aperture setting will help with the clarity of the Live View display in low light; smaller apertures reduce the amount of light reaching the sensor and force the Leica M10 to amplify the Live View display. This results in a grainier Live View image.

⌄ FOCUS PEAKING
Focus peaking outlines the sharpest areas of an image with a selected color, so it's easy to see what is in focus.

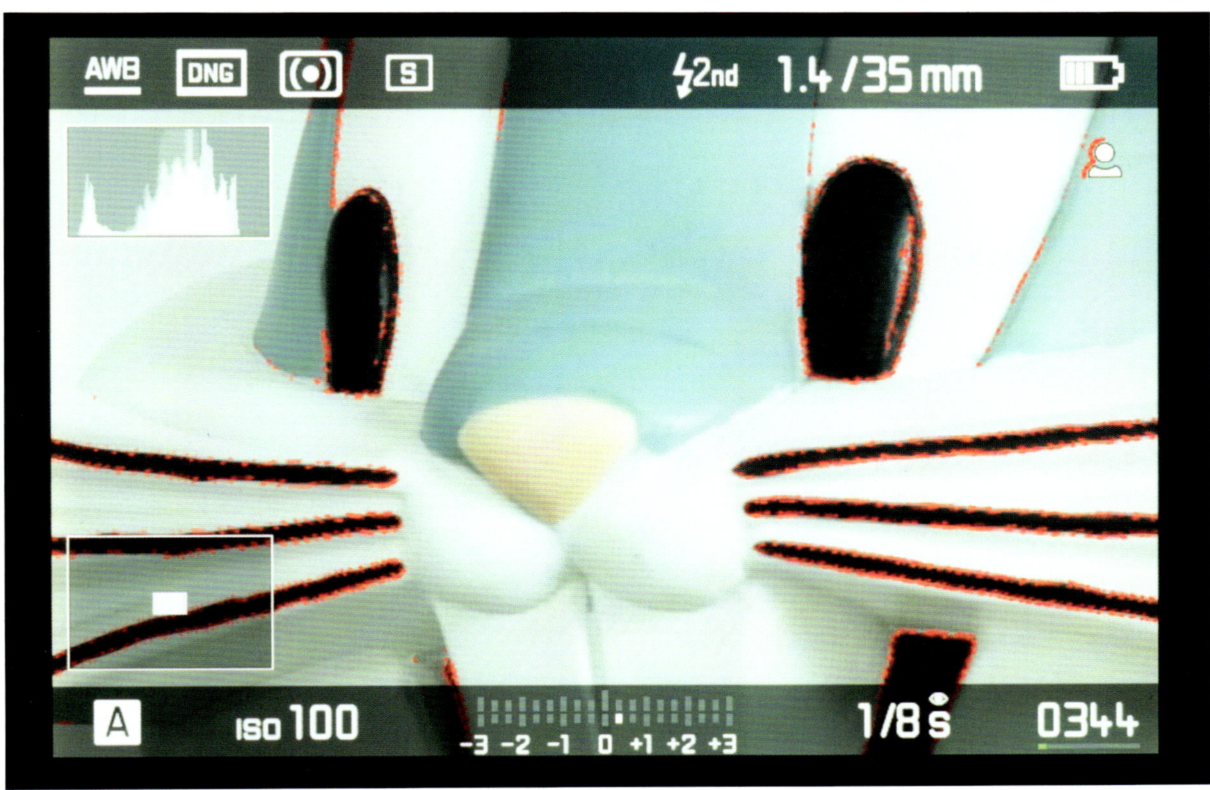

» DRIVE MODE

The drive mode determines whether a single exposure is made or a number of frames are shot when the shutter-release button is pressed down; whether a self-timer is activated; whether a specific number of images are shot over a set period of time; or whether three consecutive images are bracketed (and what the degree of exposure variation is). The drive modes are set via the **Drive Mode** page, which can be found on the Main Menu (page 1)—see page 64 for information on using the menu system.

Single (⑤)

Set to single advance the Leica M10 shoots one image with each single press of the shutter-release button. The shutter-release button must be fully released before another exposure can be made. ⑤ suits subjects that do not move, such as still life, landscapes, and posed portraits.

Continuous (▣)

Hold down the shutter-release button when ▣ has been selected and the Leica M10 can shoot at up to 5 frames per second (fps) until either the frame buffer is full or there is no longer space on the memory card.

A frame buffer is memory on a camera that is used temporarily to store images until they can be written to the card. Once the frame buffer is full, the Leica M10 will stop shooting until images have been written to the memory and the buffer begins to empty. How quickly the frame buffer empties depends on the size of the image (Raw files are larger than JPEGs and so fill the buffer more quickly) and the read/write speed of the memory card.

▣ is typically used to shoot moving subjects such as athletes, animals, or motor vehicles. In combination with a fast shutter speed and pre-focusing, ▣ is a useful tool to ensure success with these types of subjects.

Note
- When using ▣, the last picture shot in the sequence will be the one that will be displayed on the LCD in **Auto Review**.

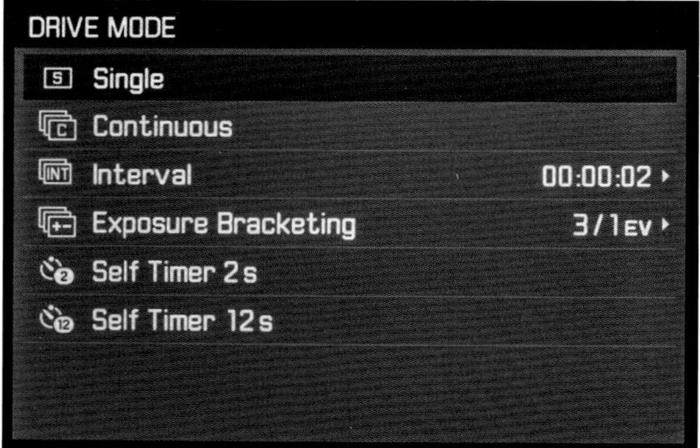

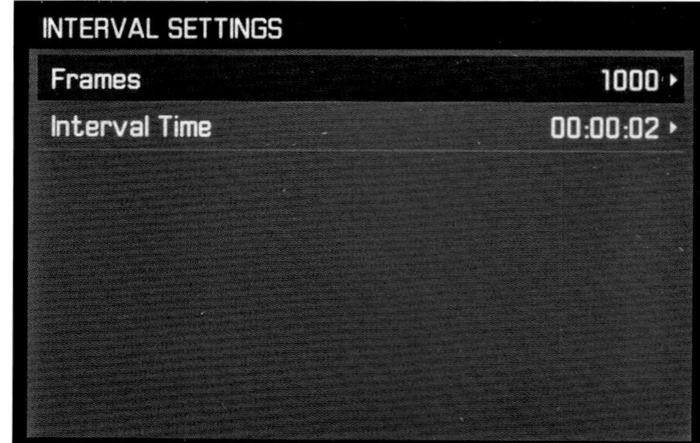

Interval (INT)

INT gives you the option of setting your Leica M10 to automatically shoot up to 9999 images over a fixed period of time—you can set up to 24 hours, 59 minutes, and 59 seconds between each image. Shooting a sequence of images like this is generally used to create timelapse movies, where the individual images shot are played consecutively. See page 168 for information about shooting with the aim of producing a timelapse movie.

Images shot over a period can also be blended together using postproduction software such as Photoshop to produce a single photograph; this technique is often used to create star trail images.

Using Interval

1) Select **Frames** on the **Interval Settings** sub-menu.

2) Use ✧ to highlight the required number of frames and press ● to add the number to the character entry bar at the top of the screen. Select ← to delete numbers if necessary. Select ✔ when you have set the correct number of frames.

3) Select **Interval Time**.

4) Press ▲ / ▼ to set the hour value (**hh**). Press ▶ to jump to the minute value (**mm**) and press ▲ / ▼ to set the required time in minutes. Press ▶ again to jump to the seconds value (**ss**) and press ▲ / ▼ to set the required time in seconds. You can use ◀ to skip backward at any point. Press MENU once all three time values are set.

5) Press the shutter-release button down to the first stage to return to shooting. Press down fully to begin shooting the sequence.

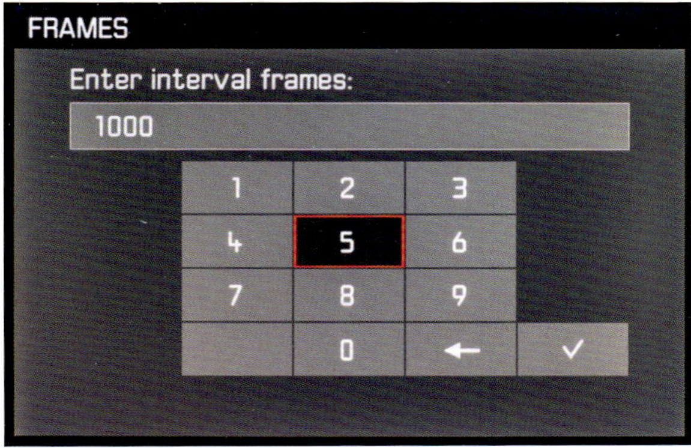

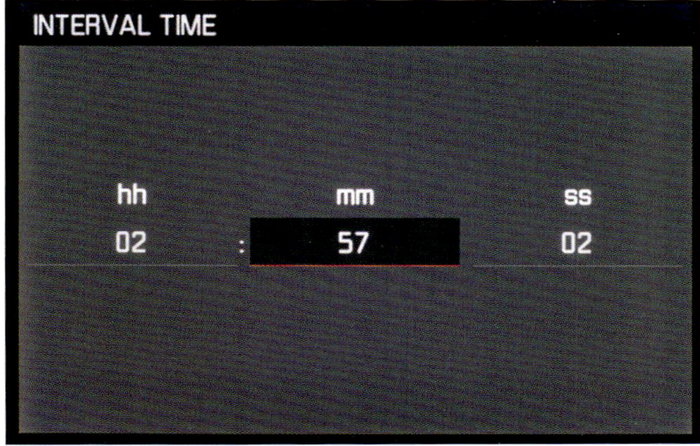

Exposure Bracketing (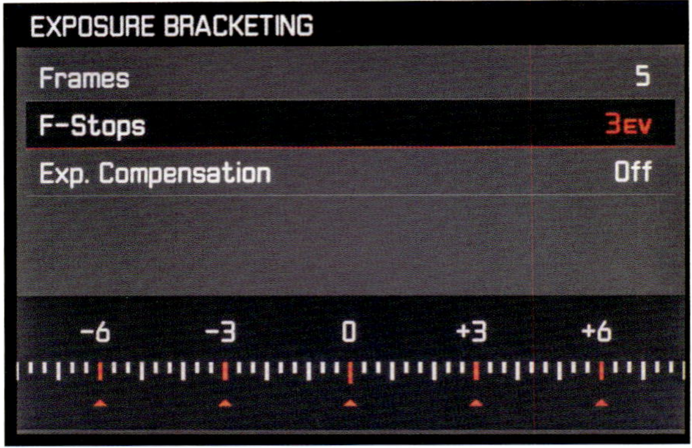)

Bracketing is a term used in photography to describe the technique of shooting two or more images of the same scene, varying one of the camera's functions as each image is shot.

The most common use of bracketing is exposure bracketing, where the exposure is varied as you shoot. This can be done manually on the Leica M10 by varying either the shutter speed or aperture between exposures, but the Leica M10's **Exposure Bracketing** option automates the process, allowing you to set the number of bracketed images, the exposure range, and whether exposure compensation is applied.

Frames on the **Exposure Bracketing** sub-menu page lets you set **3** or **5** images. Generally, **3** images are sufficient for most cases where exposure bracketing is required (one image is taken at the "correct" exposure, one is "underexposed," and the third is "overexposed'). However, if you intend to use HDR (High Dynamic Range) techniques to create an image with a wide tonal range, **5** images will expand the potential tonal range of your HDR image; from ±3 stops when shooting **3** frames to ±6 stops when shooting **5** frames.

F-Stops lets you select the difference (in stops/EVs) between each exposure in the bracketed sequence: the options are **1EV**, **2EV**, or **3EV**. You would typically use a wider range when shooting scenes that are high in contrast.

Exp. Compensation lets you shift the initial exposure by up to ±3 stops. The bracketed exposures are biased toward a sequence of brighter images when positive compensation is applied, while negative compensation results in a darker sequence.

Self-timer(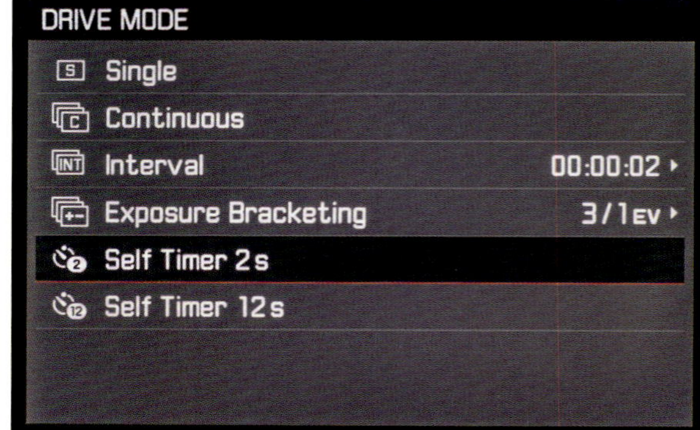)

You can set the Leica M10 to shoot 2 seconds or 12 seconds after you press the shutter-release button. This is not only useful if you want to appear in your photograph, but self-timer is an invaluable method for reducing the risk of camera shake when the camera is tripod mounted (even on a tripod there may be a slight vibration when you touch the shutter-release button). The only time this useful technique is not appropriate is when you need to shoot at a precise moment in time; it can be difficult to anticipate accurately when the self-timer should be activated, particularly when using the option.

When self-timer mode has been selected press the shutter-release button down fully to start the countdown. The LED on the front of the Leica M10 will flash every second until the shot is fired. A countdown in seconds will also be displayed on the LCD. To cancel self-timer during the countdown press MENU.

Notes

- When using **Auto ISO**, the ISO selected for the first shot in the bracketed sequence is used for all subsequent shots.

- To shoot a bracketed sequence you only need to press the shutter-release button once; the Leica M10 will shoot the sequence automatically. Exposure bracketing remains on until a new drive mode is selected.

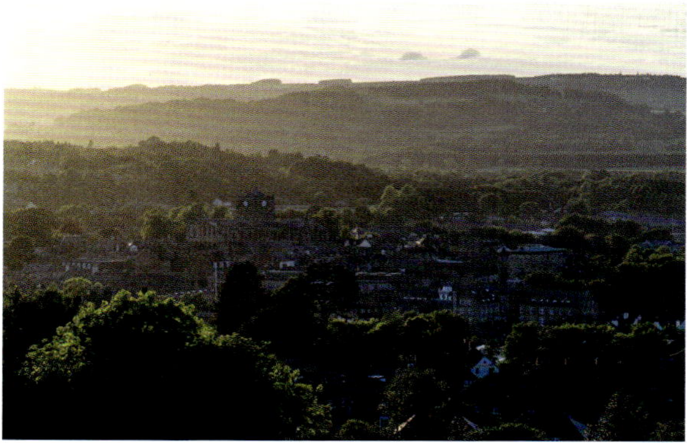

-2 STOPS (UNDEREXPOSED)

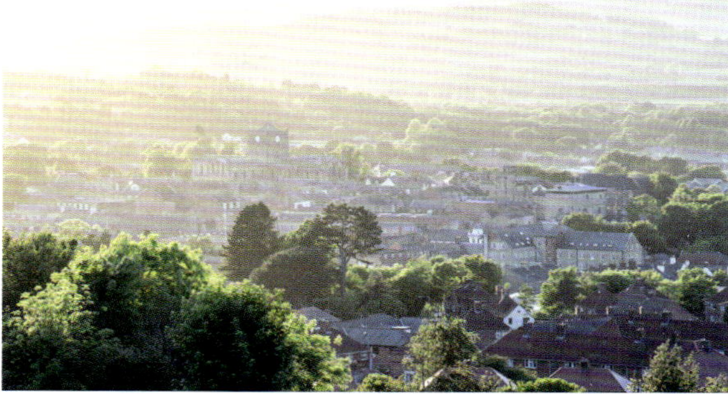

+2 STOPS (OVEREXPOSED)

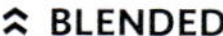 **BLENDED**

Shooting a bracketed sequence of exposures at ±2 stops helped me retain detail in both the highlights (above left), and shadows (above right), and then to produce a blended image using Adobe Lightroom (below).

⌄ BLENDED RESULT

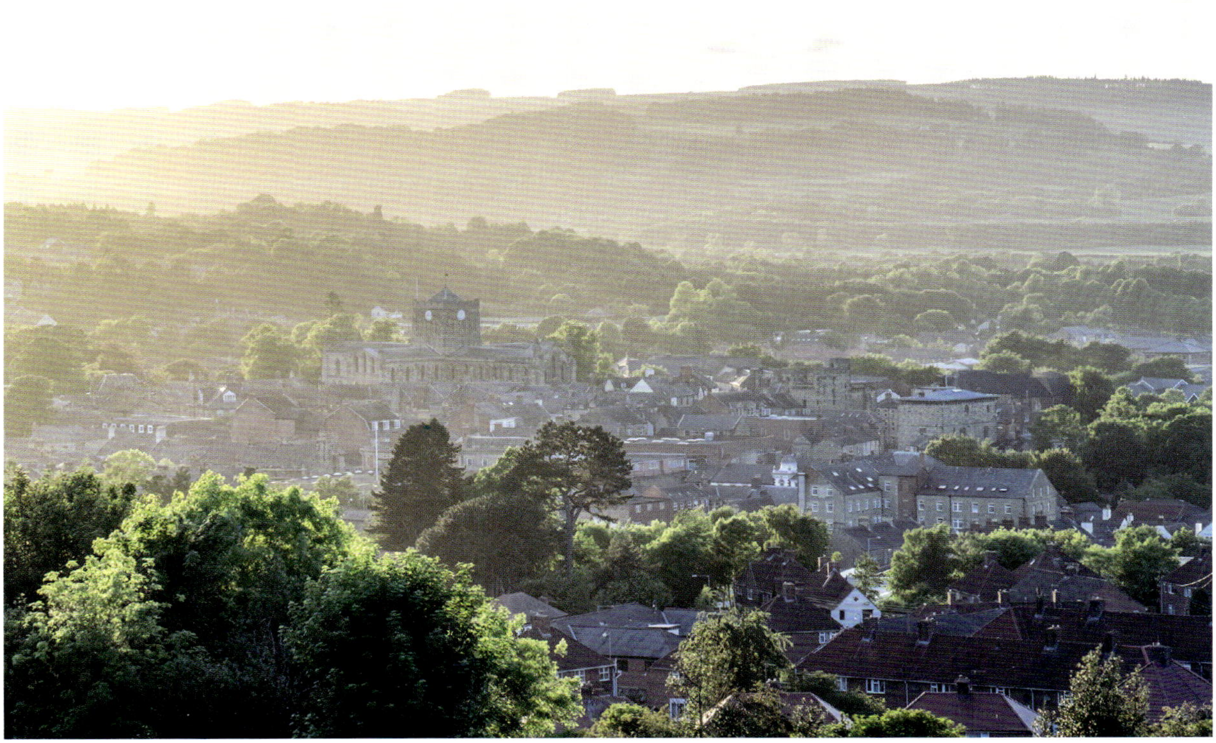

When you use the viewfinder the metering used to determine exposure is—by default—through-the-lens (TTL) center-weighted metering. Light that passes through the lens (hence TTL) is reflected from gray patches on the shutter blades to a light-metering cell inside the camera: this is used to determine the "correct" exposure.

In Aperture Priority mode, as you select the aperture the Leica M10 automatically adjusts the shutter speed based on this exposure reading. The selected shutter speed is shown in the LED display in the viewfinder. In Manual exposure mode you set both the aperture and the shutter speed. A series of indicators in the viewfinder can be used to determine how close to the standard exposure or otherwise your settings are.

With the Leica M10 switched on, the exposure meter is activated by pressing the shutter-release button down to the mid point. The meter will remain active for 30 seconds once the shutter-release button has been released. (If you change composition in Aperture Priority mode the meter will update the exposure if the light levels change as you move.) When the viewfinder indicators are unlit the Leica M10 is in standby mode.

The Leica M10's center-weighted metering pattern measures the reflected light of a scene, biasing the metering heavily toward the center. This has advantages and disadvantages and can take some getting used to, particularly if you are used to a more automated DSLR or mirrorless camera.

The big advantage of center-weighted metering is its consistency. Once you are used to how it works—and how it can be fooled in certain situations—you can anticipate and solve problems before they occur.

In general, center-weighted metering works well if your subject fills the metering area; head-and-shoulder portraits are a good example of the type of subject this metering pattern works well with.

Center-weighted metering works less well with scenes that are lit in a complex way, particularly if the main subject is outside the metering zone. In these situations you could use exposure lock to meter from one area of a scene before re-composing to shoot the desired composition (see page 46). Exposure compensation is also a useful tool when center-weighted metering produces unexpected exposures (see page 42).

⌄ BIAS

This graphic shows the metering pattern of center-weighted metering when using the viewfinder. The darker the patch, the heavier the metering bias.

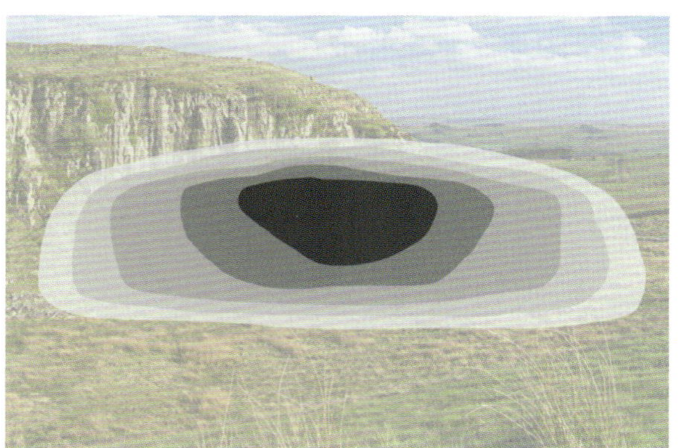

» CENTRAL

This is the type of subject center-weighted metering works well with—a central subject with a reasonably average tonal range.

Notes
- A reflective lightmeter (as used in the Leica M10) measures light that has been reflected back from the measured scene. This is opposed to incident lightmeters that measure the light that falls onto a scene. Incident meters are generally more accurate, but once you understand the principals of reflective lightmeters, their shortcomings can be compensated for. See chapter 8 for details.

- Exposure metering is not available in Bulb mode.

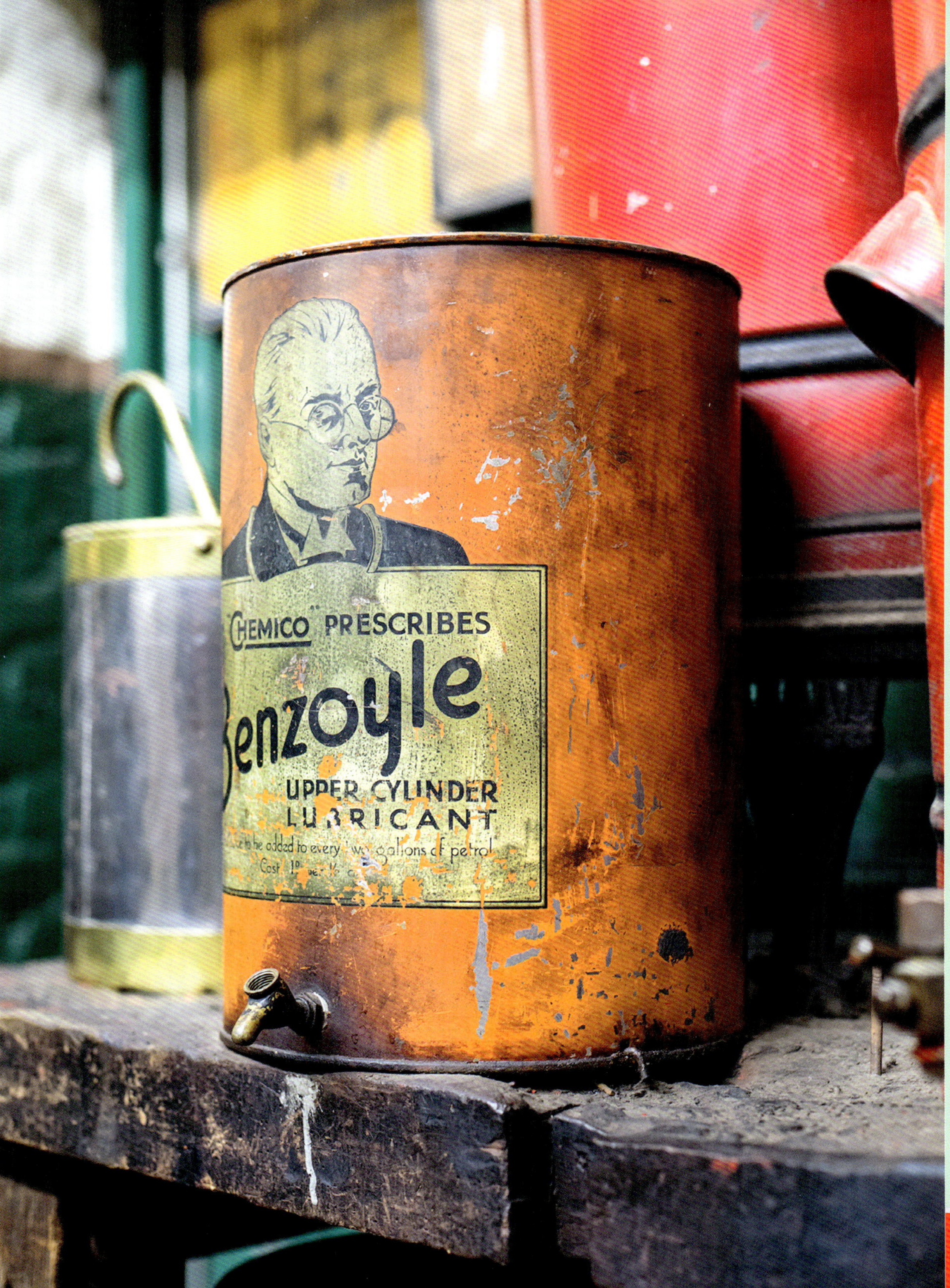
CHEMICO PRESCRIBES
Benzoyle
UPPER CYLINDER
LUBRICANT

› Live View metering options

› Metering memory lock

If you switch to Live View you can access additional metering options, as it is the image sensor that is used to determine exposure. As well as center-weighted you can opt for Multi-field and spot. These options are found under **Exposure Metering Mode** on the Main Menu (page 1).

In Live View, **Center-weighted** works the same way as the viewfinder metering.

Multi-field (the equivalent to Matrix and Evaluative metering on Nikon and Canon cameras respectively) divides the scene into a grid of zones, with each zone metered independently. This information is then assessed by the Leica M10, which attempts to predict what sort of scene you're shooting (such as a landscape or portrait) based on the distribution of areas of brightness. The final exposure is then calculated using this information. Theoretically, this should make Multi-field more reliable than center-weighted metering and this is often the case, unless you have a feel for how center-weighted metering works. However, Multi-field lacks the consistency of center-weighted metering, making it difficult to predict how the camera will meter a scene.

Finally, **Spot** metering measures a small circle at the center of the scene, shown on the LCD. Spot metering is most useful when you want to meter from a small area of the scene, such as a spotlit performer at a concert.

When shooting in Aperture Priority it is often useful to lock the exposure and then re-compose without the exposure changing. This lets you meter from one part of a scene using either center-weighted or spot metering, without the exposure being affected by the light falling on another. This is achieved on the Leica M10 using the metering memory lock. Metering memory lock works when using either the viewfinder or Live View, but it is not ideally suited to Multi-field metering when using the latter.

1) In Aperture Priority, aim the camera at the part of the scene you wish to meter from.

2) Press the shutter-release button to the midway point to activate the metering and save the reading. Keep the shutter-release button held at this point. A small dot will be displayed in the viewfinder to indicate metering memory lock has been activated.

3) Move the camera and press the shutter-release button down fully to compose and capture your shot.

›› LOCKED
Locking the exposure after taking an exposure reading from a gray card (see page 165) is a very useful technique. It is particularly useful when your central subject is not an average tone and you are using center-weighted metering.

Notes
- Metering memory lock is cancelled if you lift your finger from the shutter-release button.

- Do not change the aperture when memory lock is activated as this will cause an error in the exposure.

EXPOSURE METERING MODE

- ⊡ Spot
- ⊡ Center-weighted
- ⊚ Multi-field

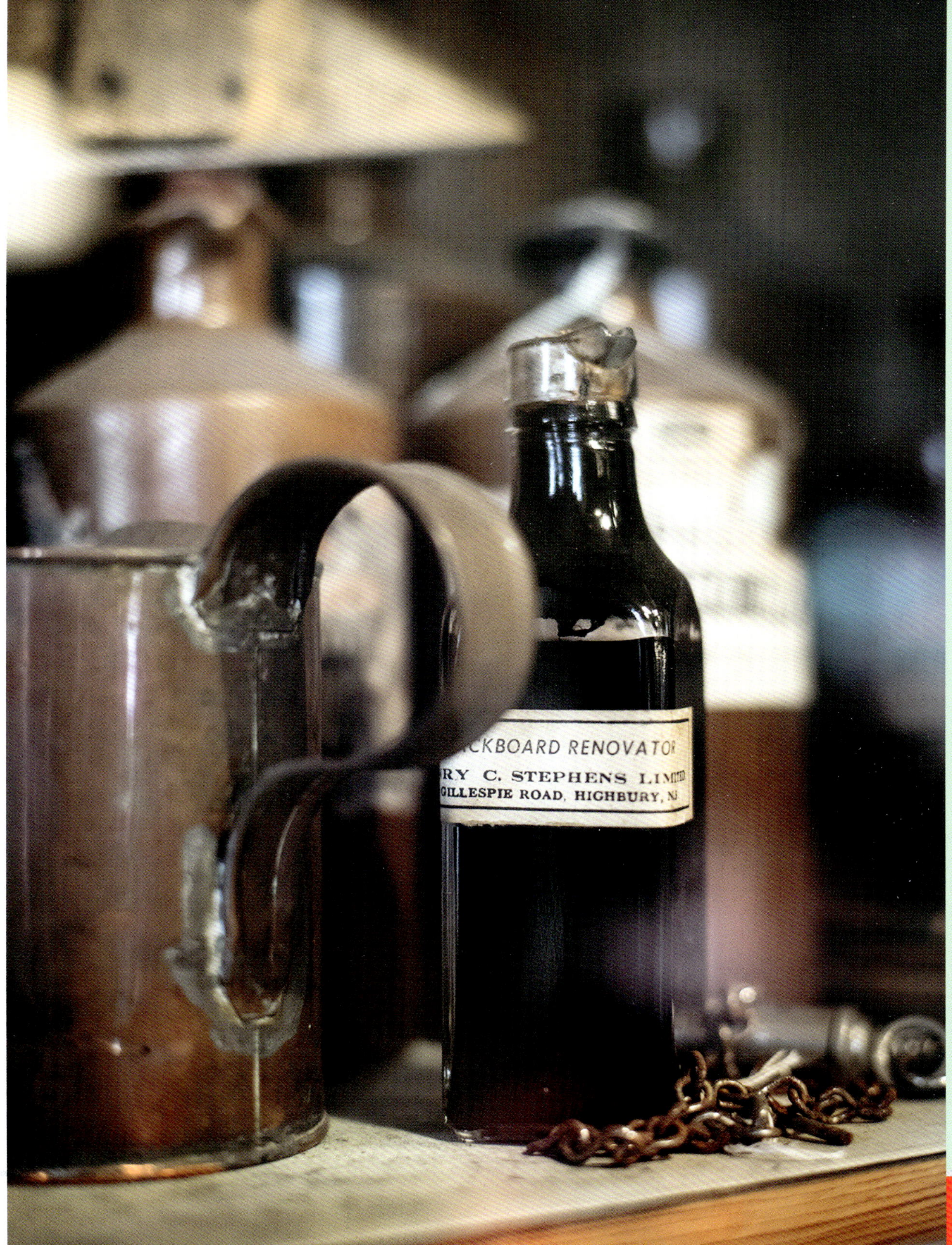

CKBOARD RENOVATOR
RY C. STEPHENS LIMITED
GILLESPIE ROAD, HIGHBURY, N.5

» ISO

ISO is an international standard that determines how much light is required by a digital sensor to make a correct exposure: the higher the ISO value, the less light is needed to make a correctly exposed image. This means that by increasing the ISO value you can set a faster shutter speed, smaller aperture, or both.

Increasing the ISO does not strictly speaking make the sensor more "sensitive" to light. An increased ISO setting amplifies the signal from the sensor to extract as much data as possible in order to make an image. However, this amplification is not perfect and causes what is known as image noise. Noise is seen as random spots of color and reduces the amount of fine detail present in the image. The higher the ISO setting—and so the greater the amplification—the more that noise is seen across the image. The ISO setting you use therefore is often a compromise between the desired shutter and aperture settings and image quality.

Increasing the ISO setting also has the effect of lowering the dynamic range of the sensor. As you increase ISO your exposures will need to be more accurate as there will be less scope later to correct exposure in postproduction. However, the Leica M10 has a thoroughly modern sensor that copes better at higher ISO settings than the Leica M9 and M Typ 240. Image quality is ultimately compromised at the highest ISO settings, but perfectly acceptable results are possible at ISO 6400 or even ISO 10,000. The lowest setting on the Leica M10 is ISO 100.

» FLEXIBILITY
Shoot at ISO 100 to maximize image quality and, perhaps more importantly, give you more flexibility to alter exposure and color in postproduction without compromising image quality.

Notes
- Dynamic range defines the ability of a sensor to capture usable image data in both the shadows and highlights before that image data is compromised by factors such as noise.

- Noise is at its most visible when an image is viewed at 100% and at the maximum resolution produced by the Leica M10. Shrink an image down (for display online, for example) and the appearance of noise is reduced. If you know that image will not be used at maximum resolution then using higher ISO settings may be less of a restriction.

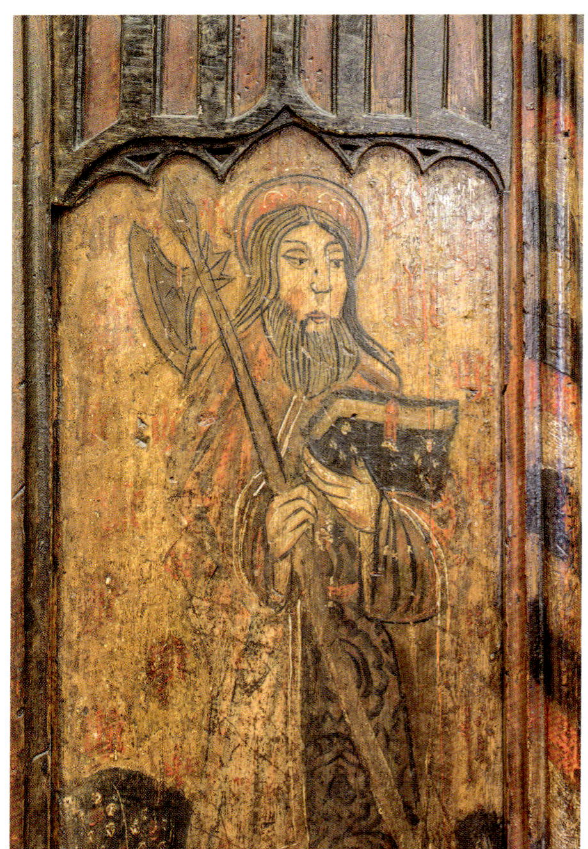

› The ISO dial

The Leica M10 has a manual dial for setting ISO, which is a design nod to Leica film cameras such as the M7 that had the film wind-on lever in a similar position. There are seven ISO values that can be selected via the dial, covering the range ISO 100–6400 in full stop increments. The dial also has an (A) Auto ISO option and (M) Manual ISO.

Auto ISO dynamically changes ISO according to the ambient light levels. Typically, Auto ISO is used when handholding a camera to reduce the risk of camera shake. There are options on the Main Menu (page 1) under **ISO Setup** that let you configure the behavior of Auto ISO—see pages 70–71. Auto ISO should not be used when shooting with ND filters (or any other exposure-altering filters) as it will automatically increase the ISO whenever such a filter is used, negating the effect of the filter. A fixed ISO is preferable.

Manual ISO sets ISO to the value chosen via **M-ISO** on the **ISO Setup** menu. The advantage of using Manual ISO rather than selecting an ISO value on the dial is choice; you can choose from a greater range of ISO values using **M-ISO**—as well as intermediate ISO values—than when using the dial.

Setting ISO

1) In shooting mode lift the ISO dial until it clicks into the raised position (a red band should be visible at the base of the ISO dial to show that it has been raised fully).

2) Turn the dial so the required ISO setting aligns with the dial index mark.

3) Push the dial back down to the lowered position.

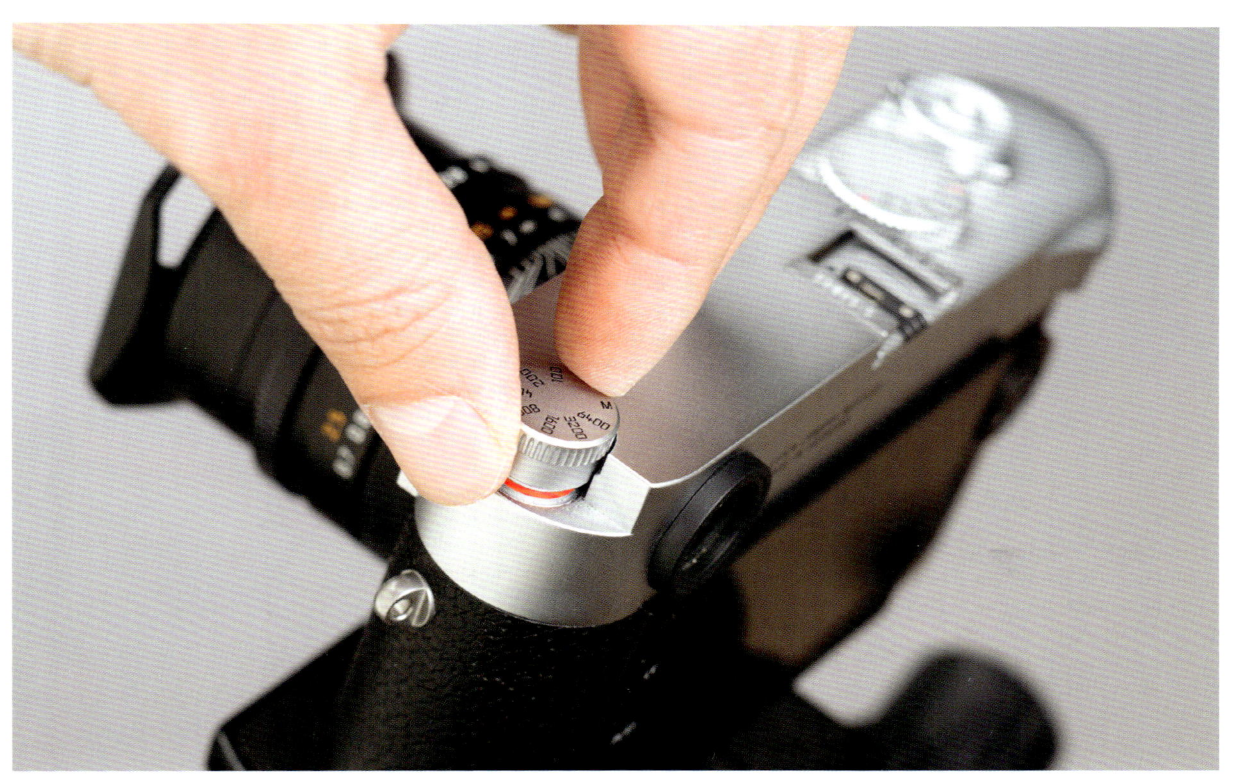

There are two types of noise: luminance and chroma. Luminance noise adds a distinctive "grain" to a picture, whereas chroma noise is seen as blotches of random color across the image. Of the two, luminance noise is usually less objectionable and can be dealt with very effectively in postproduction using noise-reduction techniques. Chroma noise is harder to remove and for that reason any ISO setting that exacerbates chroma noise is best avoided unless there is no other option. Noise reduction is a mixed blessing, though. If it is applied too heavily it can smear fine details and texture, and make an image look artificially smooth and textureless.

On the Leica M10, some luminance noise is visible at ISO 1600, but it is not objectionable and easily reduced. From that point on luminance noise increases steadily with ISO. Chroma noise also begins to appear at ISO 1600, but it too is easily reduced at this stage. For non-critical work, ISO 6400 is more than usable, although noise begins to smother fine details in the image. Above ISO 6400—when M-ISO is used to set ISO—noise is very visible and banding can generally be seen across images. ISO 50,000 should only be used as a last resort, when the available maximum aperture of your lens is too large and you need a particularly fast shutter speed.

Another drawback with using a higher ISO setting is that there's less scope for exposure adjustment during postproduction. This is particularly true if you want to increase exposure due to underexposure at the shooting stage. A 1-stop increase in exposure in postproduction is effectively the same as a 1-stop increase in ISO in terms of the visibility of noise. Therefore it is more important to expose accurately when using a higher ISO.

›› LOW ISO
Noise quickly builds in images once you start to use ISO settings above 6400. Compare the image above, taken at the almost noise-free setting of ISO 100, with the image below it, which was shot at ISO 50,000.

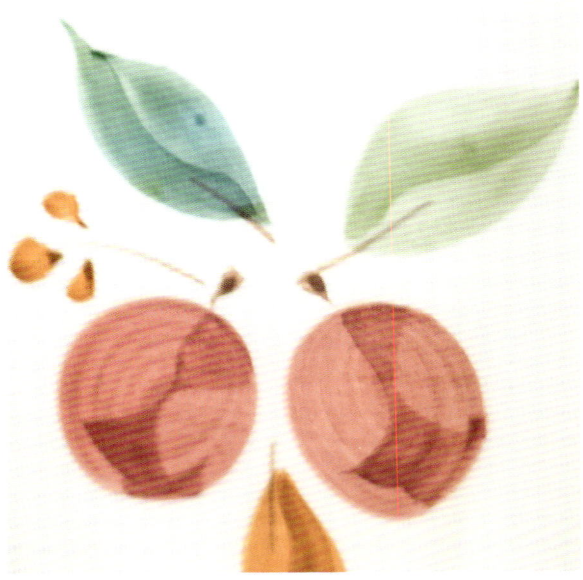

⌃ ›› **ISO 100**

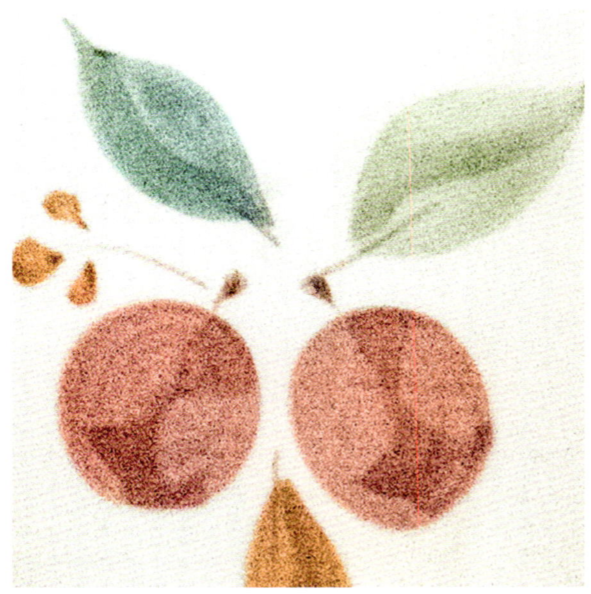

⌃ ›› **ISO 50,000**

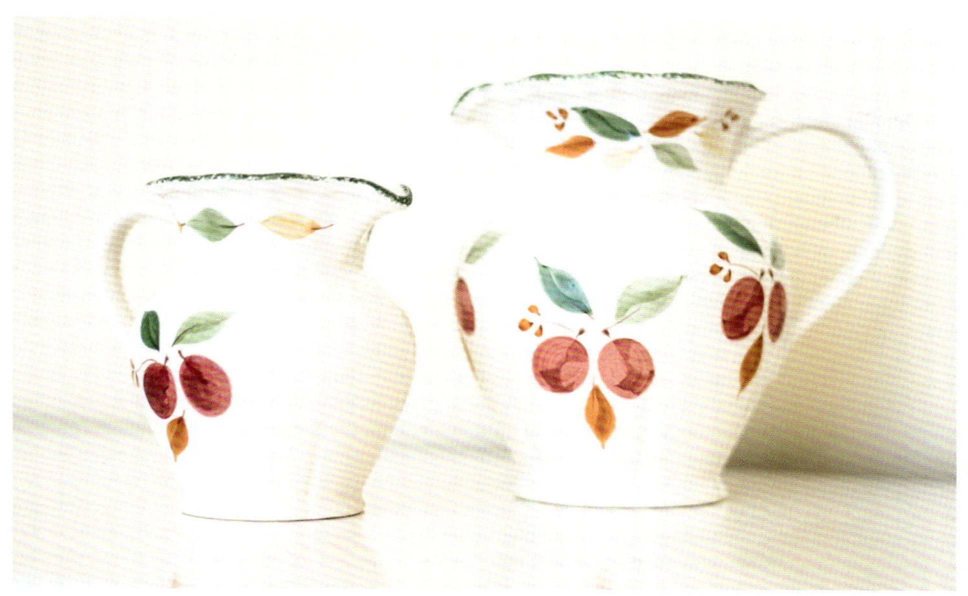

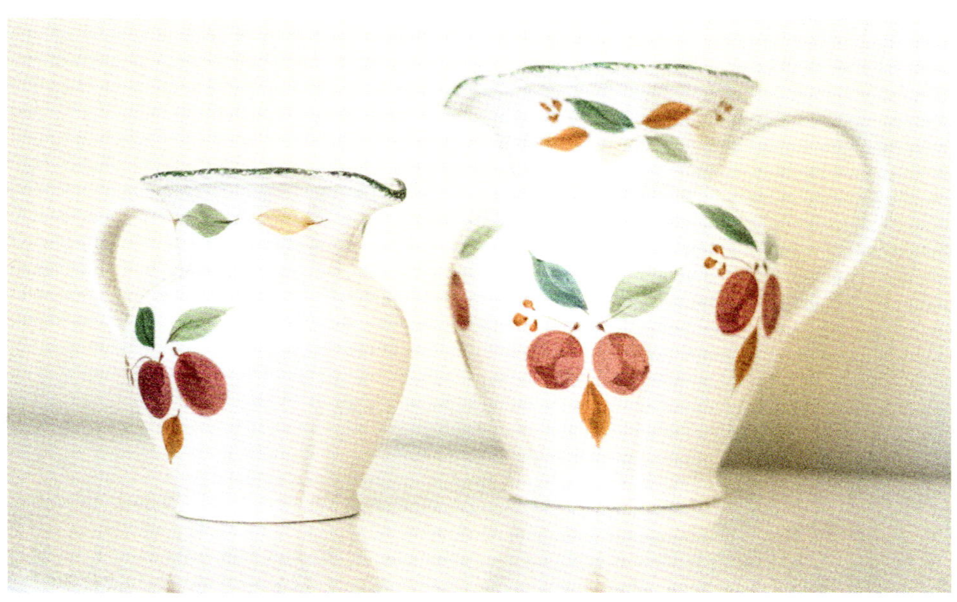

» HISTOGRAMS

The Leica M10's LCD is not ideal for assessing exposure; ambient lighting conditions can fool you into believing an image is lighter or darker than it actually is. A better—and more objective—method is to use a histogram (the Leica M10 can display a histogram in Live View and in playback). An accurate assessment of an image histogram means you can instantly see the tonal range of your images and, if required, reshoot applying exposure compensation to adjust that range.

A histogram is a graph that records the complete range of tones in an image from pure black at the left edge to pure white at the right (with the midtones in the center). There is no ideal shape for a histogram, but if possible you should avoid clipping either edge. Once a histogram has been clipped there is no tonal information there that can be adjusted later in post-production.

For example, an area of shadow that is pure black (where the pixels have RGB values of 0,0,0) will have no texture. In postproduction you could adjust those pixels so that they become dark gray instead of black, but you will not recover any image detail. The same is essentially true of the highlights, although when shooting Raw there is generally a small degree of headroom in the highlights that allows some detail to be recovered.

The vertical axis of the histogram shows the number of pixels of a particular tone in the image. It is not important if the histogram appears to be clipped at the top, this is merely an indication that you have a large number of pixels of that tone in the image.

To check the histogram of your image during playback press ● to view the detailed playback information. The Live View histogram can be switched on via **Histogram** on the **Capture Assistants** sub-menu page (see page 83).

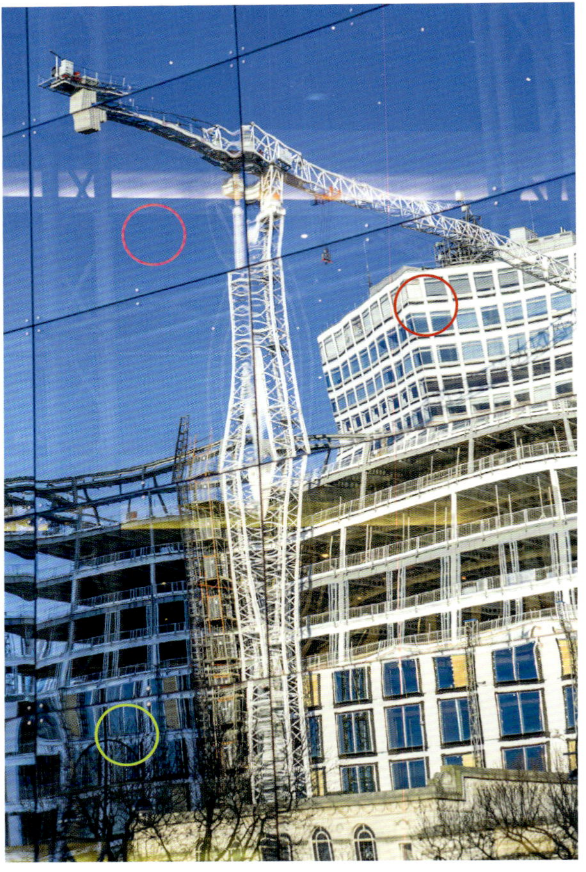

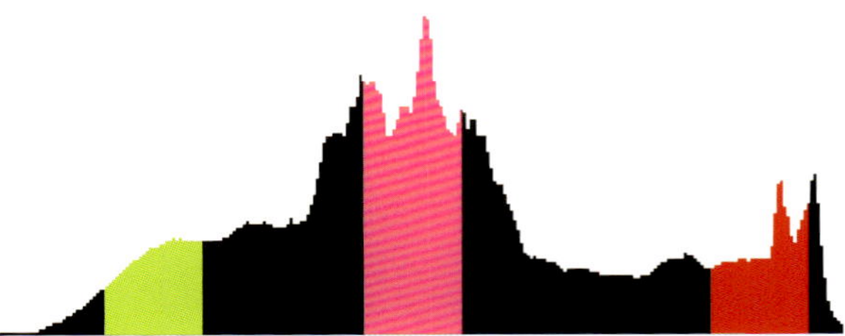

⌃ MEASUREMENT
After some practice you can start to match areas in a scene to the image histogram. In this instance the highlights are marked in red, the midtones in magenta, and the shadows in green.

› Exposing to the right

Shooting Raw gives you far more scope for postproduction correction to exposure than JPEG. However, even though the dynamic range of the Leica M10's sensor is wide, there are limits to the amount of adjustment that can be applied before image quality noticeably drops. A good example of this is noise seen when shadows are lightened in postproduction.

Accurate exposure is the key to producing pleasing JPEG images. However, Raw files can benefit from slight overexposure using a technique known as "exposing to the right" (ETTR). When using the technique, the image should be exposed so that the histogram is biased to the right, but not so far that the highlights are clipped. The resulting image will generally look washed out, but there will be more usable shadow information than there would be at the "correct" exposure. Images are then adjusted in postproduction, typically by reducing the exposure and increasing the contrast.

Notes

- ETTR is often not possible when a scene is high in contrast. In this type of scene there is little scope for exposure adjustment without compromising the highlights.

- Adding positive exposure compensation is the easiest way to expose to the right when shooting in Aperture Priority. When shooting in Manual mode you can adjust any of the exposure controls (shutter speed, aperture, or ISO).

⌄ ETTR

Low-contrast scenes are ideal for the ETTR technique. Compare the unprocessed image (below left) with the image that has been normalized and processed to taste (below right).

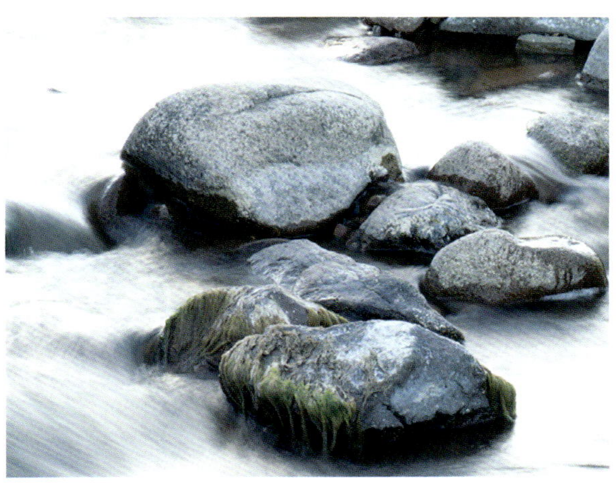
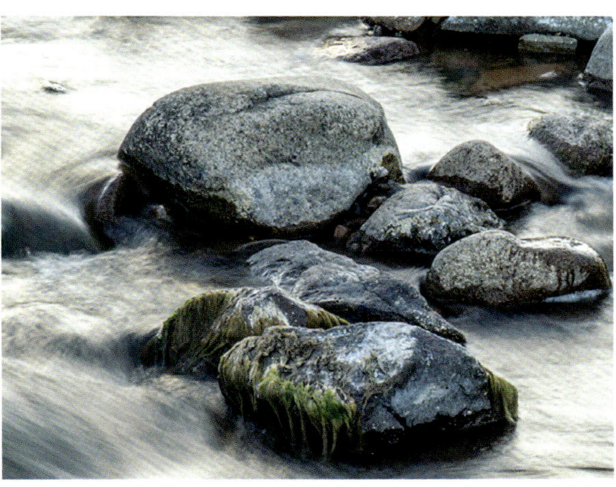

› Shutter speed dial

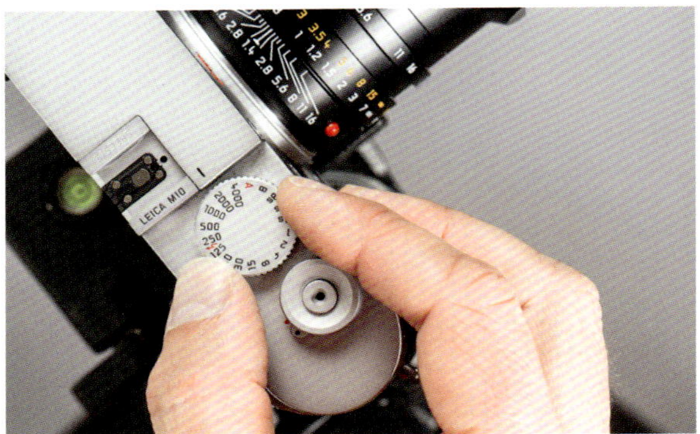

› Lens aperture ring

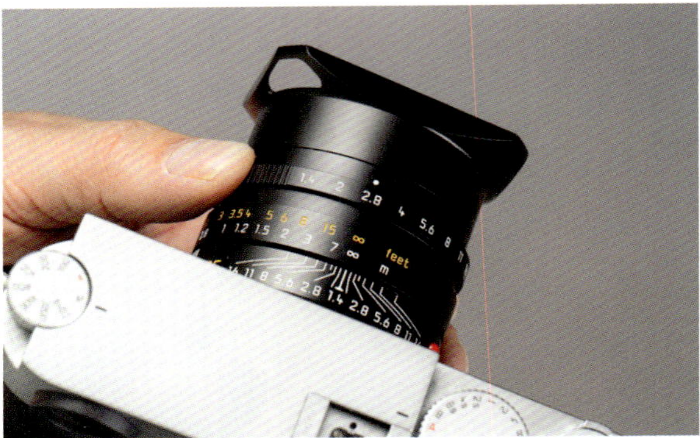

The required exposure mode or shutter speed is selected by lining up the mode letter or shutter speed value with the black line etched on the camera body at the left of the dial. The dial can be turned in both directions through 360°.

When the shutter speed dial is set to **A** the Leica M10 is set to Aperture Priority. In this mode the Leica M10's metering system—once activated by lightly pressing the shutter-release button to stage one—sets the shutter speed automatically according to the current aperture and ISO setting.

Move the shutter speed dial to **B** and the Leica M10 is set to Bulb mode. This mode allows you to set exposures manually up to a maximum of 125 seconds by holding or locking down the shutter-release button.

Selecting a specific shutter speed on the dial sets the Leica M10 to Manual exposure mode. In this mode the shutter speeds available range from 1/4000 sec.–8 seconds in ½-stop increments (only full-stop increments are shown on the dial; ½-stop values are selected by moving the dial half way between two shutter speed values). In Manual exposure mode you must set both the shutter speed and the aperture value using either exposure readings taken from the Leica M's built-in meter or measured using an external exposure meter.

The aperture on Leica M-mount lenses is set by manually turning the aperture ring on the lens. Leica M-mount lenses vary in the range of aperture values available, but it is the maximum aperture available that varies the most: the difference between the fastest Leica lens (50mm Noctilux-M f/0.95) and the slowest (28mm Summaron-M f/5.6) is 5 stops. However, the difference between the minimum apertures of Leica lenses varies by only 1 stop: the minimum setting is either f/16 or f/22.

As with the shutter speed dial, only full-stop increments are shown on the aperture ring, ½-stop values are selected by moving the ring half way between two settings.

> **Note**
> • When using flash, the fastest speed you can use is 1/180 sec. This is known as the "flash sync speed," and is marked on the shutter speed dial by the red ⚡ symbol.

› Aperture Priority

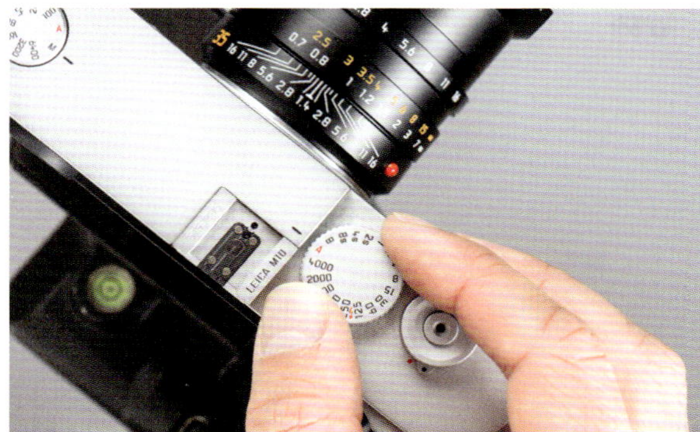

When the Leica M10 is set to A, it chooses a shutter speed between 125 seconds and 1/4000 sec. The shutter speed chosen by the Leica M10 is displayed in the viewfinder in ½-stop increments or on the LCD in Live View. Shutter speeds longer than 2 seconds will be counted down in seconds in the viewfinder after the shutter has fired.

There may be times when the required shutter speed is longer than 125 seconds or shorter than 1/4000 sec. On these occasions the required shutter speed exceeds the shutter speed range of the Leica; the shutter speed value shown in the viewfinder will flash as a warning that this has happened. You can still make an exposure (the camera will use the shutter speed shown flashing in the viewfinder), but you may find that the image is incorrectly exposed.

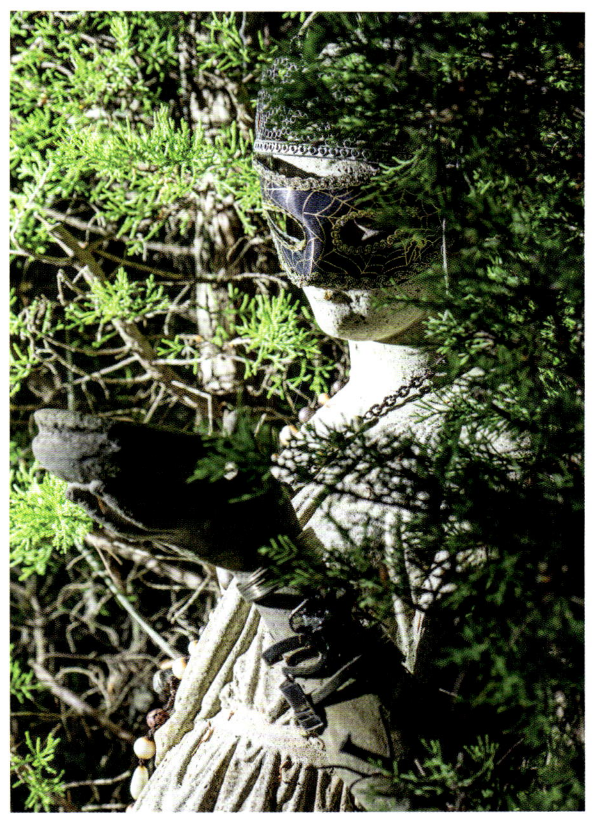

⌃ FLASH
Manual exposure is useful when shooting with flash. It means you can control the aperture and shutter speed independently, letting you control the exposure of the flash and ambient light respectively (see chapter 5 for more details).

› Manual exposure

The automation of Aperture Priority is useful in situations when there is less time to think about exposure, but when you switch to Manual exposure you are in full control of your photography.

Although this means that the chances of making an exposure error are greater, setting the exposure manually has a number of benefits. The main benefit is that you have greater creative freedom to adjust exposure to taste, including the choice of under- or overexposing an image beyond the 3-stop adjustment available when using exposure compensation.

Another benefit is consistency. Once you've set the required exposure it will not change, even if the level of reflectivity of the scene alters as you shoot. This is particularly useful when shooting sequences of images to combine into a timelapse movie or stitch together to make a panoramic image.

In Manual exposure mode you can either use a handheld lightmeter to determine exposure or use the Leica M10's internal metering as a guide to the required shutter and aperture values.

Using Manual exposure

1) Activate the camera metering by pressing the shutter-release button down to the first stage.

2) Look through the viewfinder, maintaining light pressure on the shutter-release button as you do so. Use the table below to decipher the exposure information symbols at the bottom of the viewfinder.

3) If the exposure is not correct, adjust either the shutter speed dial or aperture ring to correct for the difference until only ● is displayed in the viewfinder.

4) Press the shutter-release button down fully to take the shot.

Exposure indicator	Explanation
▶	Underexposure by 1 stop or more
▶●	Underexposure by ½ stop
●	Correct exposure
●◀	Overexposure by ½ stop
◀	Overexposure by 1 stop or more

Notes
- The direction of the arrows in the viewfinder indicates the direction you need to turn the shutter speed dial or aperture ring to correct an exposure. For example, the underexposure warning ▶ requires you to turn either the aperture ring or the shutter dial to the right to open the aperture or increase the length of the shutter speed respectively.

- When light levels are low and the meter reading is outside the exposure meter's range, the left triangular LED flashes.

› B and T settings

The maximum exposure time when shooting using Manual exposure mode is 8 seconds. For exposures longer than this the Leica M10's B (Bulb) mode lets you hold the shutter open for up to 125 seconds.

To shoot using B you hold the shutter open by keeping the shutter-release button physically pressed down, releasing it to end the exposure. However, this is a slightly clunky method and runs the risk of knocking or moving the camera during the exposure. Shooting B is best achieved using a cable release, holding the plunger down with the locking collar to keep the shutter open.

An additional mode—T (Time)—is made available when B mode is used in conjunction with self-timer. To use T press down once on the shutter-release button to activate the self-timer. Once the self-timer countdown is complete the shutter opens and remains open until you press the shutter-release button once more. Again, this is something that is best done with a cable release (although you would not need to lock the cable release plunger as with B).

As exposure metering is disabled when the Leica M10 is set to B (and T) it is up to you to determine how long your exposure should be. The digital display in the viewfinder shows the time elapsed as an exposure is made.

Note
- Aperture Priority mode lets you use an exposure of up to 125 seconds, but you are limited to setting the exposure in ½-stop increments.

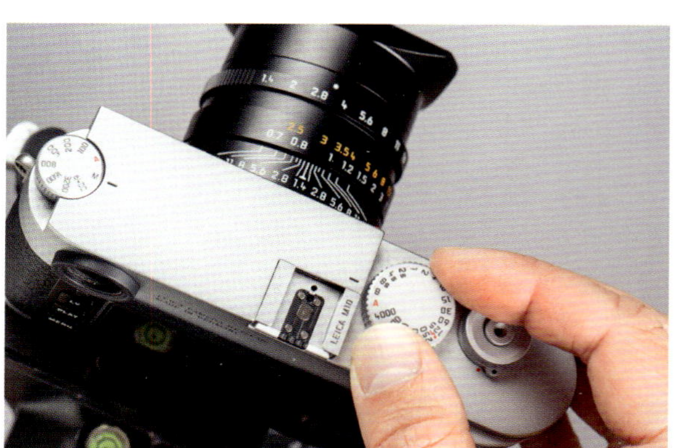

› Long exposure noise reduction

The sensor in a digital camera generates heat; the longer it is active, the greater the heat build up is. This heat can start to affect image quality in the form of long exposure noise, which is seen as randomly colored pixels scattered across an image. Long exposure noise gradually increases over time, and with a sufficiently long exposure the number of "hot" pixels can make an image unusable.

The solution is called "dark-frame subtraction." This is applied automatically to exposures longer than 1 second (and cannot be turned off). Dark-frame subtraction relies on the fact that long exposure noise patterns tend to be consistent over a set period of time.

When you shoot a long exposure, the Leica makes a second exposure of exactly the same duration, but the shutter is not opened. Theoretically, this second exposure should be completely black. However, if any "hot" pixels are present, they can be detected by the Leica M10, which then digitally subtracts them from the original exposure.

⌄ FILTRATION

A common way of forcing extended shutter speeds is to use a neutral density (ND) filter. A 10-stop filter was used here to extend the shutter speed from 1/30 sec. to 30 seconds.

In practical terms this means that you have to allow for a doubling of the time it takes to shoot a long exposure (your Leica M10 will not be ready to shoot again until both exposures have been completed). The message *Attention Noise Reduction* and a countdown of the time required will be displayed on the LCD. As the exposure time is doubled, the drain on the battery is higher, so it is a good idea to start with a freshly charged battery and/or have a charge spare handy.

Note
- You can turn off the Leica M10 during the noise reduction process. However, the camera will not fully power down until noise reduction is complete.

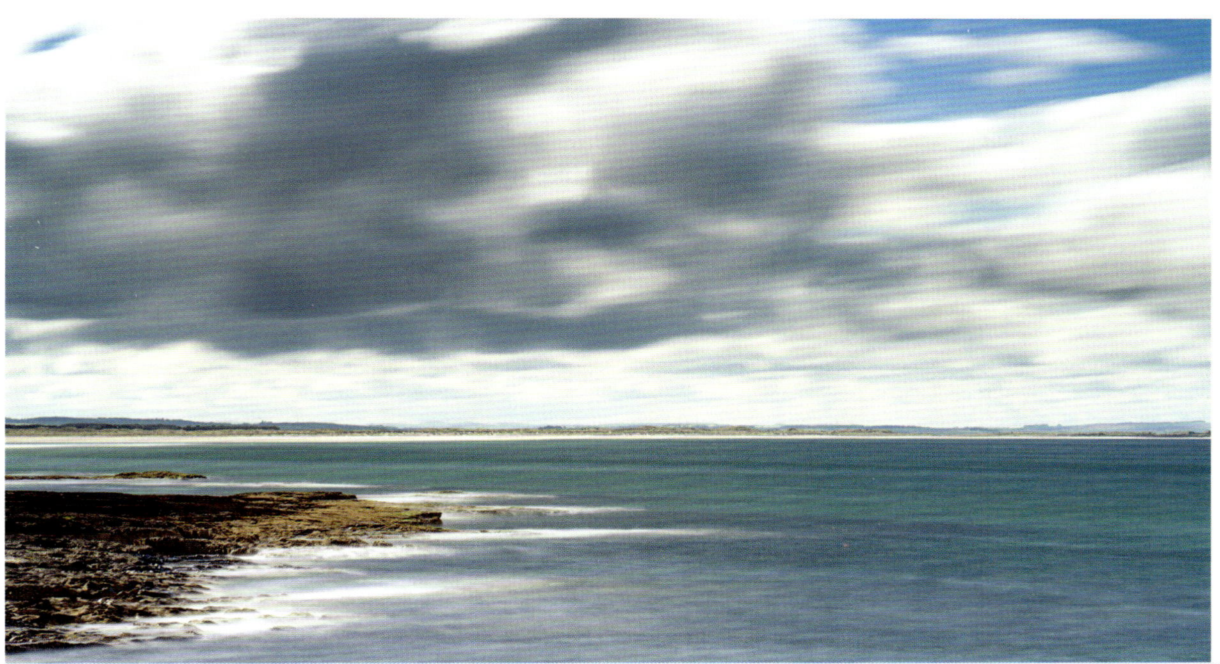

» IMAGE PLAYBACK

Once an exposure has been made and the image has been written to the memory card, the image will be displayed automatically on the LCD for five seconds. This length of time can be altered—or automatic playback switched off entirely—by selecting **Auto Review** on the Main Menu (page 2). Automatic playback can also be cancelled by pressing lightly on the shutter-release button.

You can view images at any point (even if **Auto review** is set to off) by pressing PLAY. There are two ways to view an image, which can be toggled by pressing ● during playback. The first view shows a clear view of the image, while the second overlays shooting information on the image, including the degree of exposure compensation applied, histogram, and the lens used to shoot the image (when a lens has a 6-bit identification code on the lens mount). This view also shows a blinking warning when areas of the image are over- or underexposed; overexposed areas blink red, while underexposed areas blink blue.

By pressing ◀ / ▶ you can skip through and view all the images on the memory card; pressing ◀ skips chronologically backward, pressing ▶ skips forward. Holding down ◀ / ▶ for two seconds or longer will increase the rate at which the images skip. Once you reach one end of the images on the card, the Leica M10 will loop round and start again from the other.

› Magnifying images

Magnifying an image in playback is a useful way to check if it is acceptably sharp. By turning ○ to the right the central section of the image is enlarged. You can then use ✧ to move around the magnified image. The transparent gray box at the bottom left corner of the LCD represents the image as a whole and the light gray rectangle within this box shows the proportion of the image that is being displayed and your current position within the image. Turn ○ to the left to zoom back out until the entire image is shown on the LCD once more.

When an image is magnified it is still possible to jump between images on the memory card. Hold down PLAY and press either ◀ / ▶. The next image you jump to will be displayed at the same magnification.

Notes
- Press ▲ to add a rating star to an image and ▼ to remove the rating. Ratings can be used to protect images from deletion.

- Typically you would see either the underexposure warning or the overexposure warning. Seeing both together is an indication that a scene is high contrast; producing a usable image means reducing this contrast. This could be achieved through the use of extra lighting (to add light to the darkest areas of the scene), or through the use of a filter such as a graduated ND filter (to lower the intensity of a bright sky in a landscape, for example).

- The playback histogram can be turned **On** or **Off** by setting **Capture Assistants** > **Histogram** on the Main Menu (page 2).

- The exposure warning is turned **On** or **Off** and the sensitivity of the warning adjusted via the **Capture Assistants** > **Exposure Clipping** screen.

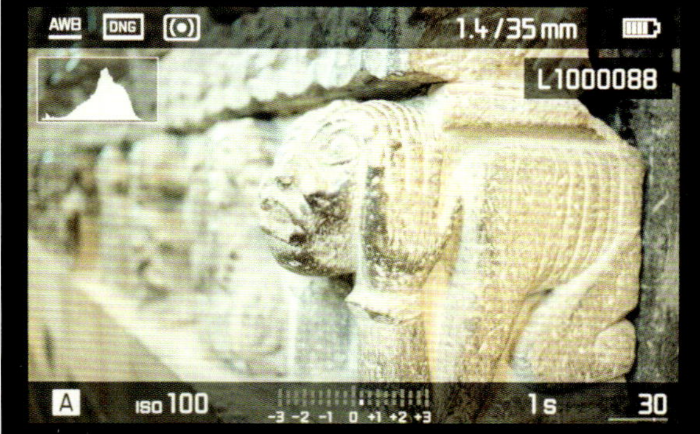

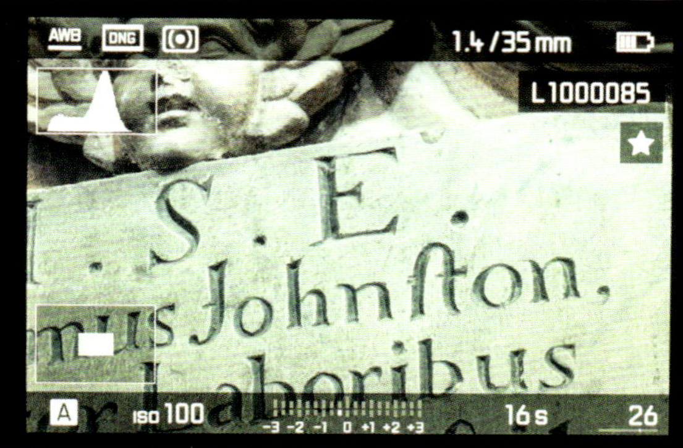

Note

- A lack of sharpness is typically the result of either a focusing error or camera shake. Incorrect focus is something that is generally more common when using a large aperture and/or a long focal length lens. Camera shake is more likely when handholding the camera and using a slow shutter speed.

› Image index

In non-magnified image playback, turning **O** once to the left will show an index of 12 small image thumbnails. Turn **O** to the left once more and an index of 20 smaller thumbnails will be displayed. In both cases the currently selected image is outlined in red.

You can highlight any of the thumbnail images using ✧ and press ● to display the selected image full screen. Use ▲ / ▼ to navigate multiple screens of thumbnails.

You can also return to full screen display by turning **O** once to the right when in 12 image view (or twice to the right in 20 image view).

When viewing the 20 image thumbnail screen, turning **O** to the left once more will highlight all the thumbnails. You can then use ◄ / ► to scroll more quickly through the images on your memory card. Turn **O** to the right to enable individual image selection.

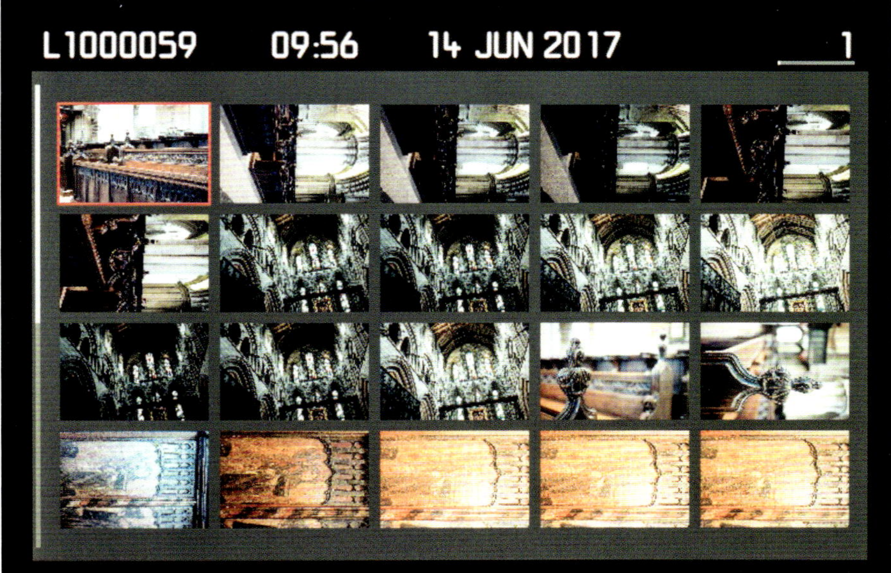

Warning!

If the memory card does not contain images shot on the Leica M10 *Attention No media file to display* will be shown on the LCD.

Note

- The detailed image view including histogram is not available when viewing image thumbnails.

› The PLAY button

Pressing PLAY has different effects depending on what is currently displayed on the LCD during playback. See the grid below for details.

Situation	Result after pressing PLAY
Image playback	LCD is turned off
Magnified image/Image index	Currently selected image is displayed full screen
Play Menu is displayed	Play Menu is cancelled

› Deleting images

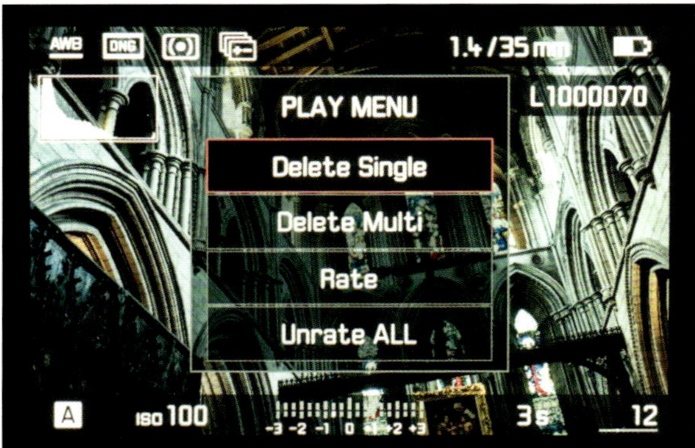

When viewing images in playback you can delete images individually or as a group. Once an image has been deleted it cannot be restored by the Leica M10, so care must be taken to ensure that images are not deleted accidentally. Should this happen it is usually still possible to recover these images using commercially available data-recovery software, but this must be done before you create further images as they may permanently overwrite the deleted files.

Deleting individual images

1) Press PLAY and find the image you want to delete.

2) Press MENU once the required image is displayed on the LCD.

3) Highlight **Delete Single** on the Play Menu and press ●. The image will be instantly deleted from the memory card. Note there is no "are you sure?" confirmation step that would allow you to change your mind when deleting single images.

4) Navigate to other images you want to delete and repeat step 3.

5) Press MENU to return to standard playback.

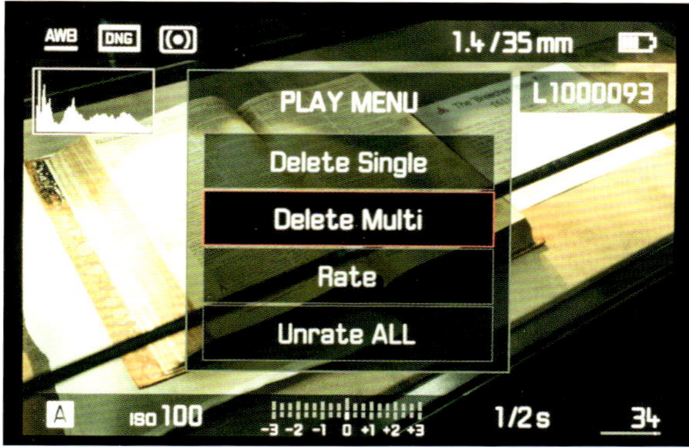

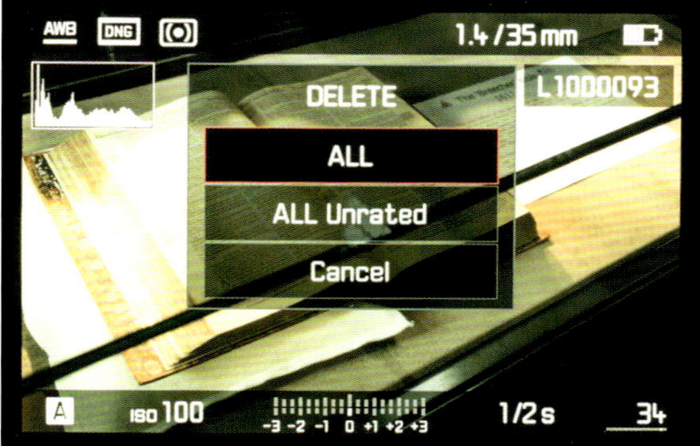

Deleting multiple images

1) Press PLAY followed by MENU.

2) Select **Delete Multi** from the Play Menu.

3) Select **ALL** to delete all the images on the memory card. Select **Yes** to complete the deletion process or **No** to return to the **DELETE** options menu.

4) Select **ALL Unrated** to delete images that have not had a rating star applied. Select **Yes** to complete the deletion process or **No** to return to the **DELETE** options menu.

5) Select **Cancel** to return to the Play Menu without deleting any images.

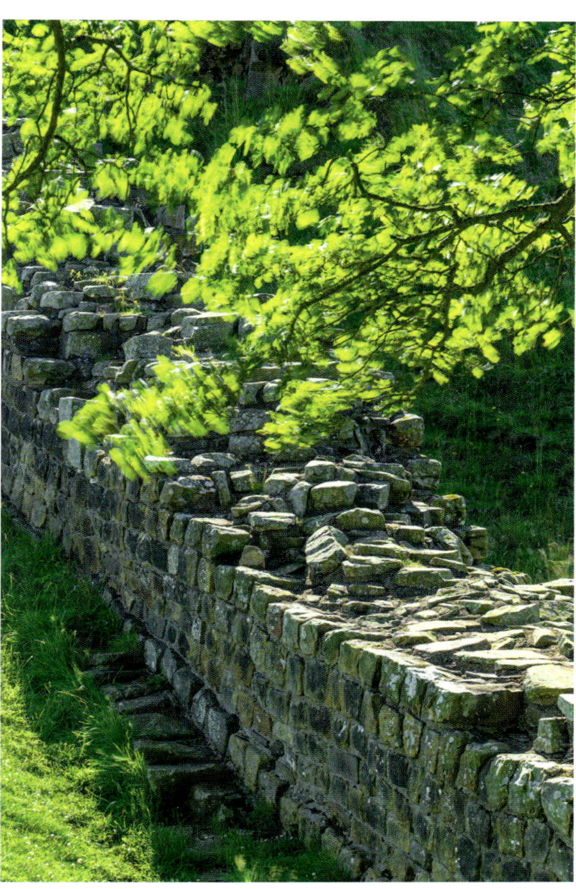

⌃ RANDOM MOVEMENT
When you shoot a subject that moves in a "random" way, such as tree branches blowing in the wind, you may need to take multiple shots before you get the perfect one. I do not delete images in-camera, preferring to look at a sequence on my computer monitor before I make a decision about which image works best.

CHAPTER 3
MENUS

The Leica M10's menu system is used to set the non-mechanical functions of the camera. It is well worth familiarizing yourself with the menu system as it will help you get the most out of your camera.

The Leica M10 essentially has two menus. The first is the Favorites menu, where frequently used menu options can be "stored" as a shortcut. The second menu is the Main Menu, which features all of the options available to tweak the camera to your specific needs.

Although the Main Menu is comprehensive, it is arguably in an eccentric order, which is why the Favorites menu is so useful. Once your Leica M10 has been set up to suit your needs you will find less need to access the menus, although there will be occasions when you are presented with unique photographic challenges; a working knowledge of the menu system will be invaluable in helping you rise to those challenges.

›› CAN YOU CLEAR THIS AWAY?
Mastering the technical side of photography means you can spend your time looking for photo opportunities rather than thinking about how to shoot them.

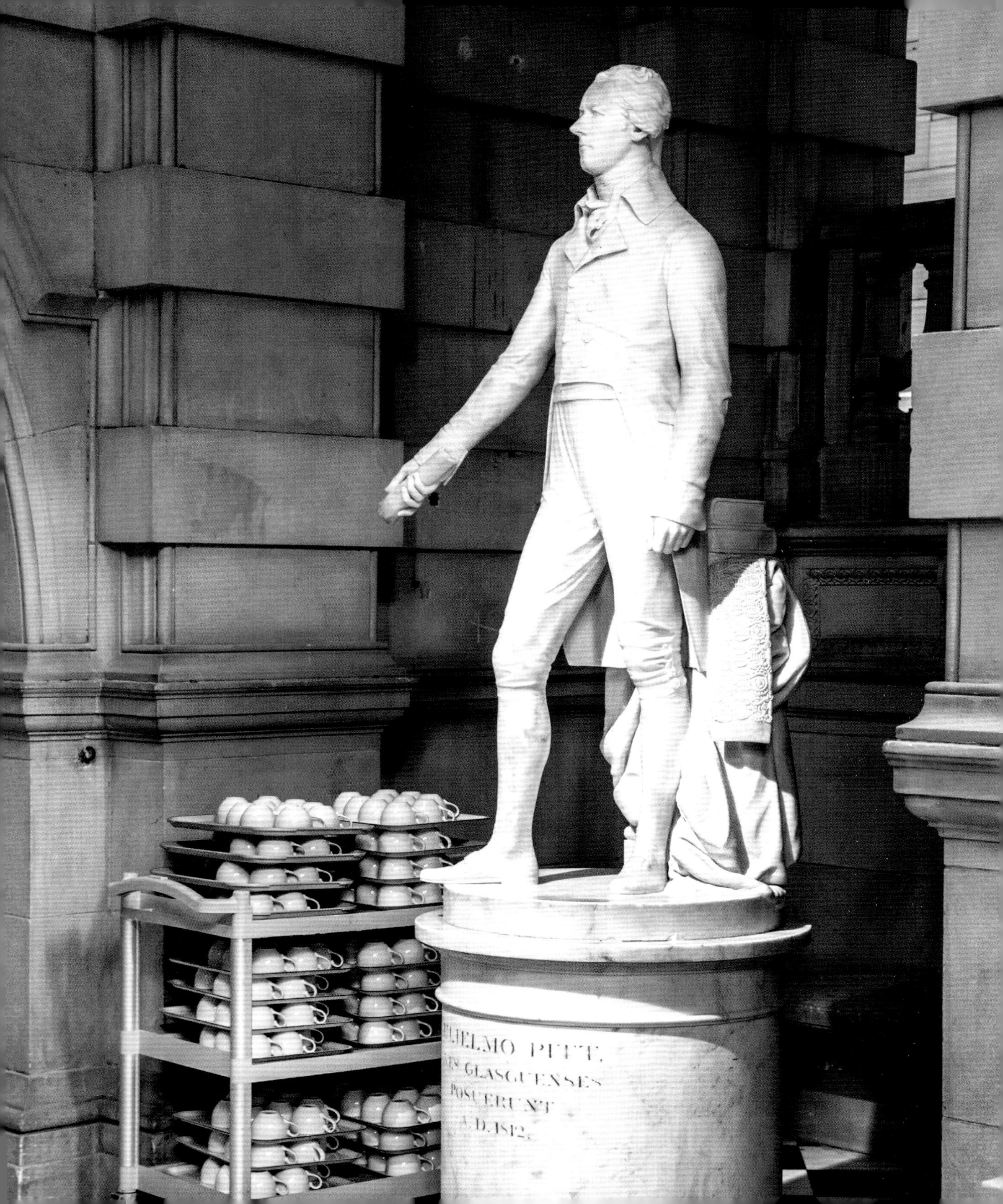

GULIELMO PITT,
CIVES GLASGUENSES
POSUERUNT
A.D. 1812.

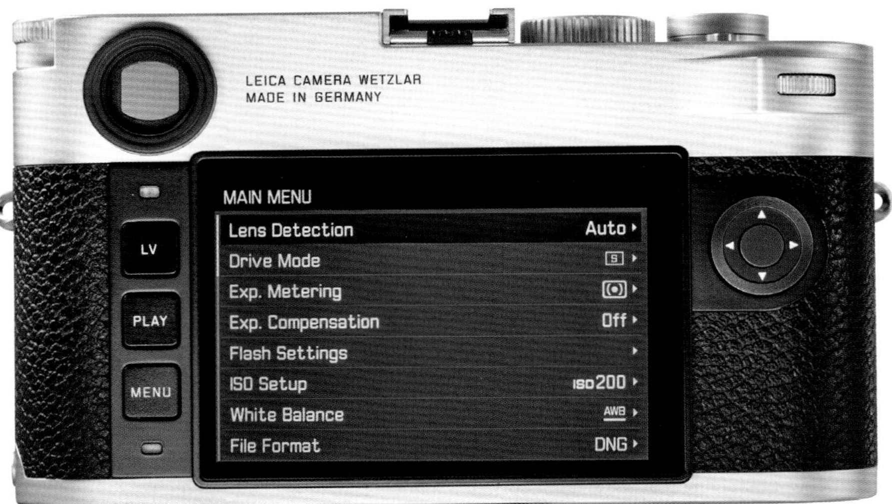

« MENU SYSTEM
The M10 only has four pages of menu options, which means it is quite easy to remember where a particular option can be found.

Using the menu system

1) Press MENU.

2) Press ▼ so Main Menu is highlighted and press ●.

3) Press ▲/▼ or turn ○ to move up or down the options on a menu page. There are four menu pages. When you reach the bottom (or top) of a page the Leica M10 will jump to the next page.

4) When the option you want to select is highlighted, press either ▶ or ● to view the sub-menu page.

5) Press ● to select an option or swap between two alternatives. If ▶ is shown at the right of the option description, press ▶ to view further options.

6) Once you have made your selection press the shutter-release button to return to the shooting mode.

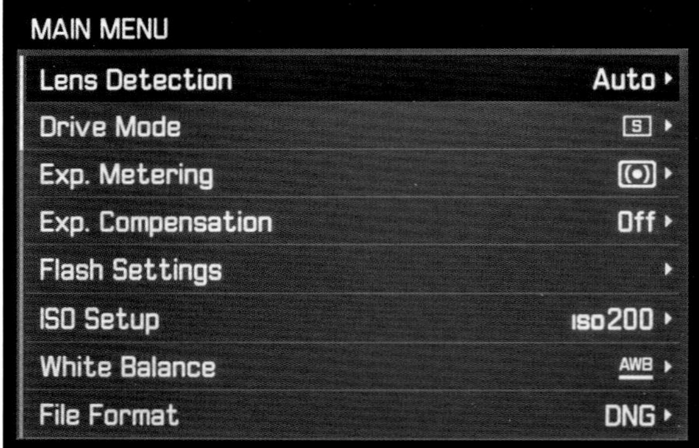

Notes
- Any options that are not available will be grayed out and cannot be selected.

- Pressing MENU or ◀ on a sub-menu page will take you back up a level.

- Some of the menu options, such as **Exposure Compensation** or **Copyright Information** have specific ways of making changes. These are described in detail later in the chapter.

MAIN MENU (PAGE 1)	OPTIONS
Lens Detection	Off; Auto; Manual M (M-series lens selection from list); Manual R (R-series lens selection from list)
Drive Mode	Single; Continuous; Interval (Frames; Interval time); Exposure Bracketing (Frames; F-stops; Exp. Compensation); Self Timer (2sec; 12sec)
Exposure Metering Mode	Spot; Center-weighted; Multi-field
Exposure Compensation	±3 stops in 1/3-stop increments
Flash Settings	Flash Sync Mode (Start of Exposure; End of Exposure); Max. Flash Sync Time (1/f; 1/(2f); 1/(4f); 1/125s; 1/60s; 1/30s; 1/15s; 1/8s; 1/4s; 1/2s); Flash Exposure Compensation (Off; ±3 stops in 1/3-stop increments)
ISO Setup	M-ISO (ISO Auto; ISO 100–50,000); Maximum Auto ISO (ISO 250–50,000); Maximum Exposure Time (1/f; 1/(2f); 1/(4f); 1/125s; 1/60; 1/30s; 1/15s; 1/8s; 1/4s; 1/2s)
White Balance	AWB Auto; Daylight; Cloudy; Shadow; Tungsten; Fluorescent Warm; Fluorescent Cool; WB Flash; Graycard; K Color Temperature (2000K–13,100K)
File Format	DNG; DNG+JPG; JPG

MAIN MENU (PAGE 2)	OPTIONS
JPG Settings	JPG Resolution (L-JPG [24MP]; M-JPG [12MP]; S-JPG [6MP]); Contrast (Low; Standard; High); Sharpness (Low; Standard; High); Saturation (Low; Standard; High); Monochrome (On; Off)
Auto Review	Off; 1s; 3s; 5s; Hold
Capture Assistants	Focus Peaking (Off; Red; Blue; Green; White); Histogram (On; Off); Exposure Clipping (Clipping enabled; Lower limit; Upper limit); Grids (Off; 3x3 Fields; 6x4 Fields); Exposure Simulation (Permanent; Release half pressed); Focus Aid (Automatic; Manual)
EVF/Display Control	Play Screen Target (Auto; EVF; Display); LV Screen Target (Auto; EVF; Display; LV disabled); Auto Review Screen Target (Auto; EVF; Display)
User Profiles	Load Profile (Standard Profile; User 1–4); Save as User Profile (User 1–4); Rename User Profile (User Profile 1–4); Export to Card (Yes; No); Import from Card (Yes; No)
Customize Control	Edit Favorites; Customize Wheel (Off; Exposure Compensation; LV Zoom)
Display Brightness	Low; Medium Low; Medium; Medium High; High; Auto
EVF Brightness	Low; Medium Low; Medium; Medium High; High; Auto

MAIN MENU (PAGE 3)	OPTIONS
Auto Power Saving	Off; 2 minutes; 5 minutes; 10 minutes
WLAN	Function (On; Off); Connection (Join WLAN; Create WLAN); Setup (SSID/Network Name); Password
GPS	On; Off
Date & Time	Auto GPS Time (On; Off); Time Zone; Daylight Saving Time (On; Off); Date Setting; Time Setting
Language	English; German; French; Italian; Spanish; Russian; Japanese; Traditional Chinese; Simplified Chinese; Korean; Portuguese
Reset Camera	Yes; No
Format SD	Yes; No
Image Numbering	New folder; Change Filename; Reset Image Numbering (Yes; No)

MAIN MENU (PAGE 4)	OPTIONS
Sensor Cleaning	Open Shutter; Dust Detection
Camera Information	Camera Firmware; Regulatory Information; Copyright Information (Copyright [On; Off]; Information; Artist)

» MAIN MENU (PAGE 1)

› Lens Detection

The Leica M10 has a built-in 6-bit optical sensor on the lens mount. This means that when you mount a compatible lens to the Leica M10—and **Lens Detection** is set to **Automatic**—the optical sensor reads the barcode on the lens to determine the lens type. Most modern Leica lenses now have a barcode, while those that don't can be retrospectively fitted with one.

The information read from the barcode is used in a variety of ways, including correcting the effects of corner light fall-off (a problem commonly seen when lenses are used at their maximum aperture); as an aid to flash exposure when using a compatible flash; and ensuring the EXIF data in the image metadata is set correctly.

Lens detection should be set to **Off** or **Manual M** should be selected when you mount an M-series lens without a data barcode to your Leica M10. When **Manual M** is selected, a list of M-series lenses made before 2006 (when lens coding was first used by Leica) is shown. Select your lens if it is shown.

If you fit a Leica R-mount lens to your Leica M10 via an adaptor, select **Manual R** to select the lens (assuming it is shown on the list).

Notes

- The list of lenses available on the Manual M list only includes Leica lenses; third-party lenses such as those made by Carl Zeiss or Voigtländer are not supported.

- The LEICA TRI-ELMAR-M 16-18-21mm ASPH f/4 has three focal length settings and three separate entries on the lens list. You will need to change the setting on the Manual M sub-menu each time you alter the focal length of the lens.

- Every lens made by Leica has a unique code, which is usually found close to the lens mount. These codes follow the lens description in the Manual M list to ensure that you select the correct lens.

- R-mount lenses were designed to fit Leica R-series cameras, an SLR system produced until 2009. Although discontinued, pre-owned R-mount lenses can be found in camera stores and online.

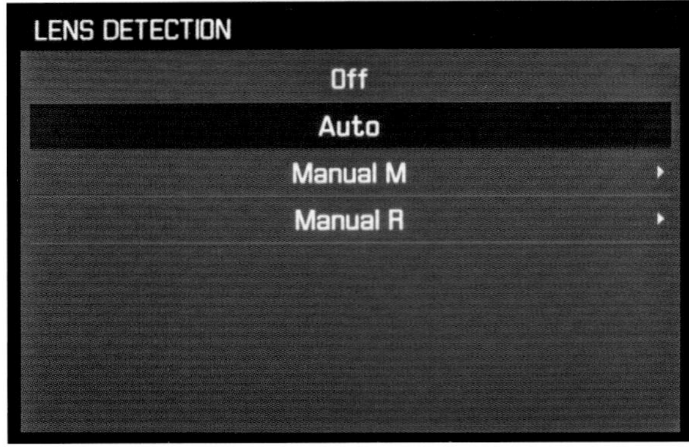

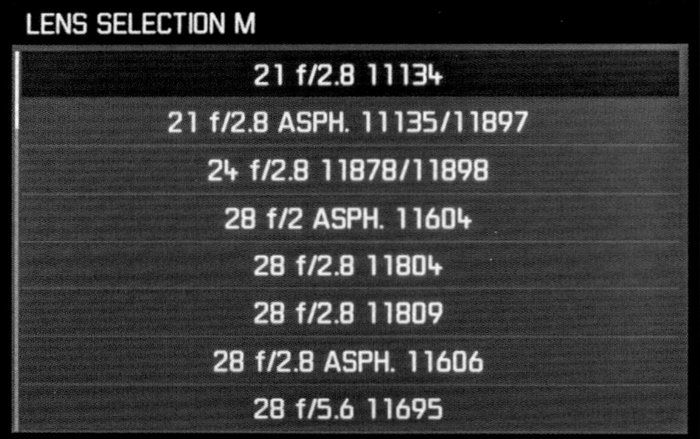

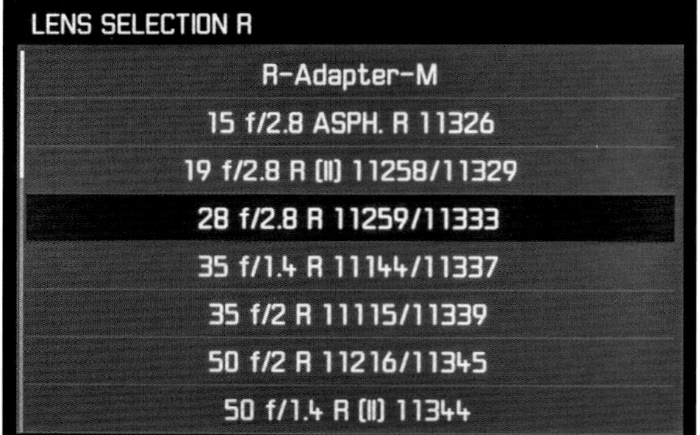

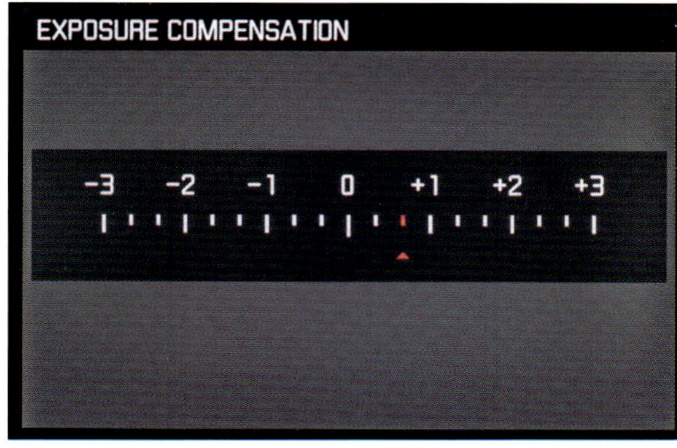

Setting exposure compensation

1) Select **Exp. Compensation** from the Main Menu (page 1).

2) Press ▶ (or turn ○ to the right) to apply positive compensation, or press ◀ (or turn ○ to the left) to apply negative compensation.

3) Press ● to set exposure compensation and return to the Main Menu.

4) Press lightly down on the shutter-release button to return to shooting mode.

› Drive Mode

Sets how the Leica M10 shoots images when the shutter-release button is pressed down. See pages 40–43 for details.

› Exposure Metering

Sets the metering mode used when shooting in Live View. See page 46 for details.

› Exp. Compensation

The exposure meter in the Leica M10 is good, but it is not infallible. Exposure compensation lets you override the set exposure when shooting in Aperture Priority mode. Exposure compensation can be set in ⅓-stop increments across a ±3-stop range. Applying positive compensation lightens an image, negative compensation darkens it.

The degree of compensation you apply is retained by the Leica M10 even when the camera is turned off and on again. Exposure compensation is a very useful option when you're shooting a series of images that require the same degree of exposure compensation. However, it is easy to get caught out and forget that you have set exposure compensation—immediately resetting exposure compensation back to 0 once it is no longer needed is a good habit to acquire.

Notes
- Exposure compensation is set to 0 (and therefore inactive) when **Off** is shown opposite **Exp. Compensation** on the Main Menu screen.

- The selected exposure compensation value is shown at the bottom of the LCD when viewing the detailed display in Live View.

- The degree of exposure compensation is also shown in the viewfinder.

- The thumbwheel can be set to allow exposure compensation via **Customize Control** (see page 89) bypassing **Exp. Compensation**.

› Flash Settings

Sets the options available when a flash is attached to the Leica M10. See chapter 5 for more information.

› ISO Setup

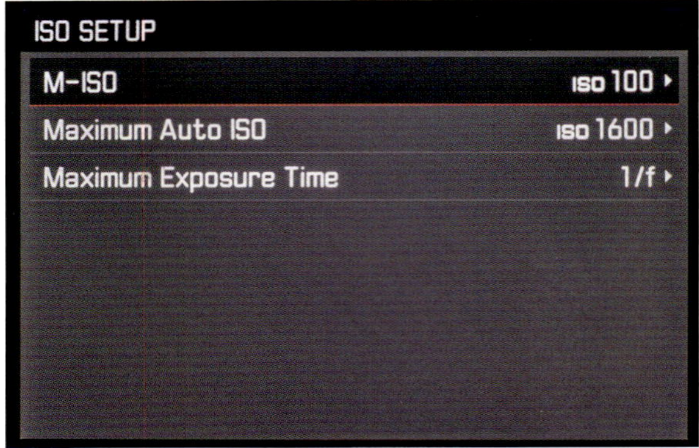

The **ISO Setup** menu is used to configure ISO behavior for M-ISO and A-ISO when the ISO dial is set to one of those two options.

M-ISO

The ISO dial can be used to set an ISO value, but switching to **M-ISO** allows you to set a greater range of values (ISO 100–ISO 50,000), including intermediate values in ⅓-stop increments and **ISOAuto**. The advantage of having this greater range is that you can refine your exposures more accurately. The disadvantage is that you will need to use the menu system when you want to change ISO.

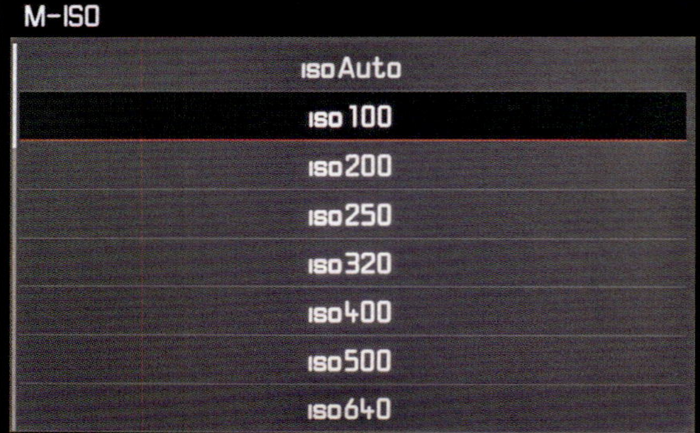

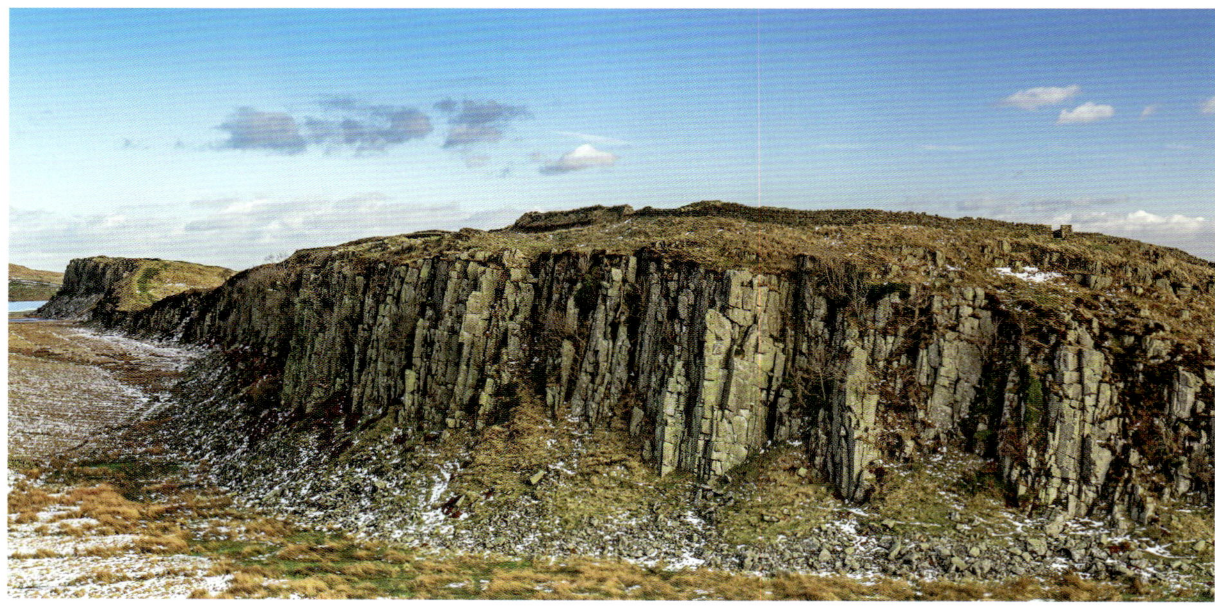

Maximum Auto ISO

This option lets you set the maximum ISO the camera will choose when Auto ISO is selected. The **Maximum Auto ISO** value you select will depend on your tolerance to noise and your ability to hold a camera steady. Although noise is not ideal, it is generally preferable to an image that is not sharp due to camera shake. Noise can be relatively easily reduced in postproduction but the effects of camera shake are far less easily dealt with. Choose between **ISO 250** at the lowest end of automatic adjustment to prioritize image quality over exposure flexibility, and **ISO 50000** to maximize exposure flexibility at the potential expense of image quality.

Maximum Exposure Time

Select this option to set whether the focal length of the lens or a particular shutter speed triggers a change to the Auto ISO setting.

A rough-and-ready rule to achieving images free from camera shake when handholding a camera is to set the shutter speed so that it matches the focal length of the lens fitted to the camera. If you use a 50mm lens then the shutter speed should be 1/50, for example. The **1/f** option ("f" standing for focal length) follows this rule. However, depending on how steady you are, you may benefit more from the shutter speed being set to twice the focal length (**1/[2f]**) or even four times the focal length (**1/[4f]**).

Alternatively you can manually select the slowest shutter speed that you want the camera to use, from 1/500 sec.–1/2 sec.

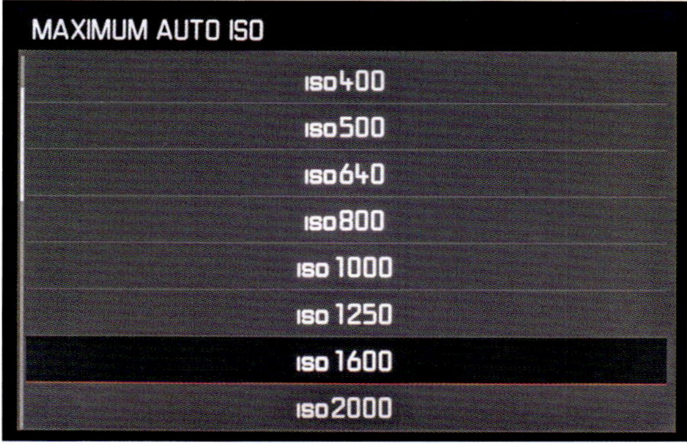

Note
- **1/f**, **1/[2f]**, and **1/[4f]** will only work when coded lenses are fitted to your Leica M10.

‹‹ CONSISTENCY
Use a fixed ISO when you need to keep the exposure consistent over a series of photographs, such as when shooting a sequence to create a stitched panoramic.

There are relatively few pure white light sources; most light sources have a color tint to one degree or another. This tint is referred to as the "color temperature" of the light, measured in degrees Kelvin (K), and is either blue (resulting in "cool" light) or red (resulting in "warm" light).

Our eyes are remarkably adept at adjusting for any color tint, so it is usually only when a light source is heavily tinted—as it is at sunrise or sunset, for example—that we really notice. A digital camera doesn't know what the color temperature of the light is, though, so when a white surface is lit by a non-neutral light source it will reflect the predominant color of the light. Without adjustment, the "white" surface could appear quite blue or quite orange, depending on the color temperature of the light.

White balance is simply the name given to the camera function that allows you to compensate for any color variation in the light and render white as neutral once more. The Leica M10 has a number of white balance presets that adjust an image to compensate for the color temperature of a particular light source. As an example, tungsten bulbs (also known as incandescent light sources) emit a very red-orange light. To correct this the Leica

M10's ☀ preset adds blue to the image to cancel out the color tint of the tungsten bulb.

The key to using white balance presets is correctly matching the preset to the type of light illuminating your subject. If in doubt, the **AWB** white balance preset will usually apply the right degree of correction, although it is less accurate when a light source is particularly warm or cool.

For greater accuracy you can also set the white balance to a Kelvin value of 2000K–13,100K by selecting a specific **K** **Color Temperature**. It is often possible to find the exact Kelvin rating of an artificial light source either from the packaging of the light or the manufacturer's website.

Alternatively, you can create a custom white balance on your Leica M10. This is desirable when the greatest color accuracy is required, as is often the case with product photography.

The method you use to adjust the white balance will depend on your shooting style. However, there is far less scope for white balance correction later when shooting JPEG than when shooting Raw. White balance is effectively "baked" into the JPEG image and cannot be easily altered later; Raw files can be easily adjusted later if white balance was incorrectly set at the time of shooting.

Symbol	Description	Color temperature (approx.)
AWB	White balance is determined automatically	–
☀	Daylight; normal sunny conditions	5500K
☁	Cloudy; outdoors on an overcast day	6500K
⛱	Shadow; open shade with no direct light	7000K
☀	Tungsten; incandescent bulbs	2700K–3000K
☰	Warm fluorescent lighting	2700K
☰	Cool fluorescent lighting	4000K
⚡WB	Flash; light from external flash	5500K
⚲	Graycard; WB determined using a neutral gray surface	–
K	Select specific Kelvin value	–

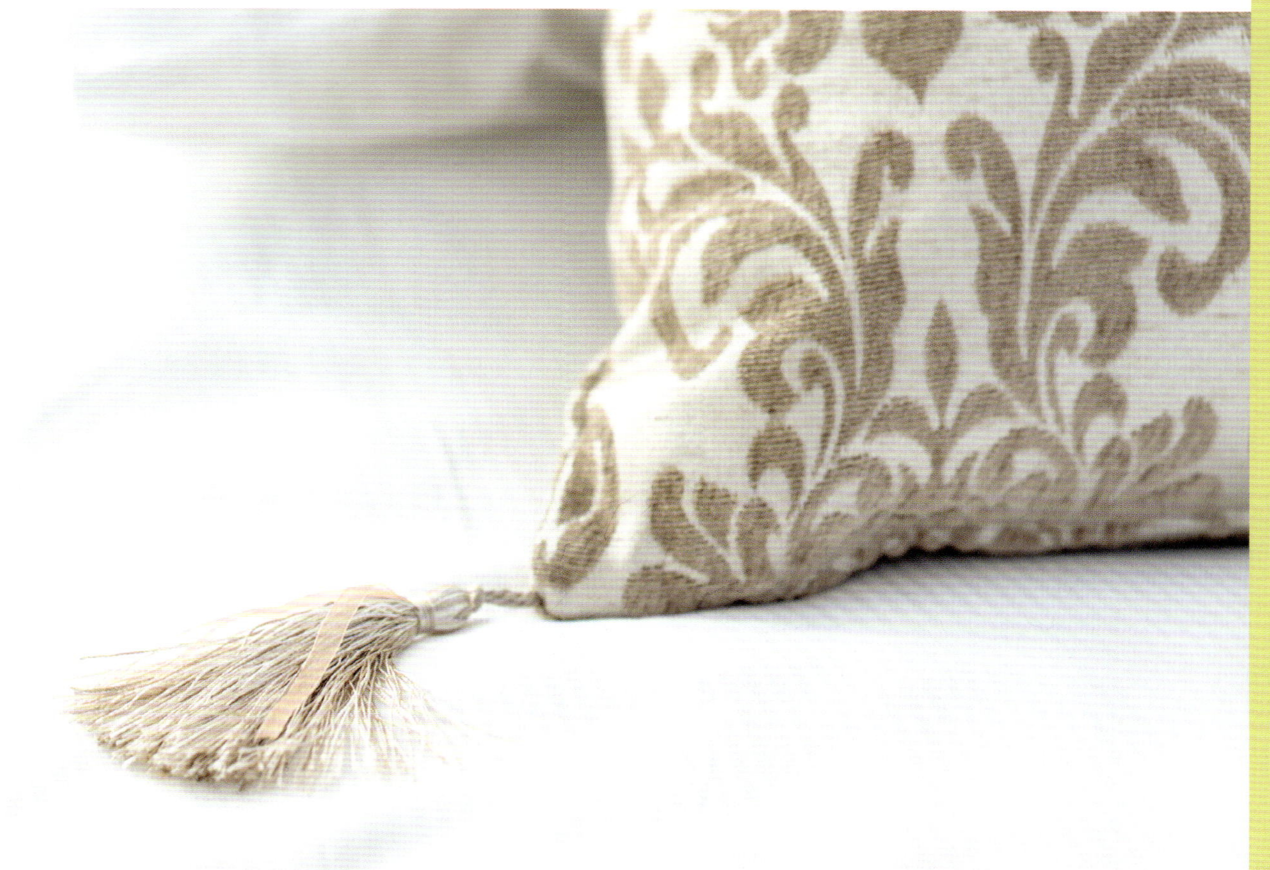

⌃ COLOR

Although a simple shot, the colors of this cushion and bedspread had to be accurate (the white of the bedspread in particular). This meant creating a custom white balance before shooting.

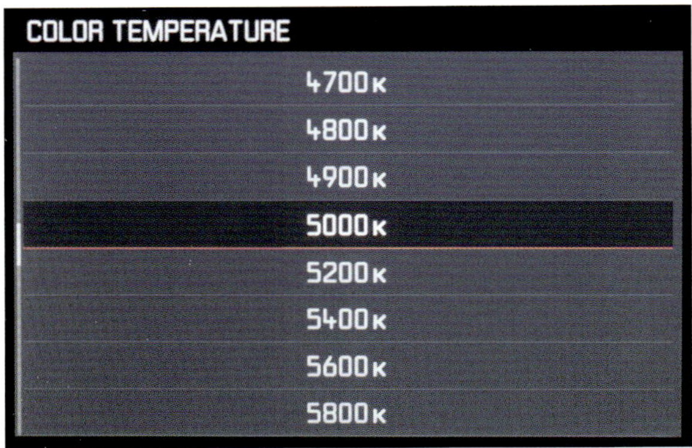

Using a white balance preset

1) Press ● and select **White Balance**. By default, **White Balance** is shown on the Favorites menu as well as the Main Menu.

2) Select the required white balance preset using the grid on page 72 as a guide.

3) Press lightly down on the shutter-release button to return to shooting mode.

Setting a specific Kelvin value

1) Press ● and select **White Balance**.

2) Select **K** **Color Temperature**.

3) Press ▲ to reduce the Kelvin value (making an image cooler) or ▼ to increase the Kelvin value (making an image warmer). The values range from 2000K–5000K in increments of 100K; 5000K–8000K in increments of 200K; 8000K–13,100K in increments of 300K.

4) Press ● to set the highlighted Kelvin value and return to the **White Balance** menu page or press MENU to return to the **White Balance** menu page without altering the original setting.

Setting white balance manually

1) Press ● and select **White Balance**.

2) Select ✦ **Greycard**.

3) The message **Please take a picture for setting the white balance** will be displayed on the LCD. Aim your camera at a neutral white or gray surface (such as a piece of card) and press the shutter-release button to create a reference image. Try to fill the image with the white surface, but do not worry about focusing.

4) The white balance will be set using the area of the image under the crosshairs that appear on screen, so use ✤ to move the crosshairs to the most neutral part of the image. Press ● to preview the new white balance setting. If the white balance doesn't look correct move the cursor and repeat. When you're happy that white balance is correct press ● to save the custom white balance setting and return to the **White Balance** menu.

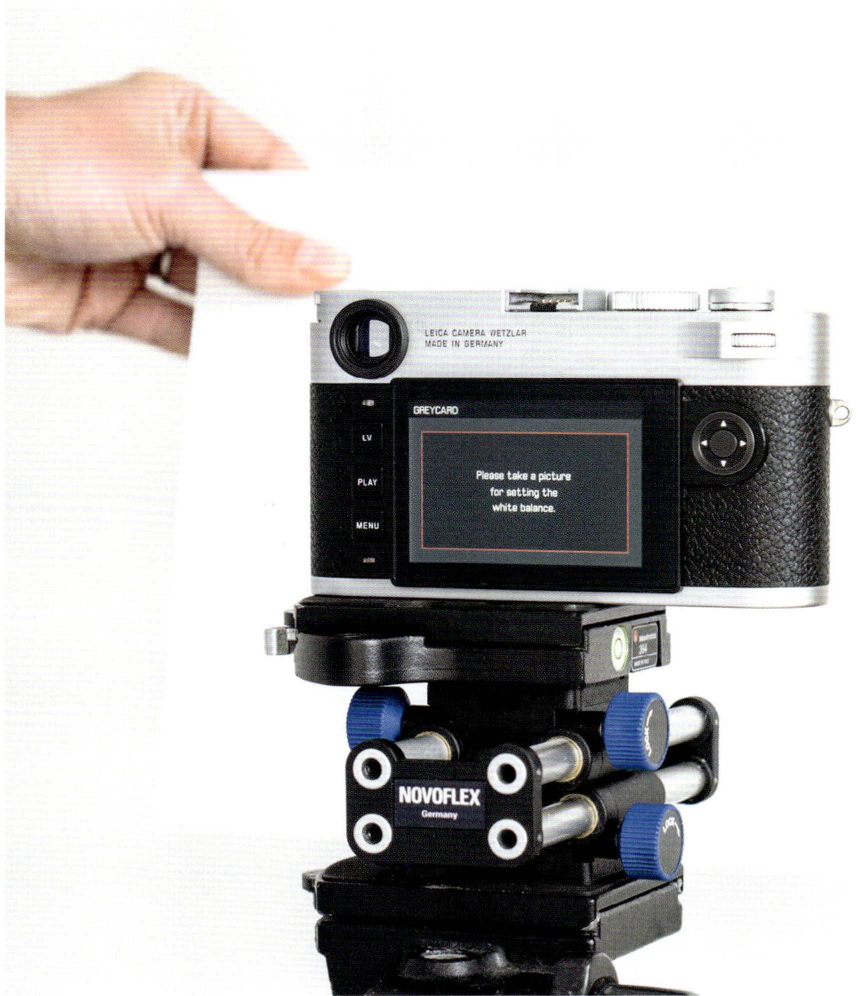

⌃ MANUAL WHITE BALANCE

Setting the white balance using a neutral target ensures accuracy, but only for that specific lighting situation: if the lighting changes, your white balance should be updated.

The Leica M10 can save images in two different file formats: JPEG and Raw. There is no right or wrong answer as to which file format you should use, as both have strengths and weaknesses. Generally, JPEG will be the most appropriate option if you need a "finished" photograph almost immediately after shooting, while Raw is worth considering if you are prepared to spend time working on an image in postproduction (in much the same way that a photographer works on a print in a darkroom). Fortunately, if you are undecided—and have a sufficiently large memory card—you can choose to shoot both together. This is the most flexible option as you will have a JPEG ready for use immediately, with a high-quality Raw file for processing.

A fundamental difference between the two is that JPEG images are "compressed" to reduce the file size. This means that more image files in JPEG format can be fitted onto a memory card than equivalent Raw files. However, this reduction in file size comes at a price: fine detail in the image is reduced, lowering the overall quality of the image. The heavier the compression, the smaller the file size, but the greater the loss of fine detail. Shooting JPEG is therefore often a compromise between file size and image quality.

Another difference is that when you shoot JPEGs, image options such as **White Balance** and options selected on the **JPG Settings** sub-menu page are "baked" into the files. Although it's possible to alter the look of your images in postproduction you will not be able to alter those images too far without a definite reduction in image quality. This means that you have to think more carefully about how your camera is set before you shoot when JPEG is selected.

Conversely, a Raw file contains all the data captured by the camera at the time of exposure without processing; how the image is processed is entirely up to you. The advantage of this is that it is possible to work and rework your images as often as required without losing image quality—you simply export a different version of the Raw file (usually as a TIFF or JPEG) each time you process it.

Unlike JPEG there is no Raw standard. However, the Leica M10 uses the closest to a standard that has ever been developed. The DNG (or Digital NeGative) format was created by Adobe Systems in 2004. This "open" format that can be used freely by any camera manufacturer and the hope was that DNG would become ubiquitous, replacing the multitude of different Raw formats produced by camera manufacturers. So far this hasn't happened, although Leica and Pentax both support DNG.

Raw, in any form, is not compatible with anything other than Raw conversion software. This means that Raw files have to be processed and exported in a more acceptable form before they can be used with other applications (usually as JPEG, TIFF, or Adobe Photoshop PSD files).

Unlike other camera manufacturers, Leica does not supply Raw conversion software. Instead, the company recommends Adobe Lightroom (a logical choice given the use of Adobe's DNG Raw format), which can be bought outright on disk or paid for monthly or annually via Adobe's Creative Cloud subscription scheme. The advantage of the subscription route is that you always have the most up-to-date version of Lightroom; the disadvantage is that you lose access to Lightroom (but not your Raw files) if you choose to end your subscription.

›› LIGHTROOM
Adobe Lightroom is a variant of Photoshop and shares many of the features of Adobe Camera Raw. It is a well-specified piece of software, but there are alternatives, such as Phase One's Capture One.

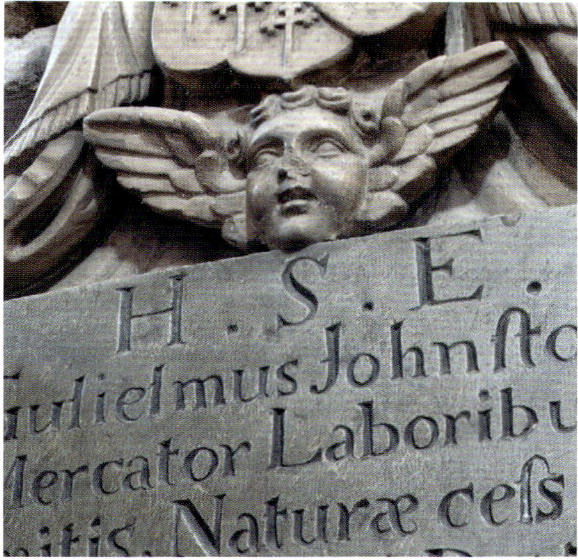 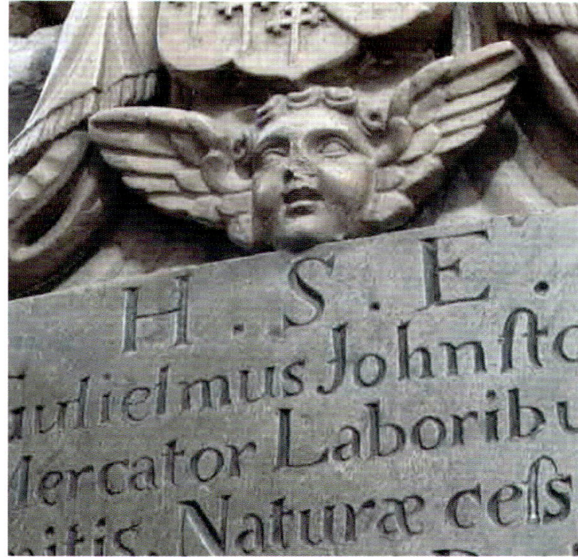

⌃ LOSSY

The compression of the Leica M10's JPEG files is not too destructive. However, every time you edit a JPEG in postproduction and then save it, more image quality is lost. Here, the fine detail of the original (left) is lost and heavy compression artifacts can be seen (right).

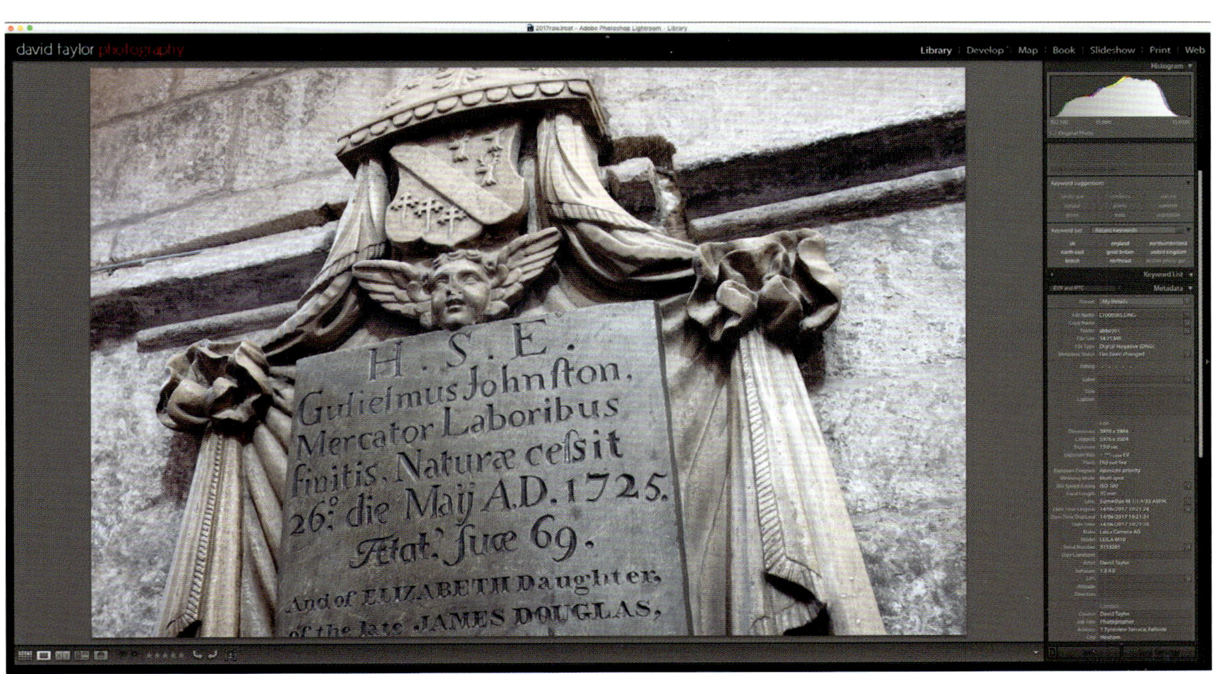

» MAIN MENU (PAGE 2)

› JPG Settings

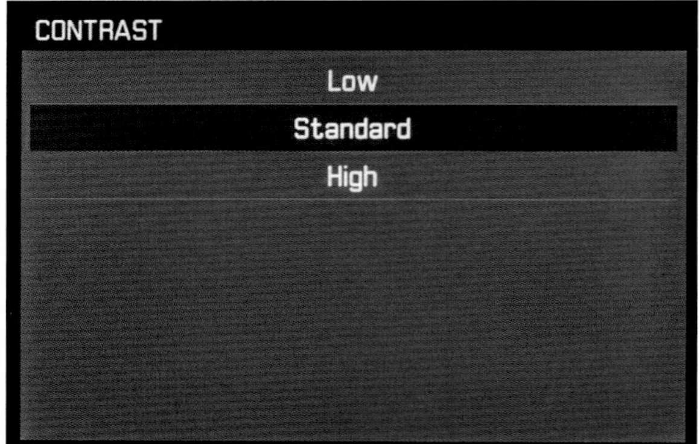

The options on the **JPG Settings** sub-menu let you alter the resolution of your JPEG images, as well as visual qualities such as contrast and color saturation.

JPG Resolution

The maximum resolution of the Leica M10 is 24 million pixels (an image size of 5952 x 3968 pixels), which is the default setting: **L-JPG (24MP)**. If you don't require the largest image size, you can reduce the resolution by choosing either **M-JPG (12MP)** (4256 x 2832 pixels) or **S-JPG (6MP)** (2976 x 1984 pixels).

The lower the resolution, the smaller the file size, and the less space it will occupy on your memory card. Resolution also affects print size. For example, at a print resolution of 300 pixels per inch (ppi), a 24mp image would produce a print measuring approximately 19.92 x 13.3in (50.6 x 33.8cm). Select **S-JPG (6MP)** and the print size at the same print resolution would drop to 9.9 x 6.6in (25.2 x 16.8cm).

Contrast

Contrast lets you control the tonal range of your JPEG images, specifically the difference in tonal value between the shadows and the highlights. When **Contrast** is set to **Low** the difference between the highlights and shadows is reduced, which can produce flat-looking images, especially if the scene you're shooting is low in contrast to start with.

When **Contrast** is set to **High** the difference between the highlights and shadows is increased. This can be used to add drama to an image, but it can be difficult to retain detail in both the highlights and/or shadows when a scene is naturally high in contrast.

Standard is roughly half way between these two extremes. As it is generally easier to add contrast to a JPEG image than remove it, **Low** or **Standard** are often the best options.

Sharpness

Sharpness sets the degree of sharpening applied to your JPEG images between **Low**, **Standard**, and **High** (with **High** applying the greatest degree of sharpening). Different methods of reproducing images require different levels of sharpening, so an image destined for printing will require more sharpening than one that will only ever be viewed on a computer screen.

Generally speaking, sharpening is best applied when it is needed, rather than in-camera, so set **Sharpness** to **Low** and use postproduction software to apply the relevant level of sharpening later. This is especially true if you intend to submit your images to stock libraries. Most libraries insist that little or no sharpening be applied to submitted images as this gives their clients more scope to choose their own sharpening levels (once it has been applied, sharpness is impossible to remove).

Saturation

Saturation lets you set the vividness of the colors in your images. Selecting **Low** will result in a relatively muted image, while **High** creates a more punchy, vibrant look. As with the options for **Contrast** and **Sharpness**, **Standard** produces results roughly half way between these two extremes.

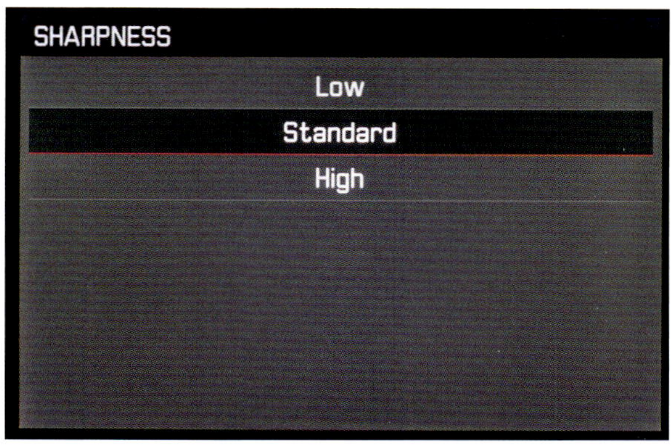

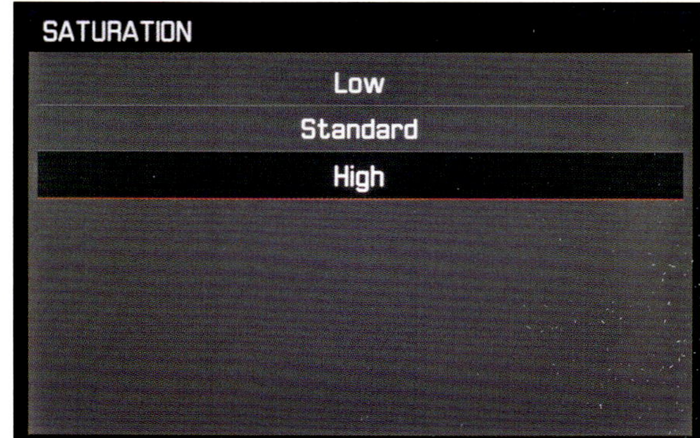

Notes
- Raw files are always saved at the maximum resolution of 24mp.

- Print resolution determines the number of pixels used per inch (or centimeter) across a print. The lower the number of pixels you have in an image (and the lower the print resolution), the lower the quality of the print.

Monochrome

The **Monochrome** option sets your Leica M10 to shoot black-and-white JPEGs. It is a simple option with no way of controlling how the black-and-white images are processed. This is unfortunate, as there is a lot more to black-and-white photography than simply removing the color from an image.

The brightness of a particular gray tone in an image is determined by the reflectivity of an object—the more light the subject reflects, the brighter the gray tone. This means that two objects that are different in color, but are reflecting similar amounts of light, will be the same shade of gray when they are photographed in black and white, which can lead to flat-looking images.

This can be overcome by using colored filters over the lens. These filters block out colors on the opposite side of a standard color wheel to the filter. For example, a red filter blocks out blue-greens, so it will lighten a red object when it is converted to monochrome, but darken blues and greens, which helps to separate the tonal values.

Landscape photographers often use yellow, orange, or red filters to darken blue skies (with red having the greatest effect), while portrait photographers are more likely to use a green filter, which helps with skin tones.

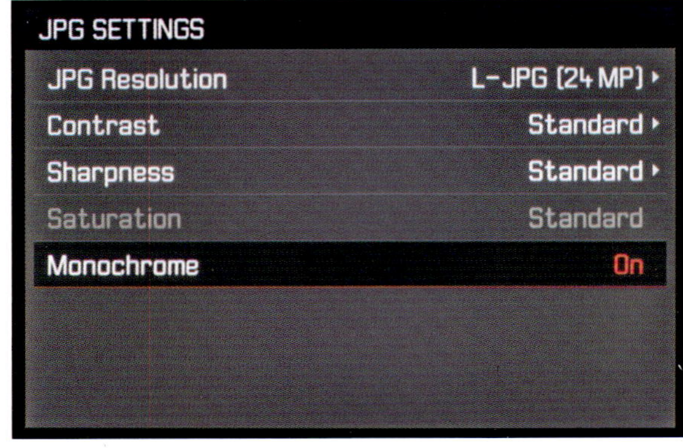

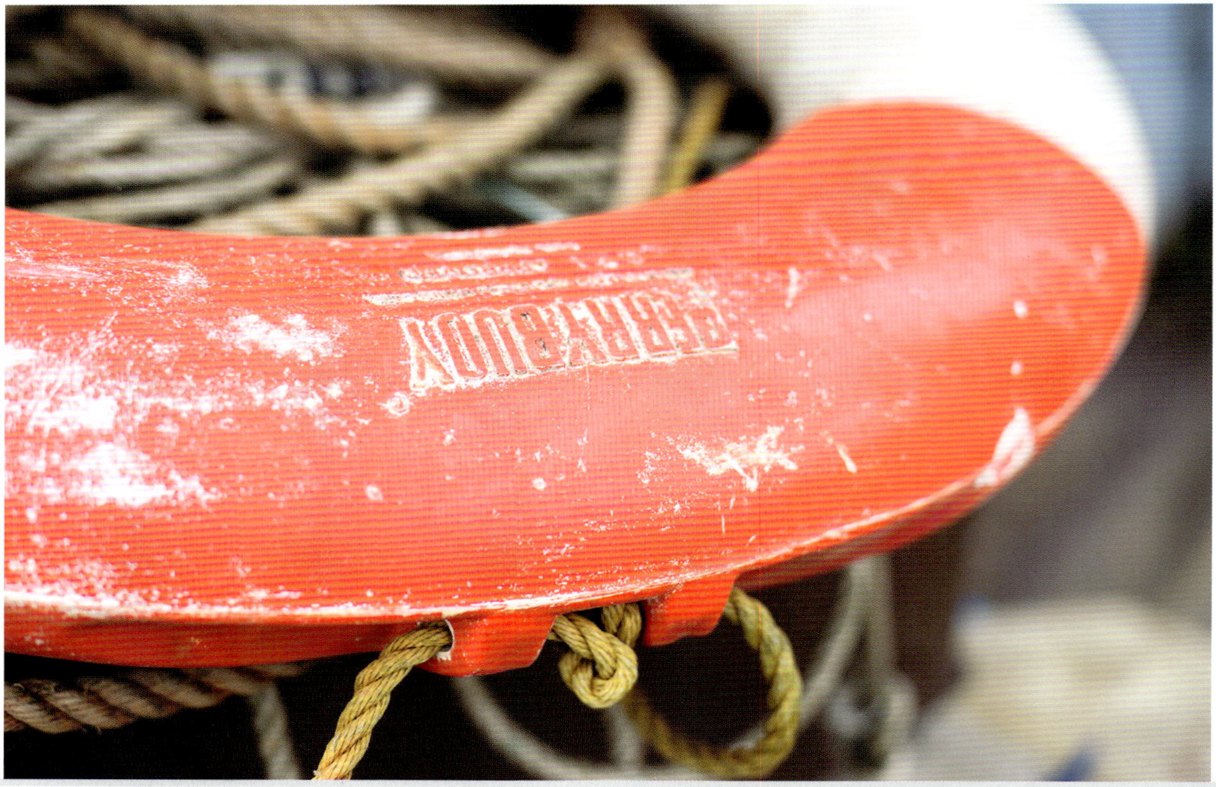

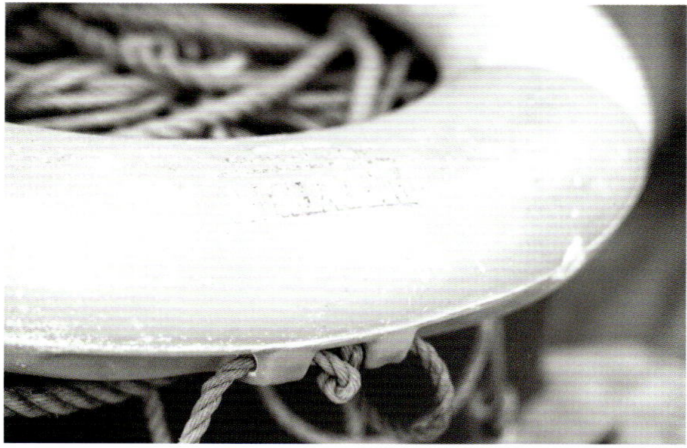

YELLOW FILTER

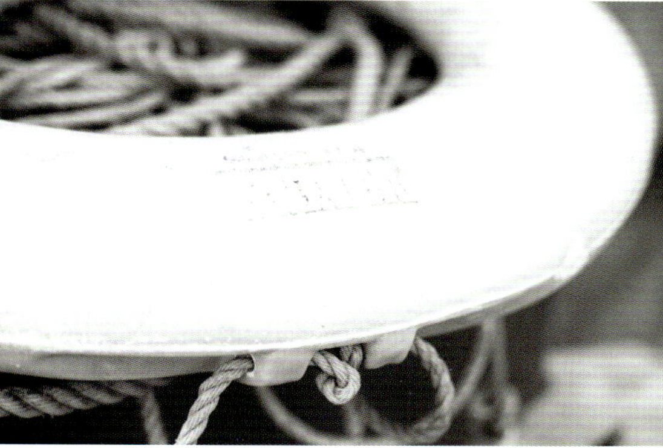

RED FILTER

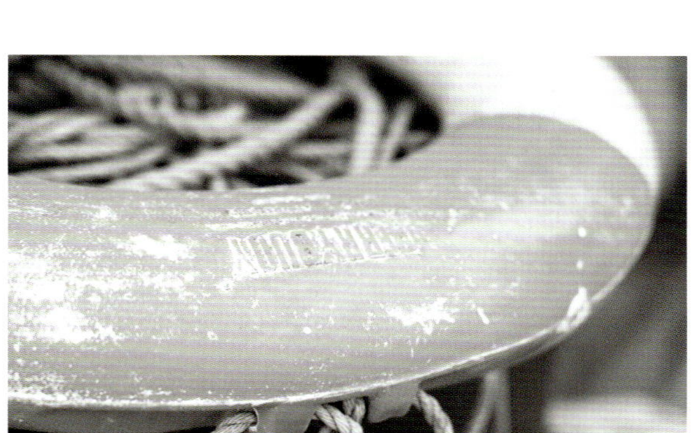

GREEN FILTER

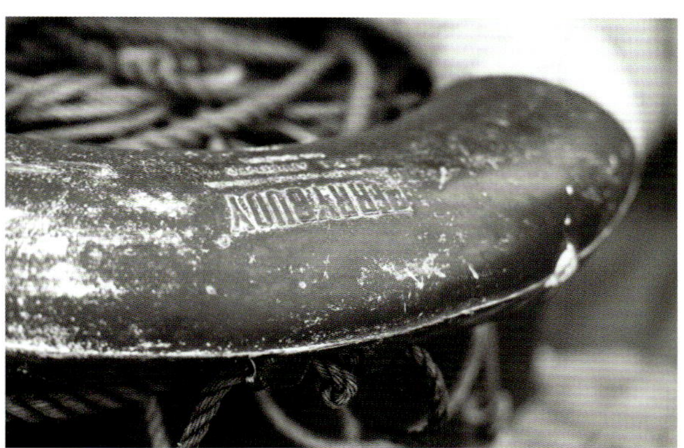

BLUE FILTER

« COLOR

Shooting in black and white means looking at the colors of a scene and deciding how you would like them to be represented in the final image. In this instance, the yellow and red filters have lightened the red of the lifebelt too much, whereas the blue has darkened it too far. For me, the green filter is the most successful, although this is very subjective.

Note
- Using colored filters only applies if you're shooting JPEGs. Raw files always retain color information, so it's easier to achieve the same effect using "virtual" filters during postproduction.

> Auto Review

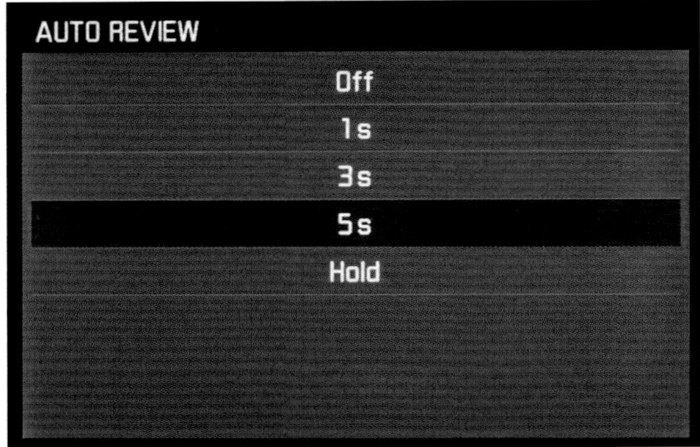

Auto Review lets you choose whether an image is displayed on the LCD immediately after it has been shot, and if it is displayed, how long it appears for.

When **Auto Review** is switched **Off**, no image is displayed, conserving battery power in the process. However, one of the big advantages of digital photography over film is that images are immediately viewable after shooting. The key is deciding how you balance this instant feedback with preserving battery power.

The biggest drain on the battery comes when you set **Auto Review** to **5 seconds** or **Hold** (so the image stays on the LCD until you press down on the shutter-release button). Setting **Auto Review** to **1 second** or even **3 seconds** is a good compromise.

› Capture Assistants

The various **Capture Assistants** options let you set visual aids that are designed to help you focus and expose your images correctly when using Live View.

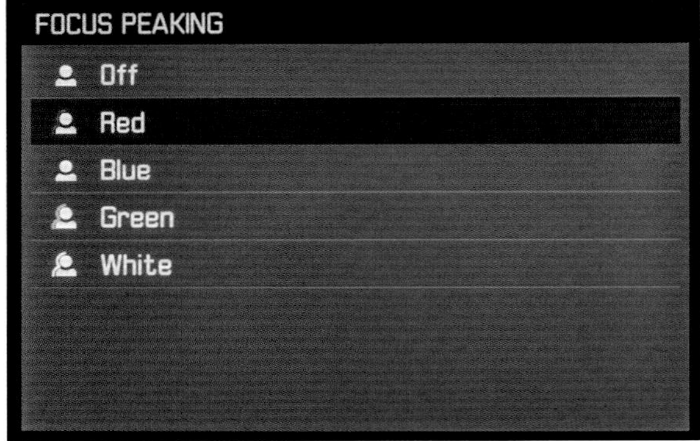

Focus Peaking

Peaking is a focusing aid derived from similar systems found on camcorders. Peaking can be set to **Off** or one of four colors: **Red**, **Blue**, **Green**, and **White**. When peaking is set to one of the colors, the Leica M10 will outline the sharpest ("in focus") areas of the image with the selected color. When selecting a color, choose one that contrasts with your subject. Red is far more visible when focusing on green foliage, for example.

There are two slight drawbacks to be aware of when using peaking, both related to the fact that peaking relies on edge contrast to detect sharpness. If you're shooting in a low-contrast scene, such as a misty landscape, peaking may be less effective or possibly not work at all. Conversely, if there are very high-contrast elements in a scene, they may trigger focus peaking long before they are in focus.

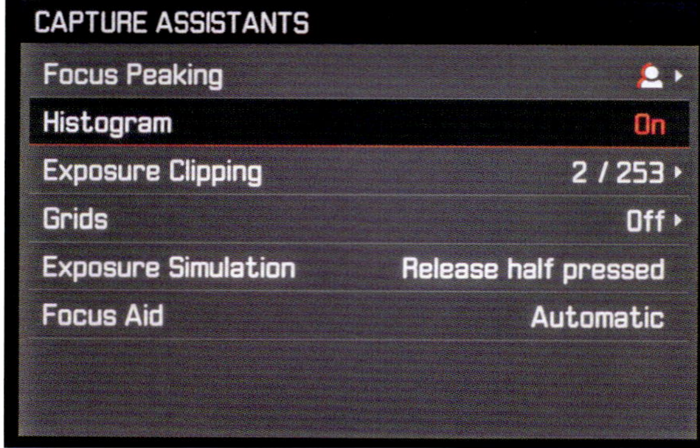

You can change the degree of underexposure or overexposure that triggers the warning system by adjusting the **Lower limit** and **Upper limit**.

Lower limit (set from **0–20**) determines the shadow clipping value, while **Upper limit** (set from **200–255**) controls the highlight clipping value. The closer **Lower limit** is to **0** or **Upper limit** is to **255** the less sensitive the clipping display is. Therefore a lower and higher value respectively is less informative, increasing the risk that exposure problems may go unnoticed.

Histogram

When **Histogram** is set to **On**, a constantly updated histogram is shown in Live View whenever the shutter-release button is pressed down to the first stage. Set **Histogram** to **Off** to disable this function.

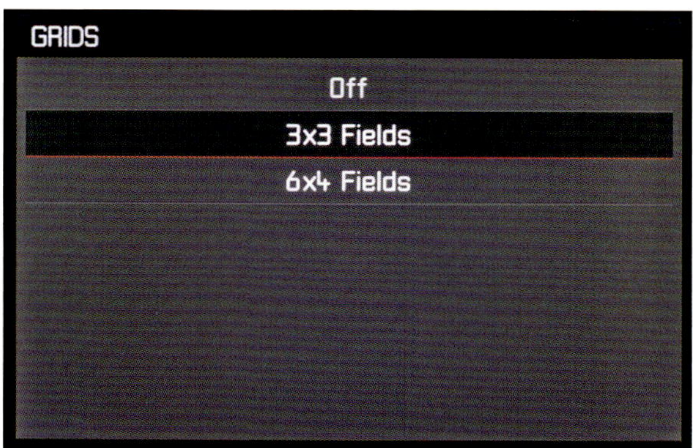

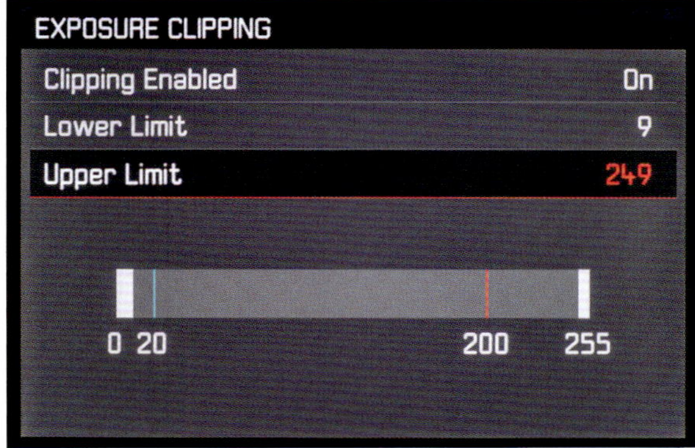

Exposure Clipping

When it is set to **On**, **Exposure Clipping** activates an exposure warning system similar to that seen in playback: underexposed areas will blink blue, overexposed areas will blink red. As with **Histogram**, **Exposure Clipping** is activated when the shutter-release button is pressed down to the first stage.

Grids

There are three **Grids** options: **Off**; **3x3 Fields**; and **6x4 Fields**.

The **3x3 Fields** grid overlays a grid across the LCD in Live View that divides the screen into thirds both horizontally and vertically. **3x3 Fields** is an aid to composition when using the Rule of Thirds. This "rule" works when the main subject is placed along one of the grid lines or at the intersection of two grid lines.

6x4 Fields adds more grid lines (four horizontal, six vertical), which is useful when shooting architectural subjects; the grid can be used to check that lines in the subject are perfectly straight.

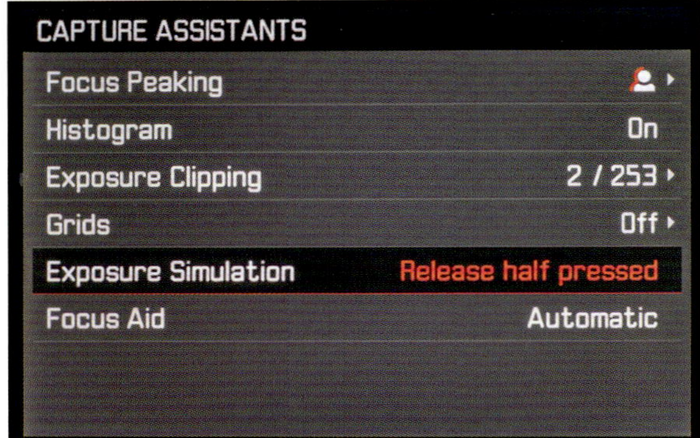

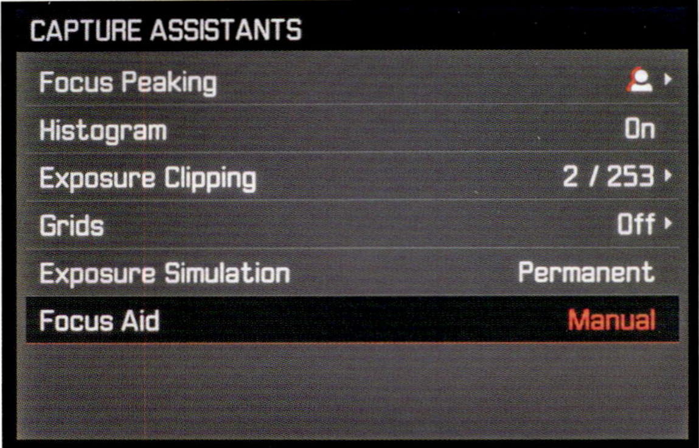

Exposure Simulation

When **Exposure Simulation** is set to **Permanent**, the brightness of the Live View display will vary as you adjust the shutter speed, ISO, or aperture in manual exposure (or vary exposure compensation in Aperture Priority). Unless the exposure is correct—or close to being correct—the display may be too bright or too dim to see your subject clearly. This is another useful (albeit slightly imprecise) way to check that exposure is correct.

However, the **Permanent** setting can be problematic in certain situations. For example, when using flash you may need to use both a small aperture and shutter speed at the sync speed of 1/180 sec. If the ambient light levels are low, the display may be so dark that it is impossible to see your subject.

If you set **Exposure Simulation** to **Release half pressed**, the display will remain at a constant brightness. It is only when you press the shutter-release button down to the first stage that the display changes brightness to reflect the exposure settings. This has the advantage that you will always be able to see the scene in front of you in Live View. However, it may mean you think the exposure is correct when it is not.

Focus Aid

When **Focus Aid** is set to **Automatic** the Live View image magnifies automatically whenever the lens focus ring is turned. The magnified image can be used to check critical focus, which is generally necessary when using a large aperture, long focal length lens, or both. The thumbwheel is used to set the level of magnification: turn to the right to zoom in; turn to the left to zoom out; and press ✥ to pan around the magnified image.

When **Focus Aid** is set to **Manual** you first have to press the focus button to magnify the Live View image.

> **Note**
> - You can set the thumbwheel to automatically zoom into a Live View image by setting **Customize Wheel** to **LV Zoom**. See page 89 for details.

› EVF/Display Control

If an optional Leica Visoflex (Type 020) electronic viewfinder (EVF) is fitted to your Leica M10 you can set which display—the LCD or EVF—shows Live View and image playback.

Play Screen Target controls which display shows images in playback (when PLAY has been pressed). **Auto** will select the display automatically: the Visoflex EVF has a built-in eye sensor, so if you look through the EVF, image playback will be sent there; if you move away from your camera, playback will switch to the LCD. Select **EVF** and image playback will always be sent to the EVF and never the LCD (unless the EVF is removed from the camera). **Display** reverses this, so playback is always directed to the LCD.

LV Screen Target sets which display the Live View image is streamed to: **Auto** makes the selection automatically; **EVF** uses the EVF for Live View; **Display** uses the LCD for Live View; **LV Disabled** turns Live View off so that no Live View is displayed, even when LV is pressed. The latter option is useful if you often find yourself accidentally pressing the LV button as you use the Leica M10.

Auto Review Screen Target offers the same options as **Play Screen Target** and controls which display shows the auto image review immediately after shooting.

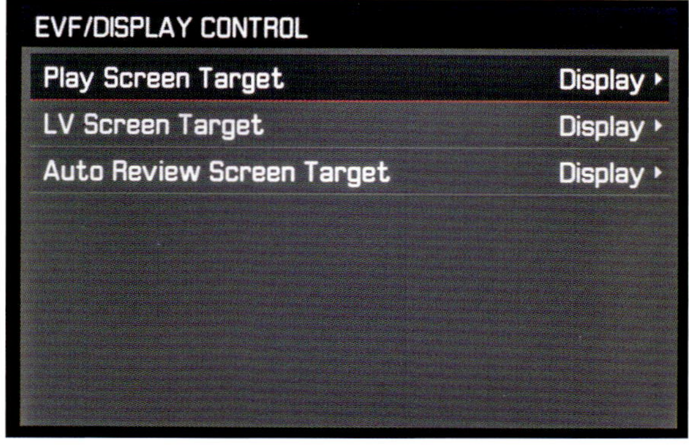

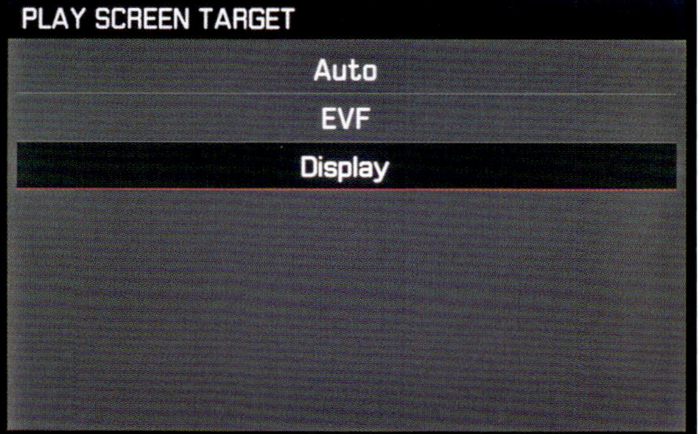

User Profiles helps to remove the strain of constantly altering menu settings as your shooting needs change. You can create and save up to four profiles that each store a particular combination of menu settings. This means you can quickly swap between different camera configurations without wading through the menus over and over again (to speed matters up further you can add **User Profiles** to the **Favorites** menu).

The four user profiles can be assigned different names, which could be used either to differentiate between different people who use the camera or between different shooting situations such as landscape or portrait. Leica has also included a **Standard Profile** that can be used to temporarily restore the Leica M10 back to its factory settings.

If you're lucky enough to own two Leica M10s you can save user profiles to the memory card and transfer it between cameras.

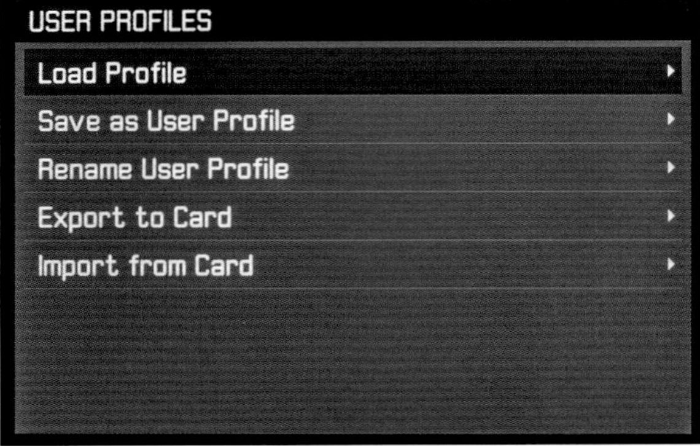

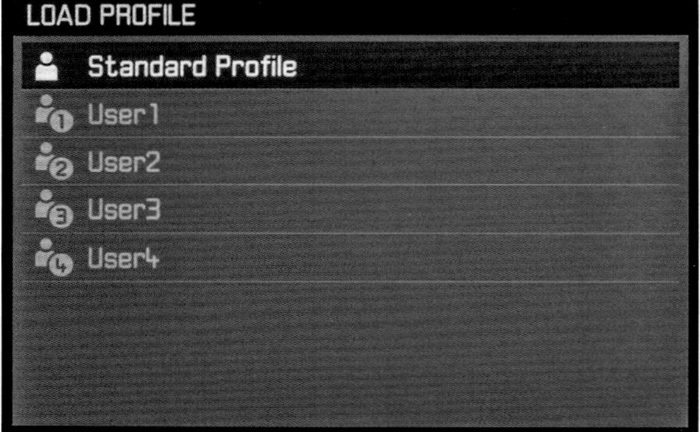

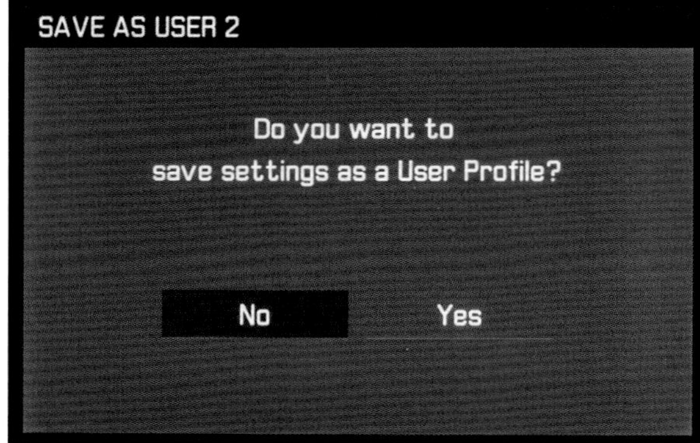

Saving a profile

1) Set the various menu options as desired.

2) Select **User Profile**, then **Save as User Profile**.

3) Select one of the four profile slots (by default these are **USER1**, **USER2**, **USER3**, and **USER4**). A free profile slot is shown as unused, a previously saved profile as used.

4) Select **Yes** to save the user profile or **No** to return to the **Save as User Profile** menu page.

5) Repeat from step 1 to create different user profiles.

Loading a profile

1) Select **User Profiles** followed by **Load Profile**.

2) Select the required profile from the list. The profile marked **active** is the profile currently in use. (Select **Standard Profile** to return the Leica M10 back to its default settings.)

3) Press MENU to return to the **User Profiles** menu page or the shutter-release button to return to shooting mode.

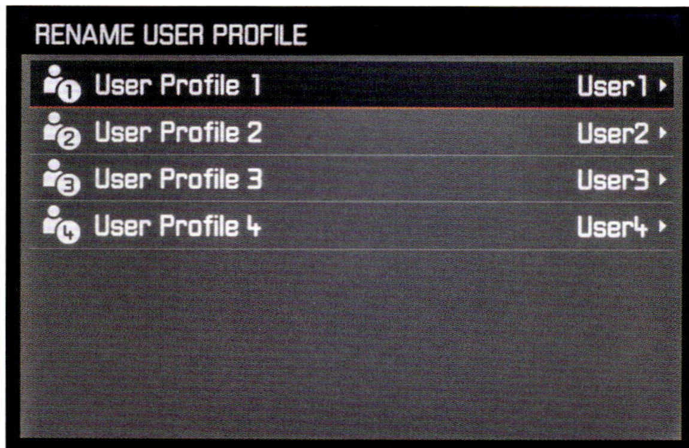

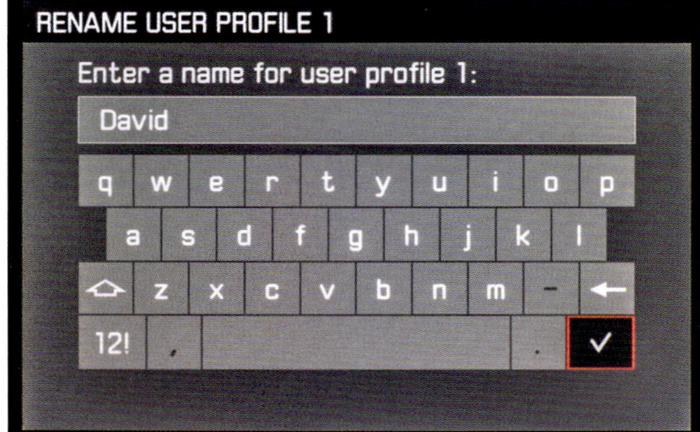

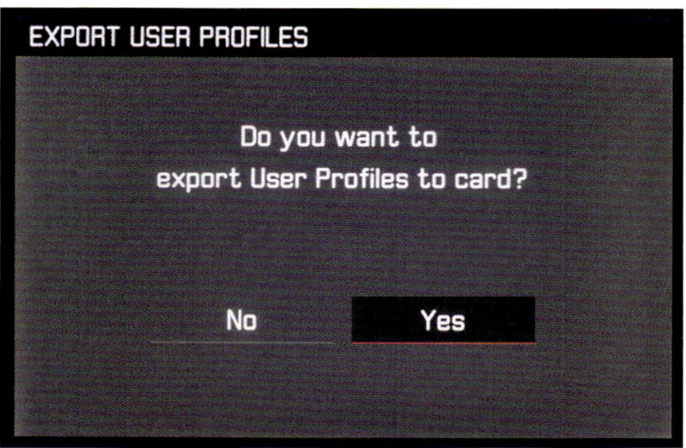

Renaming a profile

1) Select **User Profiles** followed by **Rename User Profile**.

2) Select the profile you want to rename.

3) Use the keyboard to change the name of the profile. A profile name can have 1–5 characters. Press ✥ to highlight a character and press ● to select that character. Select ← to delete a letter from the text bar at the top of the screen; ⇧ to toggle between upper and lower case lettering; **12!/Abc** to swap between lettering and number/symbol entry.

4) Select ✓ when you have entered the required user profile name.

Exporting and importing a profile to a memory card

1) Select **User Profiles** followed by **Export to Card**.

2) Select **Yes** to continue or **No** to return to the **User Profiles** menu. When **Yes** is selected, all the saved user profiles are exported to the memory card, overwriting any that have been exported there previously.

3) To import user profiles select **User Profiles**, then **Import from Card**.

4) Select **Yes** to continue or **No** to return to the **User Profiles** menu. When **Yes** is selected, the user profiles saved to the memory card are saved to the Leica M10, overwriting any that have been saved previously on the camera.

Note
⇧ changes to ~|\ on the numerical entry screen. Selecting ~|\ lets you swap between two sets of symbols. Note that you cannot use symbols in a user profile, although they can be used when entering in copyright details (see page 98).

The options on the **Customize Control** sub-menu pages are used to set the options you want saved to the Favorites menu and to customize the behavior of the thumbwheel in shooting mode.

Edit Favorites

The Favorites menu can be edited so that a selection of useful menu options are displayed immediately after you press MENU. What constitutes a useful menu option is very much a personal choice. You can alter the selection of options on the Favorites menu at any point. However, it is worth leaving the selection for a few weeks after you begin shooting with the Leica M10. This will give you a chance to work out the menu options you use most and which are rarely (if ever) used.

Changing Edit Favorites options

1) Select **Edit Favorites**.

2) Highlight the option you want to add to the **Favorites** menu. Press ● to turn that option **On**. Pressing ● again will turn the option **Off**.

3) Continue to turn options **On** or **Off** as required.

4) Press MENU to return to the **Customize Control** sub-menu page.

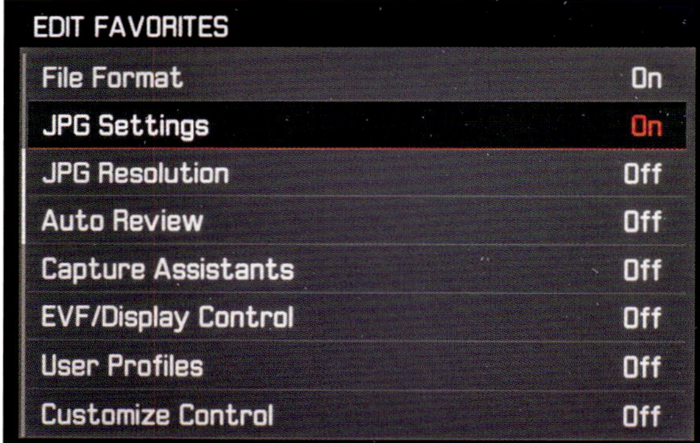

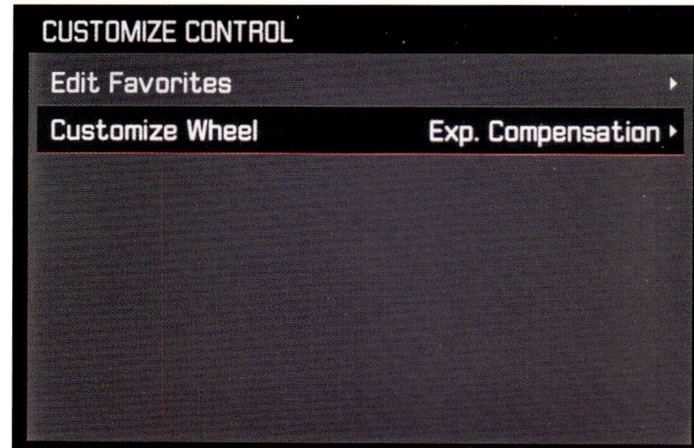

Notes

• By default, the following menu options are initially available on the Favorites menu: **Drive Mode**; **Exposure Compensation**; **Flash Settings**; **ISO Setup**; **White Balance**; **File Format**; **JPG Settings**.

• Not all menu options can be added to the Favorites menu. You cannot add the following: **Image Numbering**; **Sensor Cleaning**; **Camera Information**. Items on sub-menu pages cannot be added to the Favorites menu (with the exception of **M-ISO** when firmware update 1.3.4.0 has been installed; see page 97).

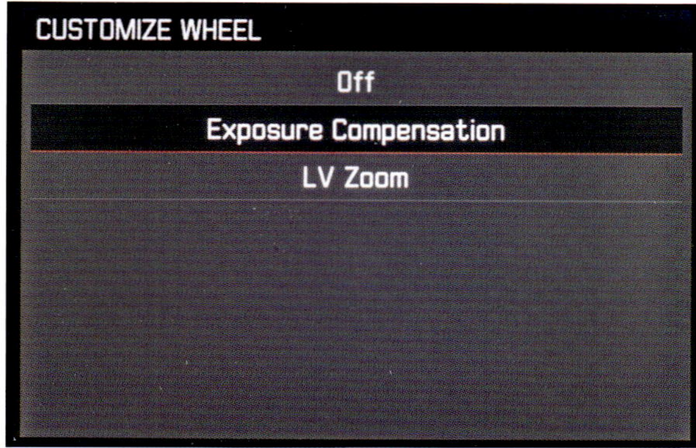

Customize Wheel

Customize Wheel lets you alter the function of the thumbwheel in shooting mode. There are three choices: **Off**; **Exposure Compensation**; **LV Zoom**.

Of the three options, **Exposure Compensation** is arguably the most useful as it allows you to make exposure adjustments quickly in Aperture Priority mode, without the need to access the option via the menu system.

LV Zoom uses the thumbwheel to magnify the Live View image, using the same control method as **Focus Aid** (see page 84). Which option you choose should be based on your shooting style.

› EVF Brightness

The principle of setting the correct **Display Brightness** also applies to the **EVF Brightness** settings when the Visoflex EVF is fitted to your Leica M10.

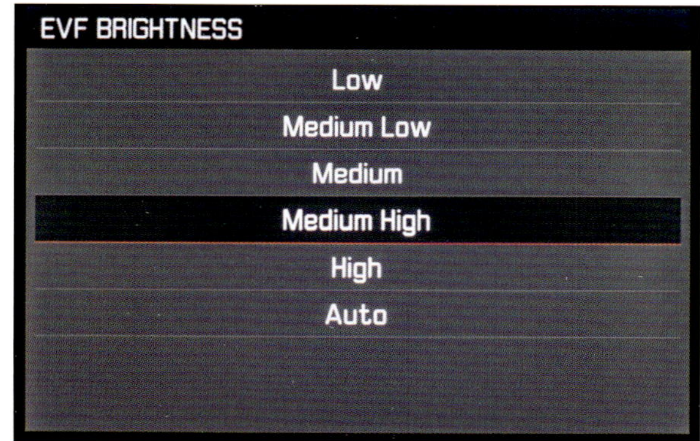

› Display Brightness

This option is used to set the brightness of the LCD. You can set this manually or let the Leica M10 decide when **Auto** is selected (if **Auto** is selected do not cover the LCD brightness sensor).

If you prefer to select the brightness manually you can choose between **Low** (the LCD is at its dimmest) and **High** (the LCD is set to its brightest level), with **Medium Low**, **Medium**, and **Medium High** settings in between.

The LCD brightness should be adjusted according to the ambient lighting conditions so that you can see the screen properly. Typically **Low** would be selected when ambient light levels are low and **High** when shooting in bright conditions. However, it's important to note that even if you have the brightness set correctly, it is not a good idea to rely on the LCD for exposure appraisal; the histogram in either Live View or playback is a far more objective and accurate way to achieve this.

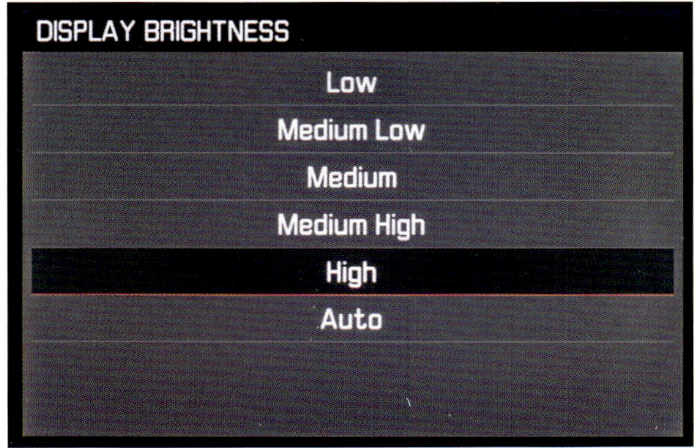

› Auto Power Saving

To conserve battery power the Leica M10 will power down automatically if it has not been used for a time. **Auto Power Saving** lets you set the duration before the camera powers down, with options for **2 minutes**, **5 minutes**, or **10 minutes**. You can also choose **Off** so the Leica M10 remains permanently on until you switch it off using the main power switch. You can wake your Leica M10 by pressing lightly down on the shutter-release button.

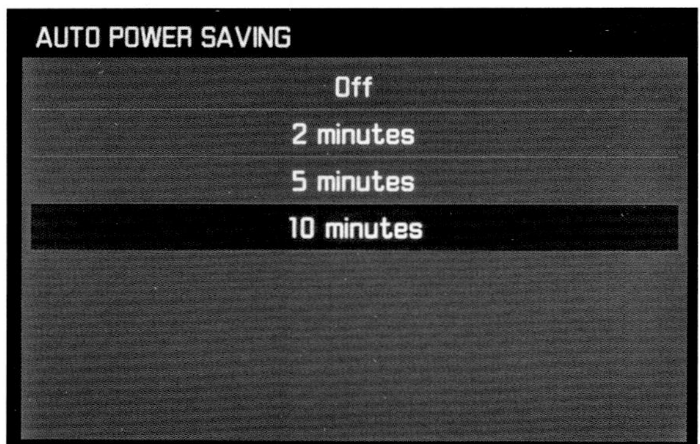

› WLAN

Sets Wi-Fi connectivity. See chapter 9 for details.

› GPS

This option is only available when the Visoflex EVF—which houses a built-in GPS—is fitted to your Leica M10. The longitude and latitude details of your current location are added to the metadata of your images as you shoot. This information can be used by software such as Lightroom to add an image's position onto a map.

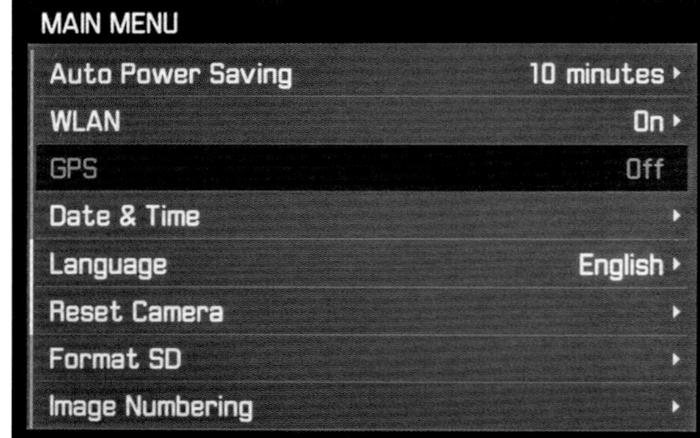

› Date & Time

The very first task when you initially use your Leica M10 is to set the default **Language** and **Date & Time**. Setting the correct time is important, as this information is embedded into the non-image metadata stored in every image file you shoot. The date and time that an image was shot is displayed on the detailed information playback screen. Your computer's operating system and image software will also be able to use the time and date metadata to sort your photographs into chronological order.

Setting Date & Time

1) Press MENU and select **Date & Time**.

2) Select **Date Setting**. Initially, **Date Format** is highlighted. Press ▲ / ▼ to skip through the three available options: **Month/Day/Year**, **Year/Month/Day**, and **Day/Month/Year**. Press ● to select a format.

3) Press ▲ / ▼ to alter the year, month, and date. Press ● to save the changes at each step.

4) Select **Time Setting**. Press ▲ / ▼ to toggle the **Time format** between **12 hours** and **24 hours**. Press ● to continue.

5) Press ▲ / ▼ to alter the hour, minutes, and set **am** or **pm** (if **12 hours** was selected previously). Press ● to save the changes at each step.

Other options

When the Visoflex EVF is fitted you can take advantage of its GPS facility to automatically keep the time and date on your Leica M10 accurate. Set **Auto GPS Time** to **On** if you think this would be beneficial (the option is ghosted out if the Visoflex EVF is not fitted).

When **Daylight Saving Time** is turned **On**, the time set on your Leica M10 will advance by one hour. When set to **Off** the time will jump back by one hour. If you intend to use this option it is advisable to set the time to the non-daylight saving time of your country.

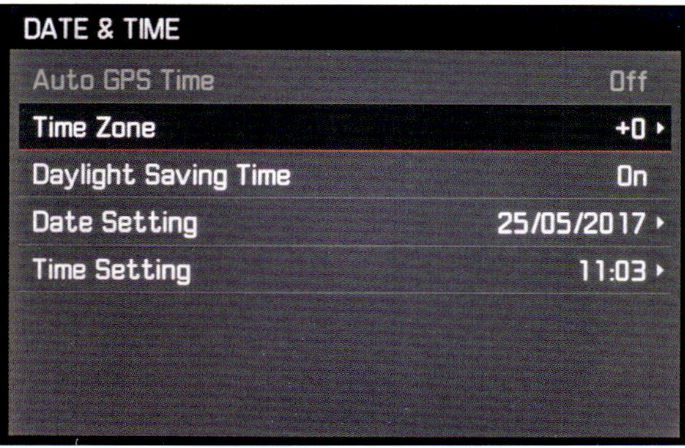

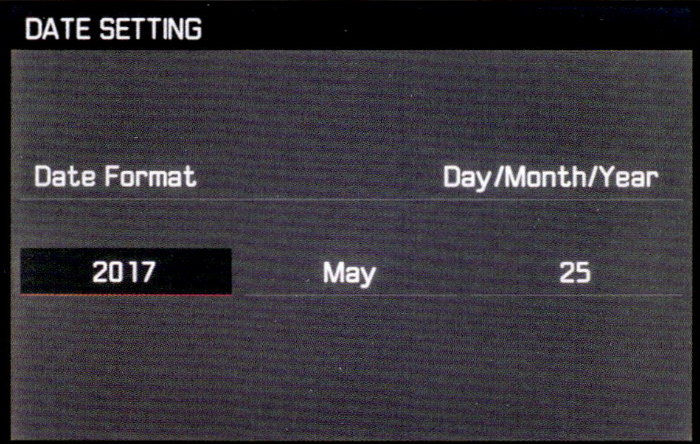

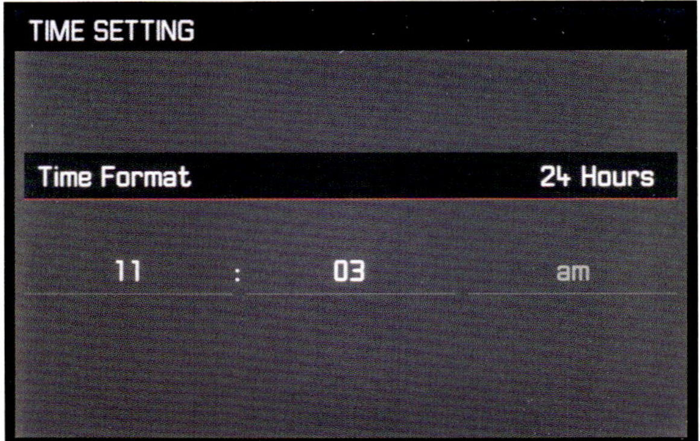

The **Time Zone** option lets you set your current time zone. Use the grid below as a guide. Each time zone is shown in relation to the number of hours ahead (+) or behind (−) it is to UTC. By selecting a different time zone you can temporarily adjust the time set on your camera. This is a useful facility if you travel a lot and is far less time-consuming than adjusting the time manually each time you enter a new time zone.

London, Casablanca	Madrid, Paris, Berlin, Wetzlar UTC +1	Athens, Helsinki, Ankara UTC +2	Moscow, Nairobi, Riyadh, Kuwait UTC+3
Teheran UTC +3:30	Abu Dhabi, Dubai UTC +4	Kabul UTC +4:30	Islamabad, Karachi UTC +5
New Delhi, Columbo UTC +5:30	Kathmandu UTC +5:45	Dhaka UTC +6	Yangon UTC +6:30
Bangkok, Jakarta UTC +7	Beijing, Hong Kong, Singapore UTC +8	Tokyo, Seoul UTC +9	Darwin, Adelaide UTC +9:30
Sydney, Guam UTC +10	New Caledonia UTC +11	Auckland, Fiji UTC +12	Tonga, Samoa UTC +13
Midway UTC −11	Hawaii, Tahiti UTC −10	Alaska, Anchorage UTC −9	Los Angeles, Seattle, Vancouver UTC −8
Denver, Phoenix UTC −7	Chicago, Houston, Mexico City UTC −6	New York, Toronto, Lima UTC −5	Caracus UTC −4.30
Manuas, La Paz UTC −4	Newfoundland UTC −3:30	Buenos Aires, São Paulo UTC −3	Fernando de Noronha UTC −2
Azores UTC −1			

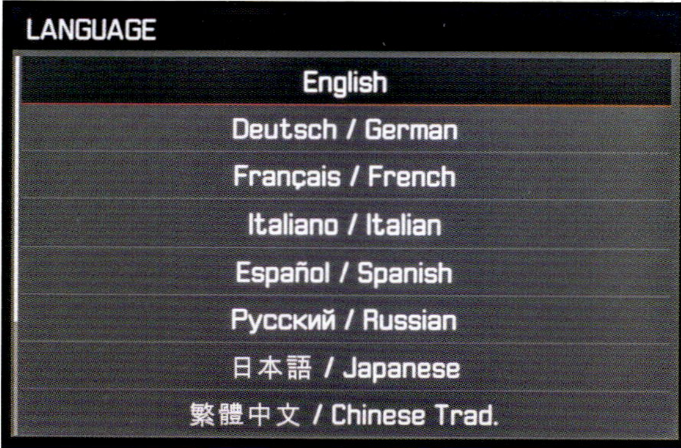

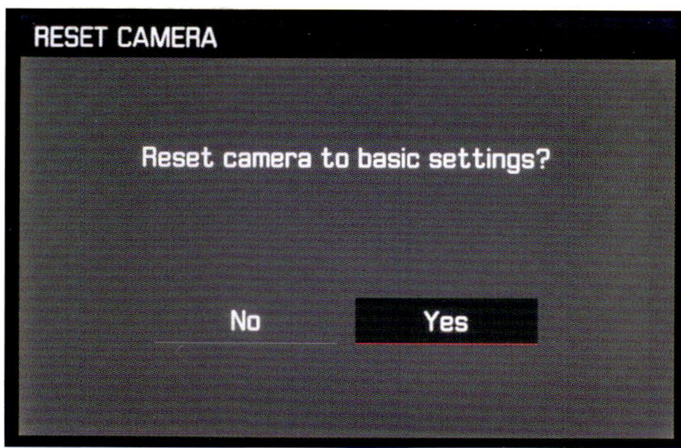

› Language

The Leica M10 can display menu options in a variety of different languages. You can choose between: **English**, **German**, **French**, **Italian**, **Spanish**, **Russian**, **Japanese**, **Traditional Chinese**, **Simplified Chinese**, **Korean**, and **Portuguese**. Tempting as it may be, be careful not to set your Leica M10 to a non-Roman language unless you speak that language—you may find locating and resetting the **Language** becomes very difficult!

› Reset Camera

You can reset your Leica M10 to its original default factory-settings. On selecting **Reset Camera** choose **Yes** to **Reset camera to basic settings** or **No** to return to the **Main Menu** without resetting the camera.

If you select **Yes**, you have the option to **Keep user profiles**. Select **Yes** if you want to retain any user profiles saved to your Leica M10 or **No** to clear all user profiles.

Next, you can select **Yes** to **Keep WLAN settings** saved to the camera, **No** to clear the WLAN settings.

Finally, select **Yes** to **Keep image numbering** or **No** to reset image numbering back to 1 for any images subsequently shot and saved to the memory card.

Press MENU to return to the previous page if you want to revise your choices at any point. Once the Leica M10 has been reset you will need to re-confirm the **Language**, **Time Zone**, **Daylight Saving Time**, and **Date & Time** settings before you begin shooting again.

› Format SD Card

It is highly recommended that you format a new memory card or one that has been used in another camera. See chapter 2 for details.

› Image Numbering

The **Image Numbering** sub-menu has a number of options that enable you to manage your image files and image folders.

New Folder

Images are stored in folders on a memory card. These folders are created automatically every time you format the memory card. By default, the folder name is a three-digit number followed by the word LEICA. The three-digit number is the folder number, starting at 100. The Leica M10 can create up to 999 folders, each one assigned a folder number that is one more than the current highest numbered folder on the memory card.

Creating a **New Folder** adds a new folder to the memory card. This could be done to separate projects or to avoid cluttering up folders with too many images. Although you can't change the folder number (this is assigned automatically) you can change the five-letter folder name if required. The name is entered using a keyboard similar to the keyboard used to rename a User Profile (see page 86). You cannot use symbols in the folder name, with the exception of _.

Change Filename

Images shot on the Leica M10 are assigned a four-letter prefix followed by a four-digit image number. Up to 9999 images can be stored in a folder starting from 0001. Once this threshold has been reached a new folder is created and the count reverts back to 0001. Select **Change Filename** and you can personalize the four-letter prefix using the Leica M10's on-screen keyboard. As with new folders you cannot use symbols, with the exception of _.

Reset Image Numbering

Choose **Reset Image Numbering** and the Leica M10 will start numbering images from 0001 again, creating a new folder to store them in.

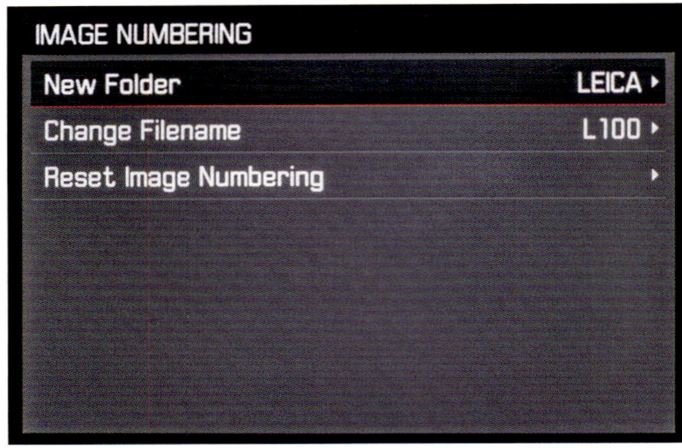

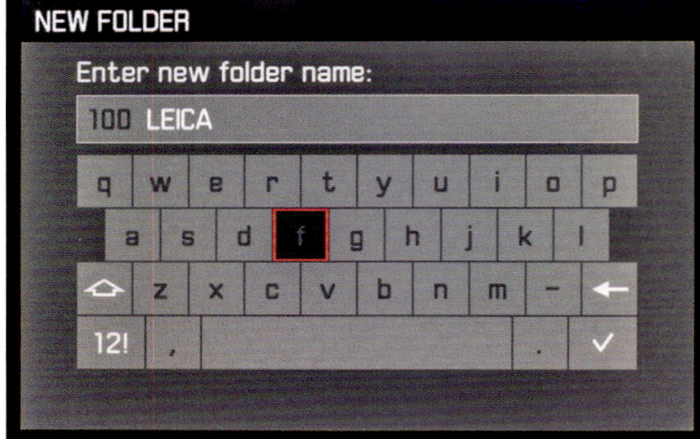

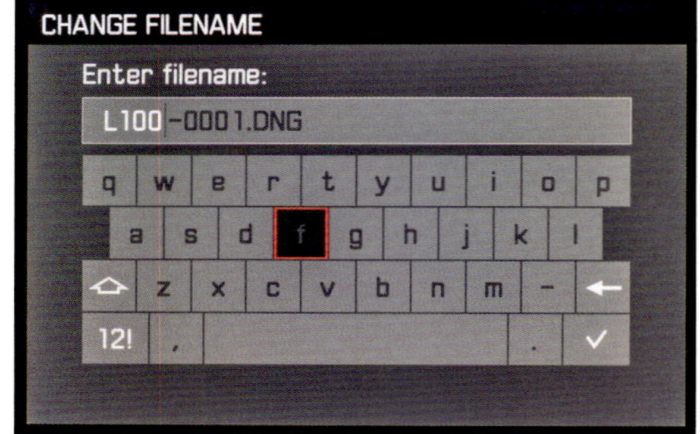

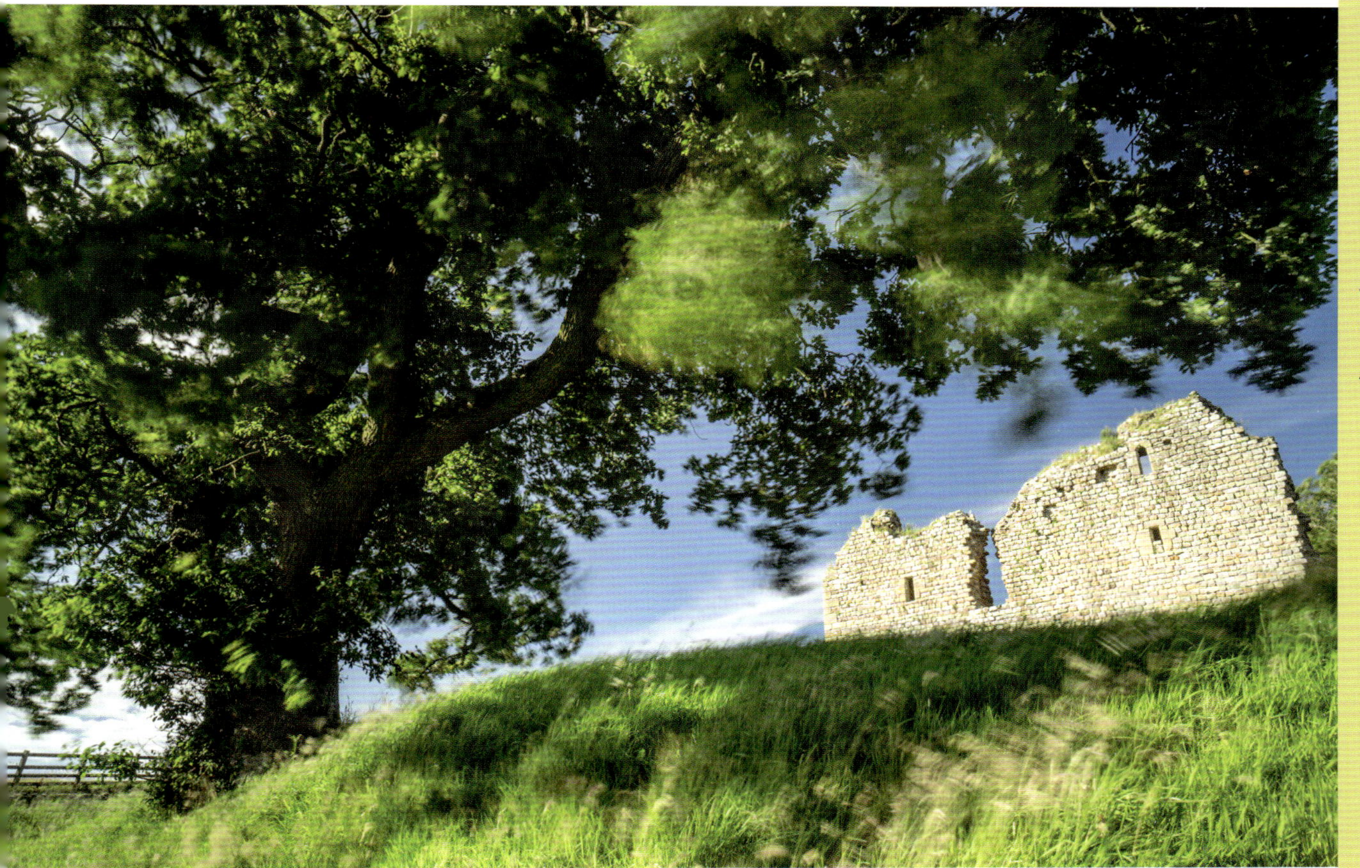

⌃ FRAMES

Accurate composition is often necessary when you're shooting a subject framed by another element in a scene. For this type of image I often use Live View so I can check that everything is OK before shooting. I may also shoot a few variations to ensure that I have something usable.

› Sensor Cleaning

Dust is the bane of every photographer's life. No matter how careful you are, dust will invariably build up on the sensor of your Leica M (keeping negatives free of dust was just as frustrating, so it is not a digital-only problem). The Leica M10 does not have an automatic dust removal system, so dust on the sensor has to removed manually.

You can assess the problem by selecting **Dust Detection.** If dust is detected it will be visible on the image displayed on the LCD (in a highly exaggerated form). The image shows you the location (and number) of dust particles found on the sensor.

Selecting **Open Shutter** holds open the shutter, exposing the sensor for cleaning. See pages 150–151 for more information about cleaning the sensor.

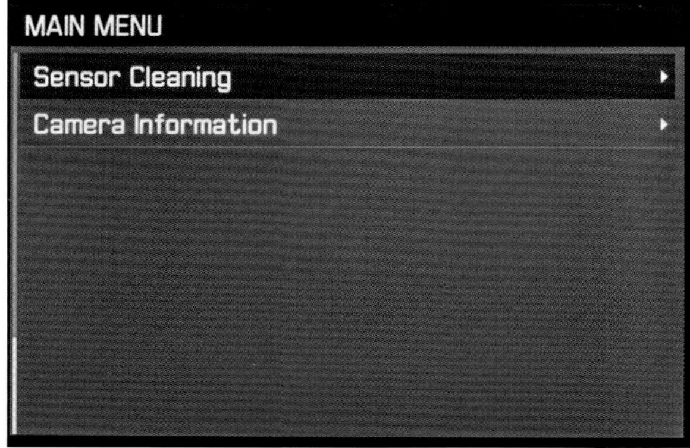

› Camera Information

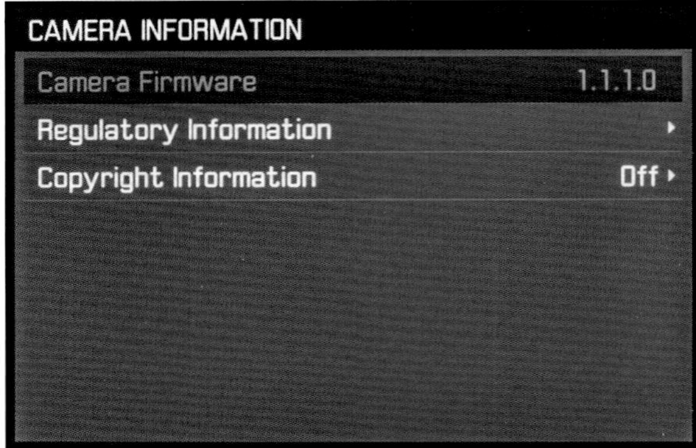

The options on the **Camera Information** sub-menu page let you update the Leica M10's firmware, view regulatory information, and set the copyright data that is embedded into the metadata of the images you shoot.

Firmware

The Leica M10 has built-in software that runs all the electrical functions. This software is known as firmware. Every so often Leica issues an update to the firmware for its cameras to fix bugs or add extra features. You'll be notified when new firmware is available after you've registered your camera. The firmware version number currently installed in your camera is shown on this menu option.

Installing new firmware

1) Download the firmware from the Leica website.

2) Insert a freshly charged battery and memory card into your Leica M10. The memory card must have at least 200MB available—formatting the memory card is a good way to ensure this, but copy any images on the card to your computer before you do!

3) Switch off your Leica M10 and remove the memory card. Insert it into a memory card reader attached to your computer.

4) Copy the downloaded file to the memory card and reinsert the memory card back into the Leica M10.

5) Turn on the Leica M10 and select **Firmware** on the **Camera Information** sub-menu page. Select **Yes** to continue updating the firmware, or **No** to return to the **Camera Information** page.

6) The firmware file will be checked by your Leica M10 and then updating will begin. Don't switch off your Leica M10 at this stage.

7) Once the firmware has been updated you will be prompted to turn off your Leica M10. Turn it off then back on again and use as normal.

Note
- When you buy a Leica from a reputable dealer it should have the latest firmware installed.

Firmware 1.3.4.0

At the time of writing, firmware 1.3.4.0 was made available. This updates a number of items on the shooting information screen and menu system including:

- A change to the color-coding of the memory card and battery status bars on the shooting information screen. The bars now change from green to yellow to red as the battery depletes or as the memory card is filled.

- An increase in the number of items that can be added to the Favorites menu. Up to 15 menu items can be selected, spread over two menu pages.

- You can now skip to the Main Menu from Favorites menu by pressing the MENU button. Pressing MENU when viewing the Main Menu lets you jump downward between the various menu pages.

- EVF/display control has changed so that it is now possible to choose between **Auto**, **EVF**, or **Display** to determine which screen **Auto Review** uses by default.

- **M-ISO** can now be added to the Favorites menu for quicker access.

- Faster return to Live View after shooting an image.

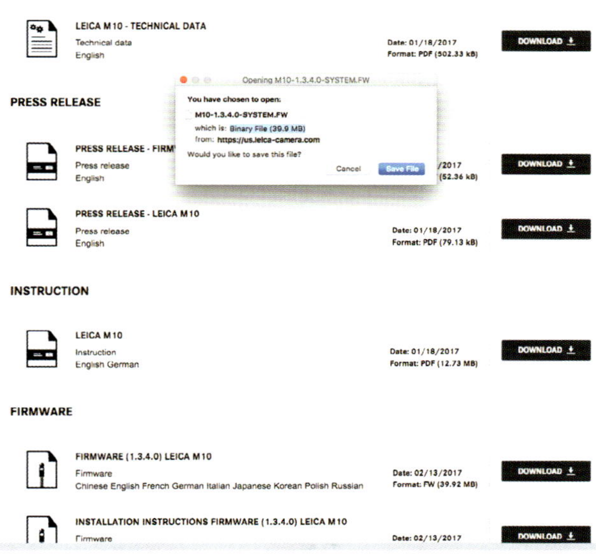

Warning!

You will not be allowed to update the firmware if the battery charge is low.

Regulatory Information

At first glance the **Regulatory Information** page looks slightly eccentric. All you see when you select the option is a series of graphics and logos relating to a variety of countries. However, there is a reason for this eccentricity. These graphics are a record that the Leica M10 complies with local laws governing functions such as Wi-Fi. However, this is largely irrelevant to how you use your camera. **Regulatory Information** is an option you may look at once (if at all) and then never view again.

Copyright Information

Every image you shoot belongs to you. It is your property and—with one exception—is no one else's. This means that if someone uses one of your images without permission you have the legal right to request payment (actually receiving the payment is another matter and unfortunately it is often not worth the time and effort pursuing minor infractions).

The first step in establishing your legal right of ownership is to add your copyright details to the metadata of your images. By entering **Copyright Information** on your Leica M10, proof of ownership is added automatically to every image you shoot.

A very current issue for photographers is the concept of the "orphan" image. These are digital images that apparently belong to no one because information about ownership has been lost. This can lead to the images being used without attribution and, more importantly, without recompense to the photographer. To avoid this happening to you it is highly recommended that adding relevant **Copyright Information** is one of the first things you do when setting up your Leica M10.

Notes
- You can assign the copyright of an image (or any created work) to anyone you wish. If you were shooting images as an employee of a company you would probably assign the company as the copyright owner.

- Some social media websites strip out the copyright information metadata from images when they're uploaded. Adding a subtle copyright watermark to your images is a good option if you are worried about others using them without permission.

› Setting Copyright Information

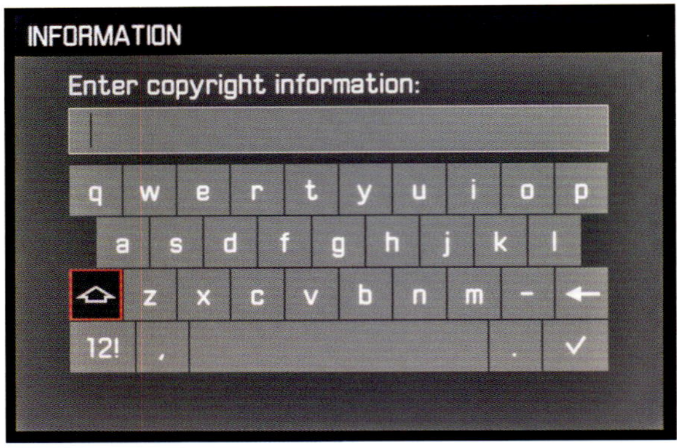

1) Set **Copyright** on the **Copyright Information** page to **On**.

2) Select **Information**. The data you enter here would typically be the copyright owner of the images shot with the camera; either you or the company that employs you as a photographer.

3) Use the keyboard to change the Information text. The copyright information can be set to anything between 1–20 characters. Press ✛ to highlight a character and press ● to select that character. Select ← to delete a letter from the text bar at the top of the screen; ⇧ to toggle between upper and lower case lettering; **12!/Abc** to swap between lettering and number/symbol entry.

4) Select ✓ when you are finished.

» COPYRIGHT

The copyright of every image you shoot belongs to you, even when you work on commission for someone else. It is only when you specifically assign copyright to someone else that it is no longer yours. Image licensing can produce a significant income for a photographer, so assigning copyright to someone else should not be done lightly.

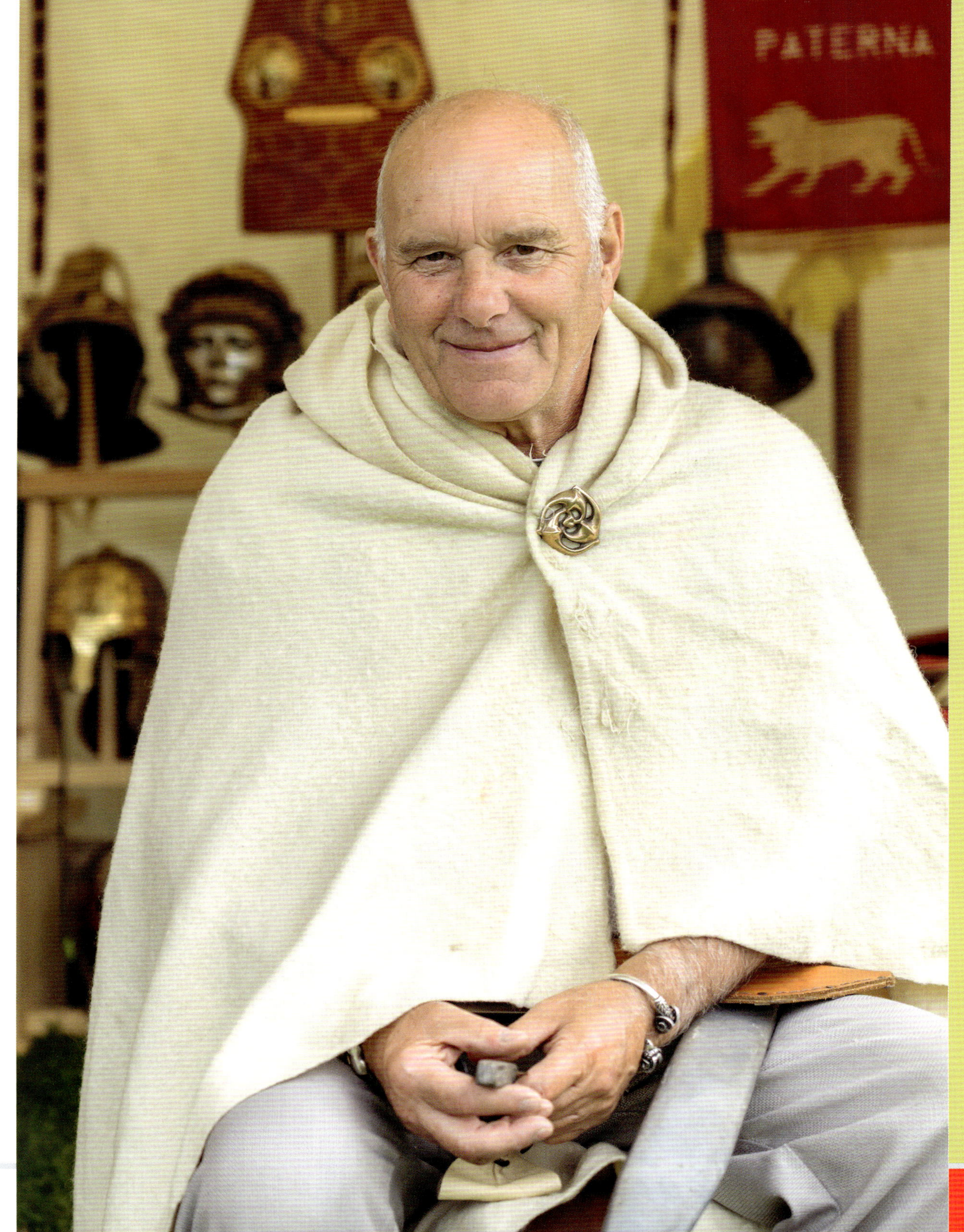

PATERNA

CHAPTER 4
LENSES

Camera bodies come and go, but a good lens is a lens for life. Leica's eminent reputation is built not just on its camera bodies, but on the optical quality of its lenses, which are often the best of their kind.

The quality of a lens will ultimately determine how sharp your images are and how free they are from aberrations (see pages 172–173). Leica's lenses have a well-deserved reputation for high optical quality and they are also a pleasure to use; from the basic engineering to the smoothness of the focusing and aperture rings, their mechanical quality is peerless.

However, there is no denying that Leica lenses are expensive compared to lenses for other DSLR and mirrorless systems. This means it is important to think very carefully about the lenses that will suit your style of photography *before* you purchase them.

To complicate matters, there is a wealth of choice when it comes to Leica lenses. As you will see in this chapter, there is repetition in the Leica lens line-up that can seem bewildering at first, so we will guide you through both Leica lenses and the various qualities of lenses in general.

» LANDSCAPE
135mm is not a focal length traditionally associated with landscape photography, but the apparent compression of space produces a more intimate effect than a wide-angle lens.

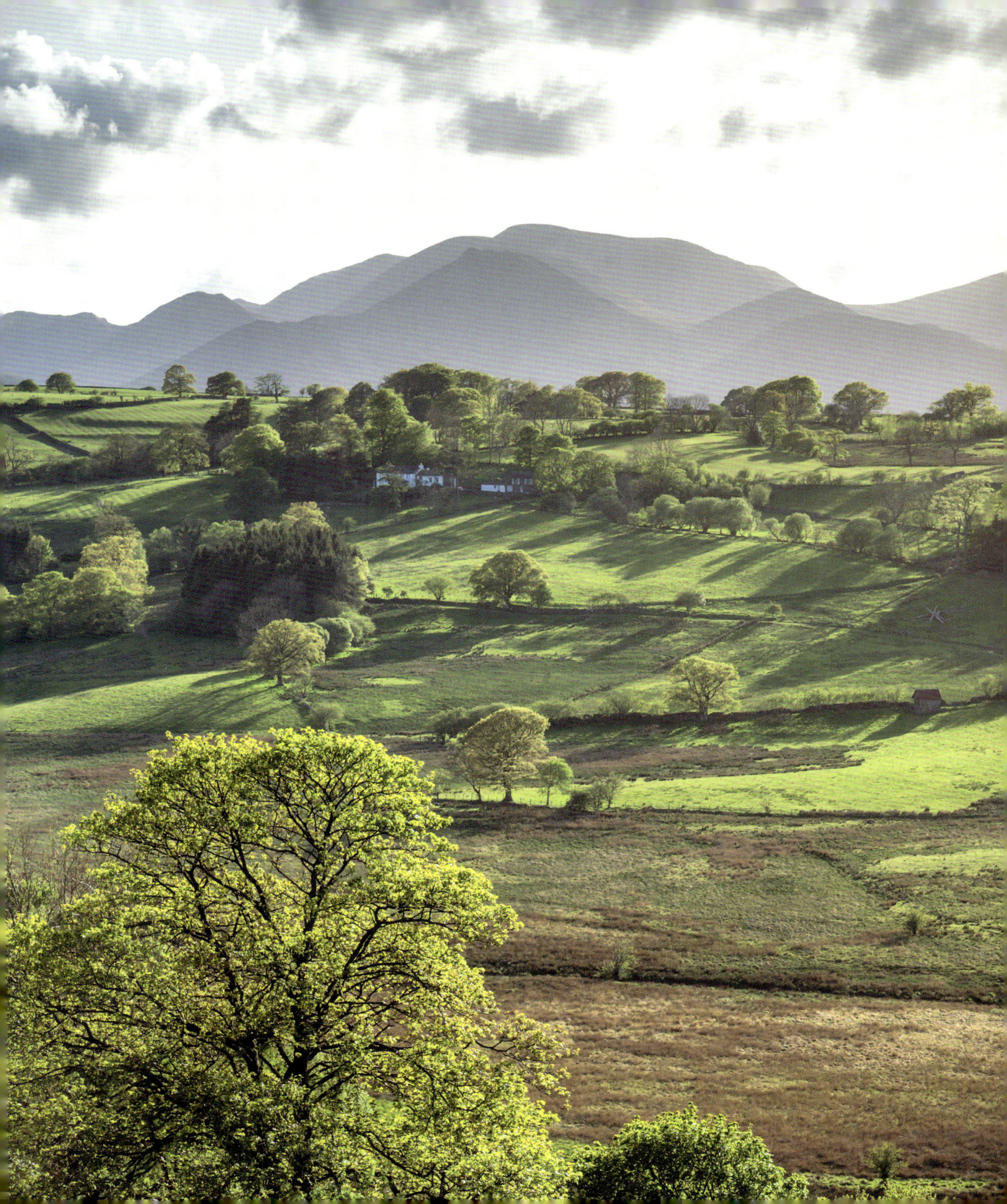

» THE LEICA M MOUNT

The history of Leica lenses is a convoluted story that is too long for this book. This chapter therefore is only a guide to what is currently available new, both from Leica and third-party manufacturers. For the curious, the Internet is a good resource for information about lenses that are now out of production but are still available used.

What is important to understand, though, is that Leica's M mount has been in use since 1954, which means you are not just restricted to modern lenses—there is a wealth of pre-owned lenses available that are compatible with the Leica M10. Although older lenses may lack technologies such as modern lens coatings, if they are in good condition they will be well worth considering.

A good reason to consider older lenses is that they often have qualities not found in their modern equivalents. For example, modern optics tend to be neutral in color (they do not add color to the image), while older lenses may be slightly warmer. This can be highly desirable when shooting portraits—providing the warmth is not removed through white balance correction.

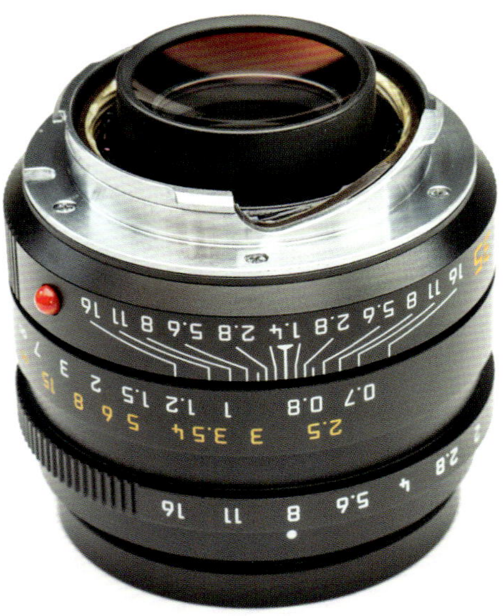

› Naming conventions

One thing a Leica owner cannot complain about is the range of lenses available for an M-series camera. Due to the longevity of the mount there is an incredible number of different M-mount lenses—both old and new—that can be fitted to a Leica M10.

However, you could be forgiven for wondering why there is so much apparent duplication of lenses: it is often possible to choose between two, three, or even four different lenses of the same focal length. The difference between these lenses typically comes down to the size of the available maximum aperture. This means that you can choose between a lighter lens with a relatively small maximum aperture (commonly referred to as a "slow" lens) or a heavier lens with a large maximum aperture (known as a "fast" lens).

Which you would choose depends on a number of factors. Landscape photographers typically shoot using small apertures, so a lens with a large maximum aperture may be irrelevant (and would add to the weight of the photographer's rucksack—an important consideration when traveling any distance on foot). However, portrait photographers or photographers who regularly shoot in low light at maximum aperture would benefit more from the faster lenses in the range.

Price is another consideration. Generally, the faster a lens is (the wider its maximum aperture), the more expensive it will be in comparison to its slower equivalents. To make life (slightly) easier for everyone, Leica uses naming conventions to help you distinguish between different lens types.

‹‹ M MOUNT
The distinctive notch in Leica's M mount moves the rangefinder coupling arm as the lens is attached.

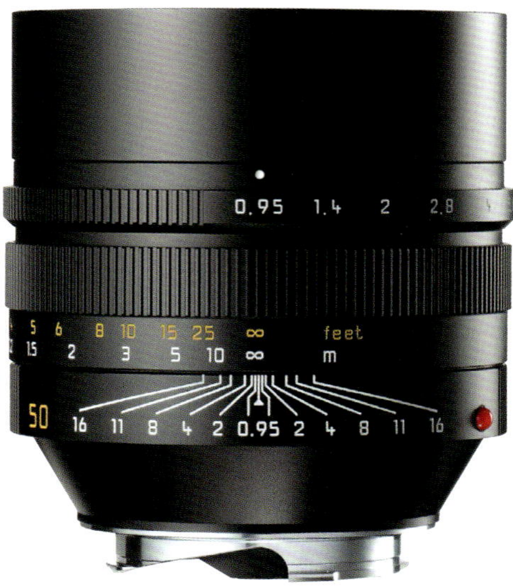

⌃ LOW LIGHT CHAMP
Leica NOCTILUX-M 50mm f/0.95 ASPH.
© Leica

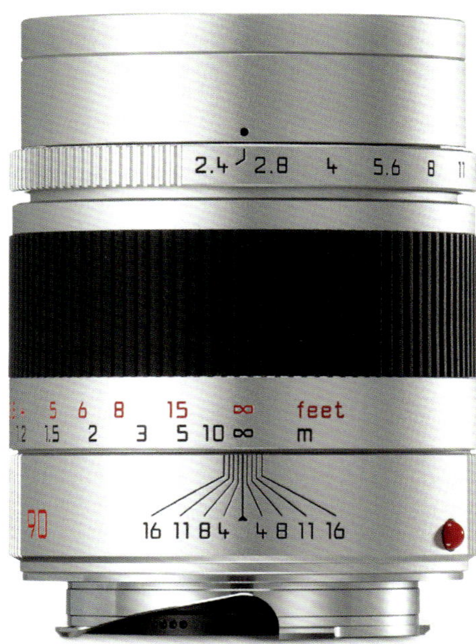

⌃ THOROUGHLY MODERN
Leica SUMMARIT-M 90mm f/2.4 silver.
© Leica

Noctilux

The Noctilux (pronounced *nok-tee-lux*) name designates lenses that have the largest maximum apertures in the Leica lens range ("Nocti" is derived from the Latin for nocturnal and "Lux" from the Latin for light). At the time of writing, Leica produces a single Noctilux M-series lens: the 50mm f/0.95 ASPH.

It is by far the most expensive and—at 1.5lb (700g)—heaviest M-series lens manufactured by Leica. However, it is not the first Noctilux lens made by Leica. Before the f/0.95 variant, Leica made a 50mm f/1.0 version (from 1976 to 2008) and an older f/1.2 design (from 1966 to 1975). Both of these older lenses are available pre-owned.

The main benefits of a Noctilux lens are the ability to shoot in very low light without a high ISO and/or slow shutter speed, or to minimize depth of field for esthetic effect. When used at or close to maximum aperture a Noctilux lens requires highly accurate focusing to ensure that the most important area of your subject is pin-sharp.

Summilux

M-series lenses in the Summilux (*soom-ih-lux*) range have a maximum aperture of f/1.4. This makes them slower than a Noctilux lens, but arguably far more useful on a day-to-day basis. Leica currently produces six Summilux lenses but, as with the Noctilux, older variants can still be purchased secondhand.

Summarit

Modern Summarit (*soom-a-rit*) lenses date back to 2007 when Leica introduced a new range of lenses for its digital M-series cameras. However, in 2015 Leica refreshed the entire Summarit lens range, increasing the maximum aperture from f/2.5 to f/2.4 and refining the optics. However, the Summarit name has much earlier origins, as Leica produced a 50mm f/1.5 Summarit from 1949–1960 (the 50mm Summilux has effectively replaced this lens).

Summicron

The Summicron (*soom-ih-cron*) name is derived from Leica's 50mm "Summar" lens (introduced in 1933) and "Krone" (the Danish for Crown), referencing the Crown glass that was used in those early lenses. Summicron lenses have a maximum aperture of f/2.0.

Elmar

Elmar (*ell-mar*) lenses are the slowest in Leica's lens range. Current Elmar lenses are either f/3.8 or f/4, as in the ELMAR-M 24mm f/3.8 and TRI-ELMAR-M 16–18–21mm f/4. Leica also produces a SUPER-ELMAR-M 21mm lens with a maximum aperture of f/3.4. The first Elmar lenses were derived from a 50mm f/3.5 Elmax lens produced in 1925 (the name is taken from **E**rnst **L**eica and **Max** Berak).

Elmarit

A derivation of Elmar, Elmarit (*ell-mar-it*) lenses have a maximum aperture of f/2.8. Confusingly, though, not all f/2.8 lenses are Elmarits: the 50mm f/2.8 "collapsible" lens, manufactured until 2007, was designated as an Elmar, rather than an Elmarit.

≽ 24MM
Two Leica 24mm lenses: the ELMAR-M 24mm f/3.8 ASPH (below left) and the SUMMILUX-M 24mm f/1.4 ASPH (below right). Although they have the same focal length they are aimed at two different types of photographer.
© Leica

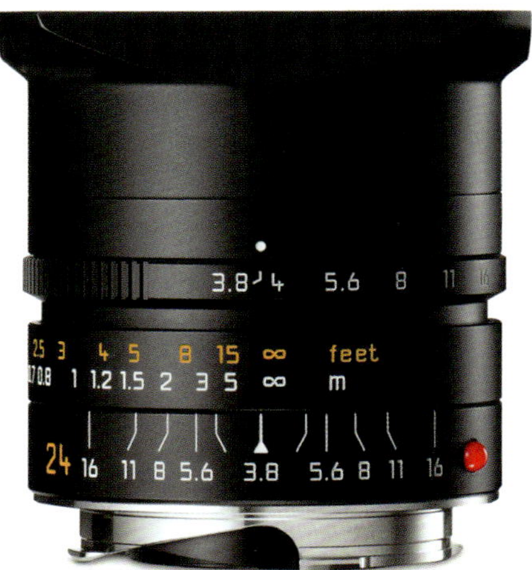

› Lens technology

Lens technology improves as new manufacturing techniques are developed, and this helps to reduce problems that older lenses can suffer from. Leica appends acronyms to lenses that use a particular technology to help differentiate new lenses from old ones.

APO

Chromatic aberration is an optical problem seen as colored fringing along high-contrast edges in images (typically either cyan/red or green/purple). Chromatic aberration is caused by the inability of a lens to focus the different wavelengths of light at the same point. Apochromatic (APO) lenses use low-dispersion glass lens elements to reduce this problem.

ASPH

One problem that older lenses can display is the uneven focusing of light across the image circle. This results both in soft image corners and chromatic aberration, particularly when shooting at maximum aperture. Leica now uses aspherical—ASPH—lens elements in a selection of its lenses.

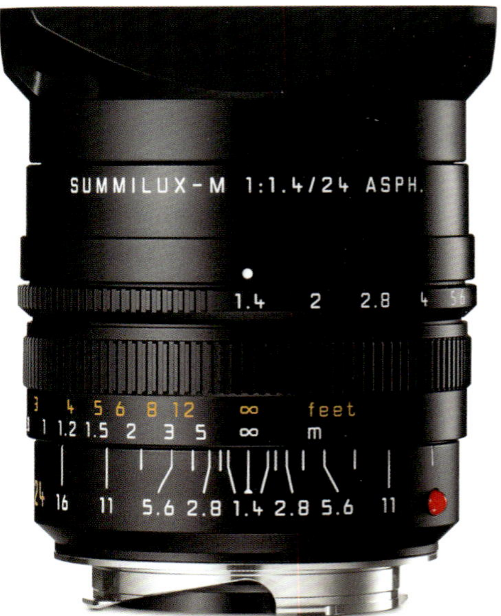

ASPH lens elements have a complex curved profile that helps focus light more evenly across the image space. This reduces the likelihood of both soft image corners and chromatic aberration. However, aspherical lens elements are expensive to design and manufacture, which is reflected in the cost of ASPH lenses compared to their simpler cousins.

TELE

Generally, the longer the focal length of a lens, the longer its corresponding physical length. Telephoto (TELE or TELYT) lenses are physically shorter than their focal length would suggest. This is achieved through the use of lens elements (known as the telephoto group) that extend the light path within the lens to create a longer focal length lens in a shorter "package."

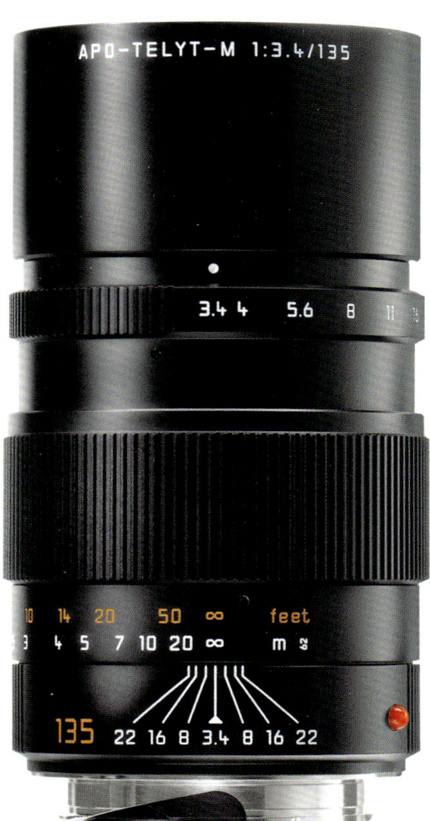

« TELEPHOTO
Leica APO-TELYT-M 135mm f/3.4.
© Leica

› Other lens information

The Leica M10 is compatible with most lenses designed for the M-system mount. However, there are several lenses that should be avoided, even though you can mount them to your camera. These lenses include:

• Zeiss Hologon 15mm f/8 (note this is not a Leica lens).

• SUMMICRON 50mm f/2 (set to close-up).

• ELMAR 90mm f/4 with retractable tube (manufactured between 1954–1968).

• Examples of the SUMMILUX-M 35mm f/1.4 (manufactured in Canada between 1961–1995) either will not mount to the camera correctly or will not focus to infinity. These lenses can be modified to work with the M10 by Leica customer services.

• Any lens with a retractable tube should only be used with the tube extended (the current MACRO-ELMAR-M 90mm f/4, is the only exception to this warning). If the tube extends inside the sensor chamber there is a real risk of damage to the camera shutter blades.

In addition, the following lenses can be used safely with the Leica M10, although TTL metering is not possible. Exposure must be set manually:
• SUPER-ANGULON-M 21mm f/4.

• SUPER-ANGULON-M 21mm f/3.4.

• ELMARIT-M 28mm f/2.8 with a serial number earlier than 2 314 921.

4 » THIRD-PARTY LENSES

Other manufacturers have produced lenses for the M mount since its introduction in 1954. Two manufacturers—Carl Zeiss and Voigtländer—are still producing well-regarded lenses for the M mount.

Carl Zeiss was founded in 1846 in Jena, Germany. The company is renowned for producing high-quality optics for applications such as medical imaging, astronomy, and—of course—photography. As well as making lenses for the Leica M mount, Carl Zeiss also supplies lenses in the Nikon F, Canon EOS, and Sony A and E mounts.

Founded in Vienna in 1759, Voigtländer is even older than Carl Zeiss (and predates the birth of photography as we know it). Voigtländer has had a slightly more checkered history than Carl Zeiss, being sold to Rollei in 1973 and Plusfoto in 1982. Today, Voigtländer lenses are made and marketed by the Japanese company Cosina.

Both companies produce lenses with focal lengths that are not produced by Leica, such as the extreme wide-angle 10mm Heliar lens made by Voigtländer. The drawback to using lenses with exotic focal lengths is that the Leica M10's viewfinder bright-line frames will not be accurate (particularly with lenses significantly wider than 28mm). To use these lenses effectively you will either need to use Live View or fit a supplementary viewfinder to your M10.

˅ **CARL ZEISS**
Selection of M-mount lenses from the Zeiss range.
© Carl Zeiss AG

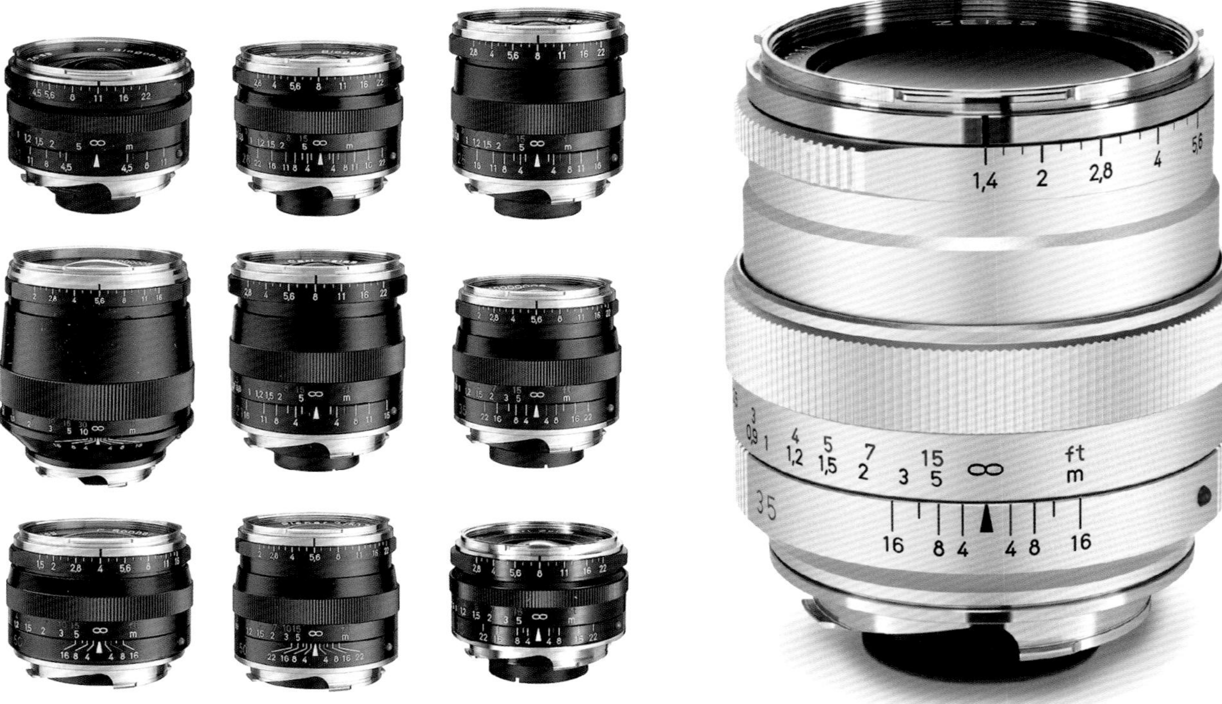

» LENS PROPERTIES

› Focal length

The focal length of a lens is the distance (in millimeters) from the optical center of the lens to the focal plane when the lens is focused at infinity. In digital cameras such as the Leica M10, the sensor is placed at the focal plane.

With the exception of the TRI-ELMAR-M 16–18–21mm, all of Leica's lenses have a fixed focal length. This type of lens is known as a "prime lens." The focal length (and the size of the image sensor) defines the angle of view of a lens, as well as the magnification of elements in a scene.

› Angle of view

The angle of view is the angular extent of the image projected by a lens and recorded by the sensor inside the camera. The angle of view is expressed in degrees and typically refers to the diagonal coverage of the lens (although horizontal and vertical measurements are used occasionally).

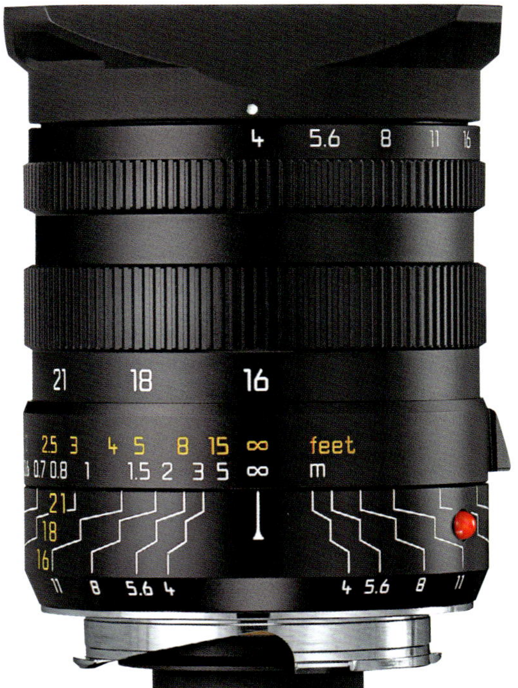

‹‹ VARIABLE FOCAL LENGTH
Leica TRI-ELMAR-M 16–18–21mm f/4 ASPH.
© Leica

» LENS TYPES

Lenses can be broadly placed into one of three categories: wide, standard, or telephoto.

› Wide-angle lenses

A wide-angle lens is generally thought of as any lens with a wider angle of view than a standard lens (see next page). On the Leica M10 this is generally considered to be any lens with a focal length wider than 35mm. The go-to wide-angle lens for Leica M photographers was once the 28mm, largely because this was the widest lens supported by the bright-line frames in the viewfinder. However, Live View and the availability of supplementary viewfinders (that fit above the lens mount in the Leica M's flash hotshoe) allow the use of ultra-wide angle lenses produced by Leica and third-party lens manufacturers.

The wider the focal length of a lens, the more unnatural the perspective of an image will look. Spatial relationships between elements in a scene are stretched, and distant objects will appear far smaller in the image than they would if you were looking at the scene in question.

Landscape photographers frequently use wide-angle lenses, as their optical properties do help to create a sense of space in an image. However, wide-angle lenses are not flattering for portraits: the increase in apparent distance between elements in an image will apply equally to a person's facial features as to a landscape.

⌄ 24MM
Wide-angle lenses are commonly used to shoot architectural subjects. The height of this crane was exaggerated by shooting upward, producing a vertiginous feel. The slightly sinister feel of the subject was increased by converting to black and white during postproduction.

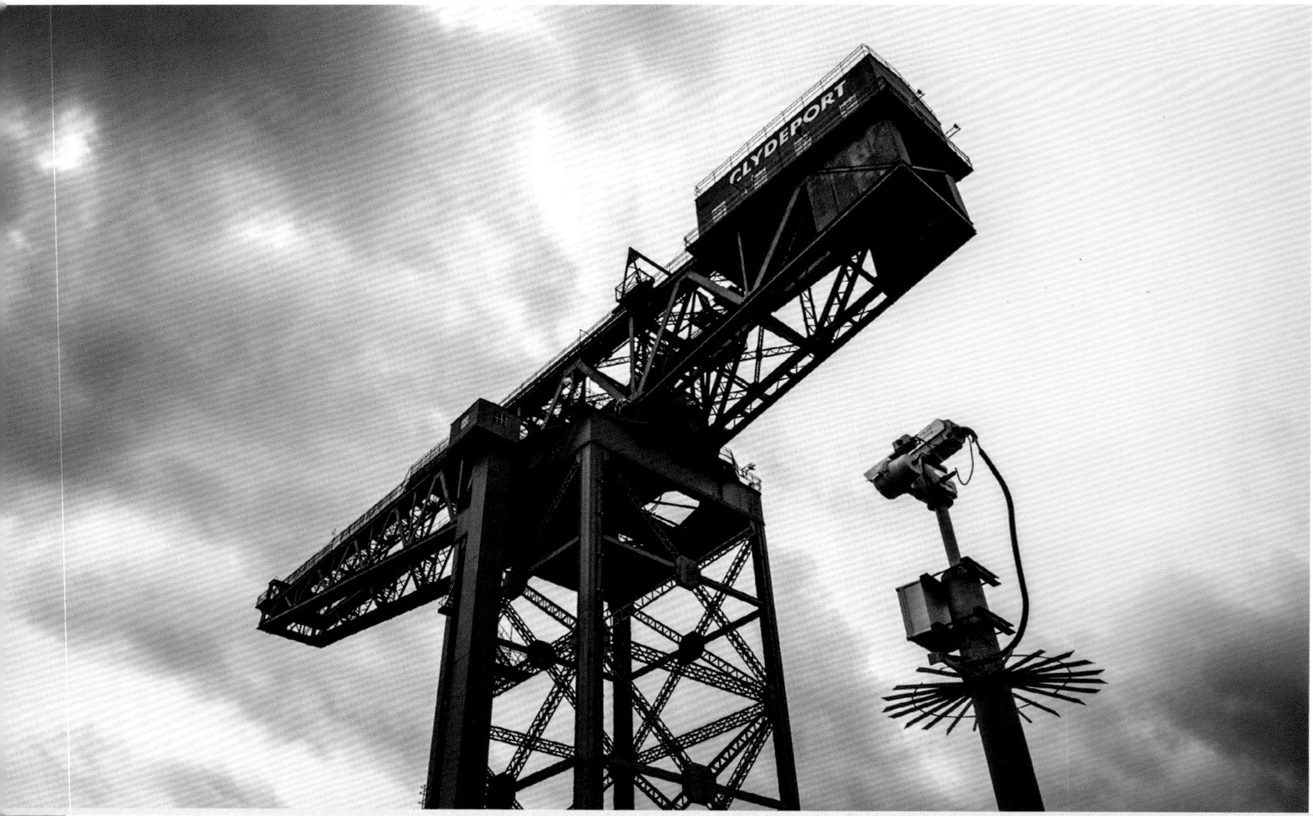

› Standard

The definition of a "standard" or "normal" lens is one that has a focal length roughly equal to the diagonal measurement of the sensor inside the camera. The Leica M10 has a full-frame sensor, which has a diagonal measurement of 43mm. However, Leica—and indeed most lens manufacturers—do not make a 43mm lens. The closest Leica equivalent is 50mm (although Voigtländer produces a 40mm), which is generally regarded as the "standard" lens for full-frame cameras.

The angle of view of a 50mm produces naturalistic images that lack the spatial distortion of wide-angle lenses and the magnification of telephoto lenses. Because of this, 50mm lenses are often underrated. However, they should not be dismissed. A 50mm lens is often the optically finest lens in a manufacturer's lens line-up due to its relatively simple optical construction (particularly when compared to extreme wide-angle lenses).

A 50mm lens is also a great "walkaround" lens. They tend to be reasonably light (with the notable exception of the Leica's Noctilux) and the focal length allows an intimate photographic style (you can keep a reasonable distance from your subject, but still fill the frame in a way that is impossible with a wide-angle lens). For these reasons a 50mm lens is often the go-to focal length for street and documentary photographers.

⌄ 50MM
When you want a lens that produces images that look natural then a "standard" lens cannot be beaten.

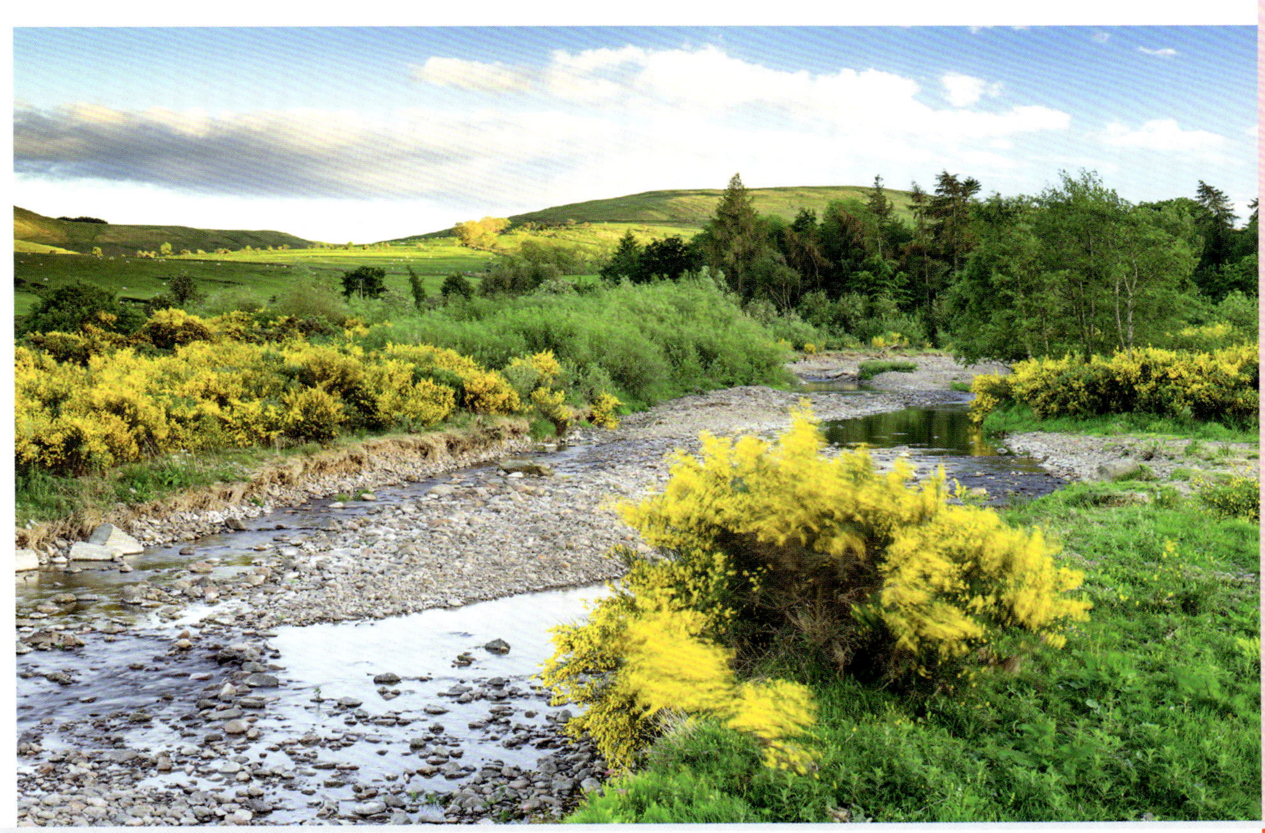

› Telephoto lenses

The longest M-mount focal length lens currently produced by Leica is 135mm, which is a comparatively short focal length compared to the extreme telephoto lenses available for most other DSLR/mirrorless system cameras. The main reason why Leica's lens range stops at 135mm is the difficulty of using long focal length lenses with a rangefinder viewfinder. Use Live View however and it is immediately easier to compose (although longer lenses will need to be fitted via a suitable lens adaptor).

Telephoto lenses restrict the angle of view and magnify distant objects, allowing you to work at a distance from your subject. Leica's 135mm lens is arguably too short for subjects such as nature photography, but it is an ideal portrait lens, as it enables you to stand back from your subject to create a flatter, more pleasing perspective, and throw the background out of focus by using a wide aperture setting.

› Macro lenses

Technically, a macro photograph is one shot at a magnification ratio of 1:1 or greater, so the subject projected onto the image sensor is life size or larger. One of the drawbacks of a rangefinder camera like the Leica M10 is that the closer the subject is to the camera, the more difficult it is to correct for parallax error. This makes it difficult to compose macro images as they require very precise framing. Live View solves this problem and also makes it easier to achieve critical focus too.

Leica produces only one truly close-focusing lens: the MACRO-ELMAR-M 90mm f/4. It can be used either on its own to achieve 1:6.7 magnification or with the optional Leica Macro-Adaptor M to achieve 1:2 magnification. Strictly speaking, neither are macro magnifications, but it does allow you to shoot striking close-up imagery.

Because depth of field diminishes as the distance from the camera to the subject is reduced, achieving overall image sharpness can be problematic. The MACRO-ELMAR-M 90mm is one of the few Leica lenses that allows you to stop the aperture down to f/22 to maximize depth of field.

⌄ CLOSE-UP
Leica MACRO-ELMAR-M 90mm f/4.
© Leica

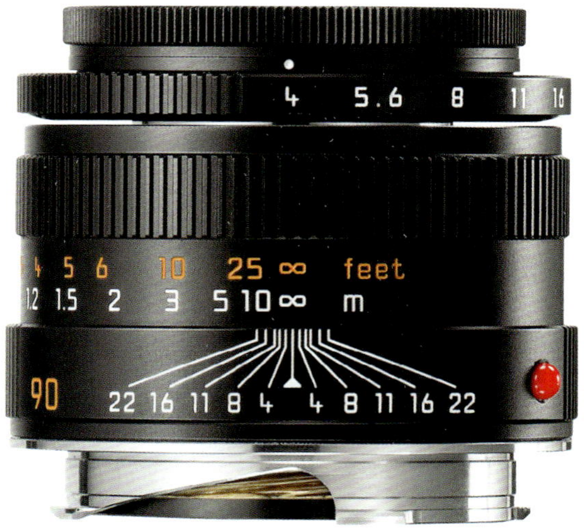

› Zoom lenses

A true zoom lens would be impractical on a rangefinder camera, as the viewfinder could not possibly display the range of bright-line frames required for compositional accuracy. However, Leica does produce a sort of "zoom lens"—the TRI-ELMAR-M 16–18–21mm. This lens comes with its own variable viewfinder, which mounts on the flash hotshoe of the M.

Unlike a traditional zoom lens, there are no in-between values when changing the focal length of the lens (the lens effectively has three specific focal length settings: 16mm, 18mm, and 21mm). Although this may seem like a disadvantage, it means that each focal length has its own depth-of-field scale marked on the lens, unlike zoom lenses designed for other camera systems.

Note

- Strictly speaking, a telephoto lens is one that uses special optical elements to make the physical length of the lens shorter than the focal length. However, telephoto is now usually used to describe any lens with a longer-than-standard focal length.

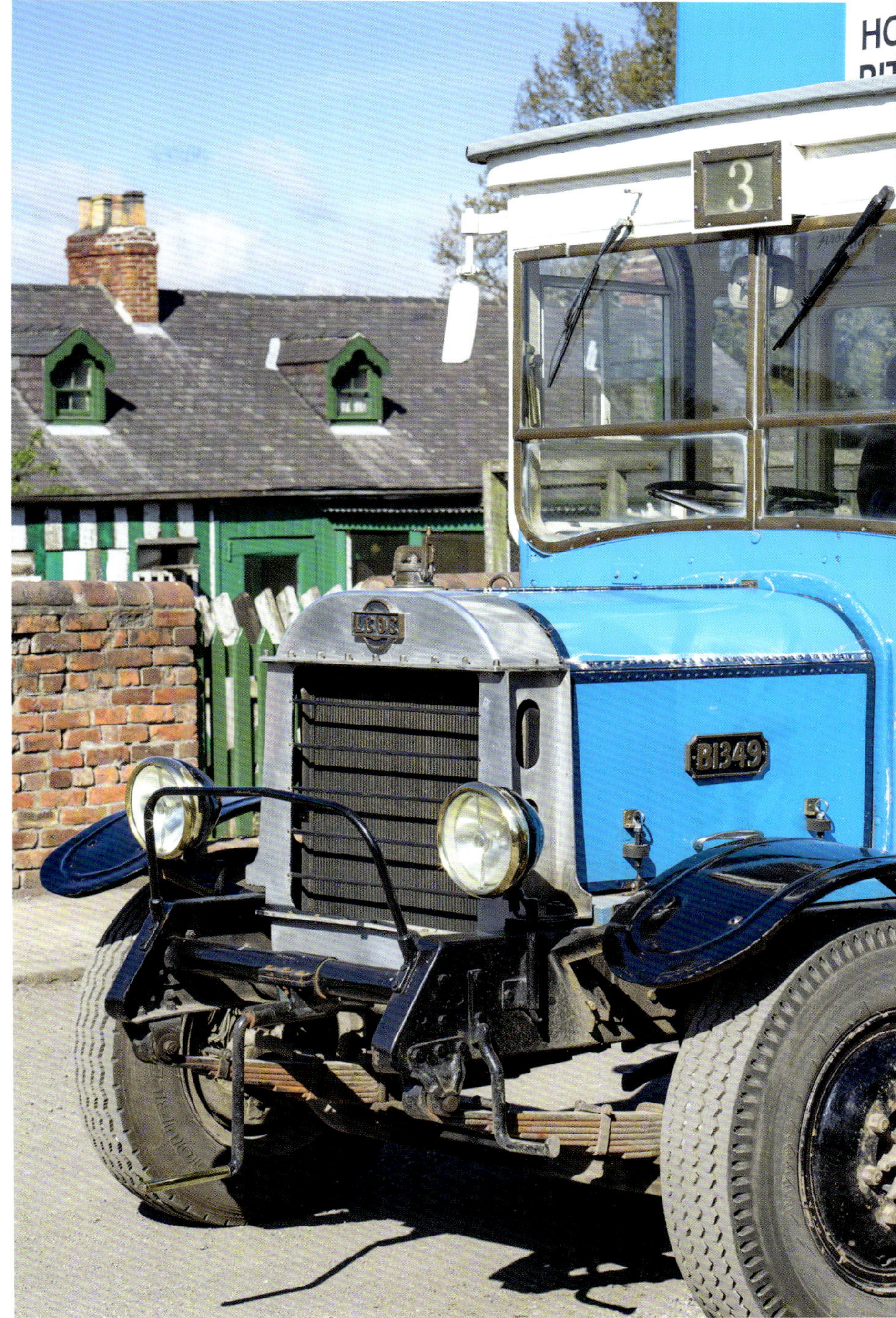

» 90MM
Telephoto focal lengths are ideal when you want the foreground of a shot to relate strongly to the background, thanks to the apparent spatial compression of a scene.

›› LENS ADAPTORS

Lenses are designed to suit a particular camera system. This is largely due to the specific flange focal distance of a camera system. This is the distance—usually measured in millimeters—from the lens mount to the film or sensor inside the camera. The flange distance of a camera system has to be taken into account when creating a lens so that the lens is able to focus at infinity (∞) correctly.

The flange focal distance of Leica M cameras is 27.8mm. This is much shorter than the flange focal distances of the Canon EOS system (44mm), Nikon F mount (46.5mm), and other DSLR systems, including Leica's own R-system cameras. This is because DSLRs typically have a relatively large flange focal distance to allow for the reflex mirror mechanism.

The practical benefit of the Leica M10's relatively short flange focal distance is that—with a suitable adaptor—lenses from camera systems with a larger flange focal distance can be used with the Leica M10 and still maintain infinity focus. The job of the adaptor, apart from allowing the physical coupling of the lens to the camera, is to hold the lens at the correct flange focal distance from the Leica M10's sensor.

Leica produces an adaptor that allows you to fit its R-series lenses to the M10, while third-party manufacturers such as Novoflex has produced adaptors that let you use lenses designed for a wide range of other camera systems.

Notes

• There are a number of limitations when using adaptors. Modern lenses designed for DSLRs typically do not have an aperture ring (the aperture is usually altered electronically via a dial on the camera body). A good lens adaptor should allow control of the aperture via a ring on the adaptor itself. However, this is usually not as precise as using the aperture ring on a Leica lens.

• The flange focal distance is a very precise distance. Cheaper adaptors may not have the necessary engineering tolerances to guarantee accuracy. This will affect whether the lens can be focused at infinity or not.

• Do not use adapted lenses designed for cameras with sensors smaller than the Leica M10. The image circle projected by these lenses may be smaller than the sensor in the Leica M10. This will result in vignetting around the edges of the image frame.

⌄ R LENSES
Leica R-mount lens fitted to a Leica M10 via Leica's R-mount adaptor.
© Leica

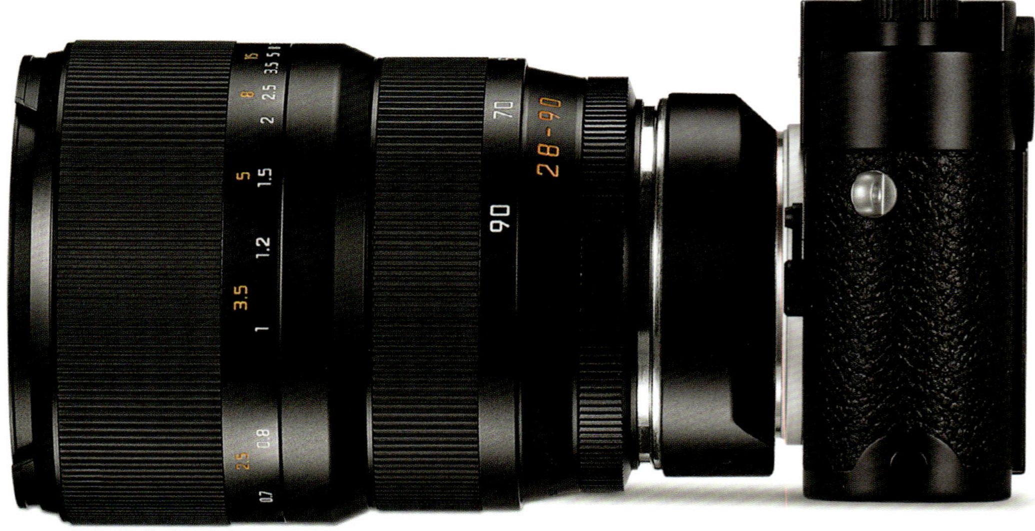

› Leica lenses on other cameras

Adaptors will also let you use your Leica lenses on mirrorless camera systems such as Micro Four Thirds or the Fuji X-series. The only difference with these systems is that—with the exception of the Sony A7 series—they tend not to use full-frame sensors. The practical effect of this is that a lens will appear "longer" on those cameras. On a Fuji X-series camera, for example, a 28mm Leica M lens will behave more like a 42mm focal length.

› M39 Lenses

The Leica M mount followed on from the Leica M39 standard used on Leica cameras before 1954. The M39 mount is a screw mount with a 39mm thread and there is a plentiful supply of pre-owned lenses of this type. If you are willing to experiment with older lenses, adaptors can be used with the Leica M10 that let you mount M39 lenses to your camera. Adaptors can be bought from third-party manufacturers such as Fotodiox.

⌄ ADAPTORS
With the right adaptor the Leica M10 can be fitted with a wide range of lenses from different manufacturers. For this shot I used an adapted 50mm lens.

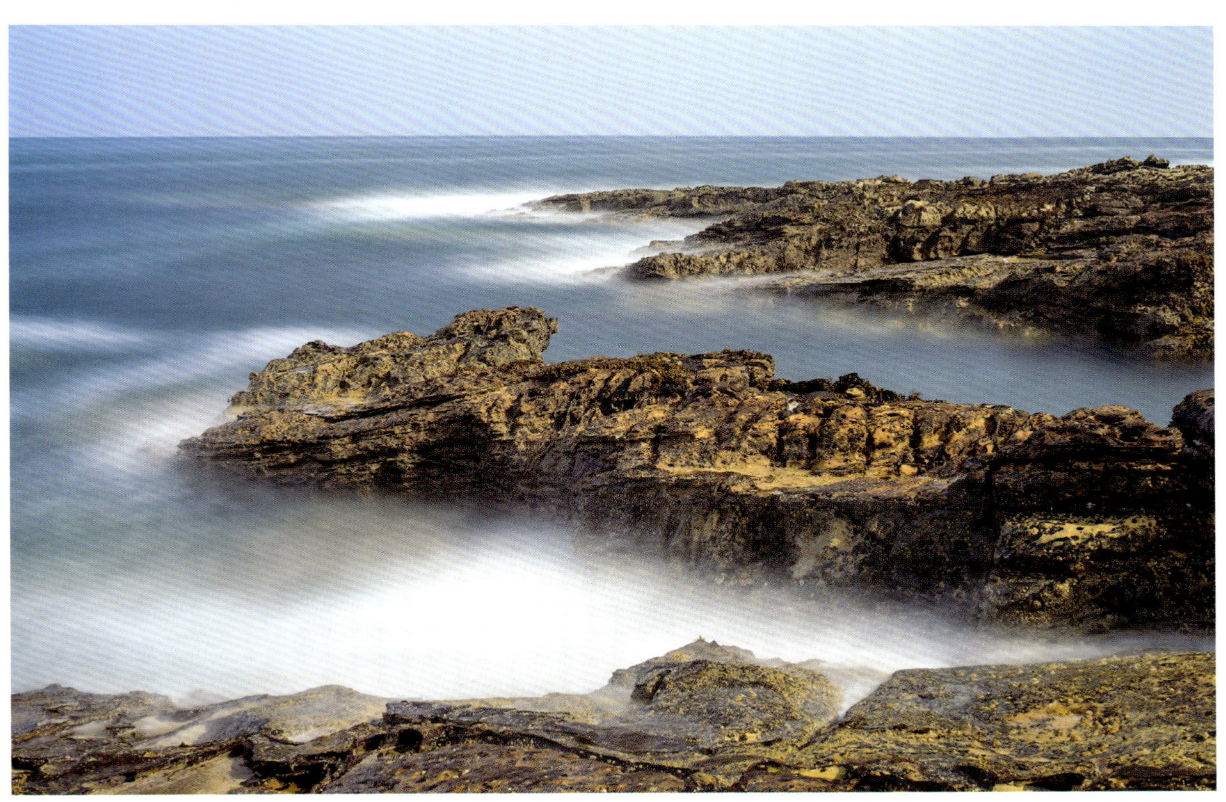

Lens	Max.–min. aperture	Min. focus distance (m)
16–18–21mm TRI-ELMAR-M f/4 ASPH	f/4–f/22	0.5
18mm SUPER-ELMAR-M f/3.8 ASPH	f/3.8–f/16	0.7
21mm SUMMILUX-M f/1.4 ASPH	f/1.4–f/16	0.7
21mm SUPER-ELMAR-M f/3.8 ASPH	f/3.8–f/16	0.7
24mm ELMAR-M f/3.8 ASPH	f/3.8–f/16	0.7
24mm SUMMILUX-M f/1.4 ASPH	f/1.4–f/16	0.7
28mm ELMARIT-M f/2.8 ASPH	f/2.8–f/16	0.7
28mm SUMMARON-M f/5.6	f/5.6–f/22	1.0
28mm SUMMICRON-M f/2 ASPH	f/2–f/16	0.7
28mm SUMMILUX-M f/1.4 ASPH	f/1.4–f/16	0.7
35mm SUMMARIT-M f/2.4	f/2.4–f/16	0.8
35mm SUMMICRON-M f/2 ASPH	f/2–f/16	0.7
35mm SUMMILUX-M f/1.4 ASPH	f/1.4–f/16	0.7
50mm APO-SUMMICRON-M f/2 APSH	f/2–f/16	0.7
50mm NOCTILUX-M f/0.95 ASPH	f/0.95–f/16	1.0
50mm SUMMARIT-M f/2.4	f/2.4–f/16	0.8
50mm SUMMICRON-M f/2	f/2–f/16	0.7
50mm SUMMILUX-M f/1.4 ASPH	f/1.4–f/16	0.7
75mm APO-SUMMICRON-M f/2 ASPH	f/2–f/16	0.7
75mm SUMMARIT-M f/2.4	f/2.4–f/16	0.7
90mm APO-SUMMICRON-M f/2 ASPH	f/2–f/16	1.0
90mm MACRO-ELMAR f/4	f/4–f/22	0.8
90mm SUMMARIT-M f/2.4	f/2.4–f/16	0.9
135mm APO-TELYT-M f/3.4 ASPH	f/3.4–f/22	1.5

Angle of view (diagonal)	Filter thread size (mm)	Dimensions (mm)	Weight (grams)
107°–100°–92°	67	54 x 62	335
100°	77	61 x 58	310
92°	–	70 x 66	580
92°	46	43 x 55	279
84°	46	57 x 41	260
84°	–	61 x 59	500
75°	39	52 x 30	180
75°	34	51 x 18	165
75°	46	53 x 40.8	270
75°	49	61 x 81	440
63°	46	52 x 34	197
63°	39	53 x 34.5	255
63°	46	56 x 46	320
47°	39	47 x 53	300
47°	60	73 x 75.1	700
47°	46	52 x 33	190
47°	39	53 x 43.5	240
47°	46	53.5 x 52.5	335
32°	49	58 x 67	430
32°	46	55 x 60.5	325
22°	55	64 x 78	500
27°	39	52 x 59	230
22°	46	55 x 67	346
18°	49	58.5 x 104.7	450

Lens	Max.-min. aperture	Min. focus distance (m)
(V) 10mm f/5.6 Hyper Wide Heliar	f/5.6–f/22	0.5
(V) 12mm f/5.6 UltraWide Heliar	f/5.6–f/22	0.5
(V) 15mm f/5.6 UltraWide Heliar	f/5.6–f/22	0.5
(CZ) 15mm Distagon T* 2.8 ZM	f/2.8–f/22	0.3
(V) 21mm f/1.8 Ultron	f/1.8–f/22	0.5
(V) 21mm f/4.0 Color Skopar Pancake II	f/4–f/22	0.5
(CZ) 21mm Biogon T* 2.8 ZM	f/2.8–f/22	0.5
(CZ) 21mm C Biogon T* 4.5 ZM	f/4.5–f/22	0.5
(CZ) 25mm Biogon T*2.8 ZM	f/2.8–f/22	0.5
(V) 28mm f/2 Ultron	f/2–f/22	0.7
(CZ) 28mm Biogon T*2.8 ZM	f/2.8–f/22	0.5
(V) 35mm f/1.2 Nokton	f/1.2–f/22	0.5
(V) 35mm f/1.4 Nokton	f/1.4–f/16	0.7
(V) 35mm f/1.7 Ultron (aluminum)	f/1.7–f/16	0.5
(V) 35mm f/1.7 Ultron (brass)	f/1.7–f/16	0.5
(V) 35 mm f/2.5 Color Skopar Classic	f/2.5–f/22	0.7
(CZ) 35mm f/1.4 Distagon	f/1.4–f/16	0.7
(CZ) 35mm Biogon T*2 ZM	f/2–f/22	0.7
(CZ) 35mm C Biogon T*2.8 ZM	f/2.8–f/22	0.7
(V) 40mm f/1.4 Nokton	f/1.4–f/16	0.7
(V) 50mm f/1.1 Nokton	f/1.1–f/16	1.0
(V) 50mm f/1.5 Nokton (aluminum)	f/1.5–f/16	0.7
(V) 50mm f/1.5 Nokton (brass)	f/1.5–f/16	0.7
(V) 50mm f/3.5 Heliar	f/3.5–f/22	0.7
(CZ) 50mm C Sonnar T* 1.5 ZM	f/1.5–f/16	0.9
(CZ) 50mm Planar T* 2 ZM	f/2–f/22	0.7
(V) 75mm f/1.8 Heliar	f/1.8–f/16	0.9
(CZ) 85mm Tele-Tessar T* 4 ZM	f/4–f/22	0.9

Angle of view (diagonal)	Filter thread size (mm)	Dimensions (mm)	Weight (grams)
130°	–	67.8 x 58.7	312
121°	–	64.8 x 59.2	283
110°	58	64.8 x 55.2	247
110°	72	78 x 86	500
91°	58	69 x 78.4	412
91°	39	55 x 25.4	136
90°	46	53 x 75	300
90°	46	53 x 56	210
82°	46	53 x 71	260
75°	46	55 x 60	244
75°	46	51 x 51	220
63°	52	60.8 x 62	470
63°	43	55 x 28.5	200
62°	46	53 x 50.6	238
62°	46	53 x 50.6	330
63°	39	55 x 23	134
63°	49	63 x 65	381
63°	43	52 x 56	240
63°	43	52 x 55	200
56°	43	55 x 29.7	175
46°	58	69.6 x 57.2	428
46°	49	53.8 x 45.7	220
46°	49	53.8 x 45.7	293
46°	27	52 x 43.2	210
46°	46	55 x 38	240
46°	43	51 x 43	230
33.2°	52	57.9 x 73.8	427
29°	43	54 x 95	310

CHAPTER 5
FLASH

You need light to make a photograph. When the ambient light levels are low you have two choices: you can either increase the exposure or you can add your own light to the scene.

The simplest and most common way to throw light on the situation is to use flash, although achieving pleasing results with flash is often seen as a bit of a dark art. Fortunately, using flash is simpler than you might think—once a few concepts have been grasped, illumination (often literally) soon follows.

The Leica M10—like every other M-series camera—does not have a built-in flash. It does have a hotshoe, though, which allows you to fit an external flash. Leica makes three compatible flashes: the SF 26, SF 40, and SF 64. Of the three, the SF 64 is the largest, best specified, and most powerful. However, any of the three can be used to add a new creative twist to an image.

This chapter serves as an introduction to using flash with your Leica M10, as well as a short guide to the steps you can take to improve your flash photography.

» LIGHT
The beauty of a flash is that—in a relatively small package—it gives you the power to control light for effect.

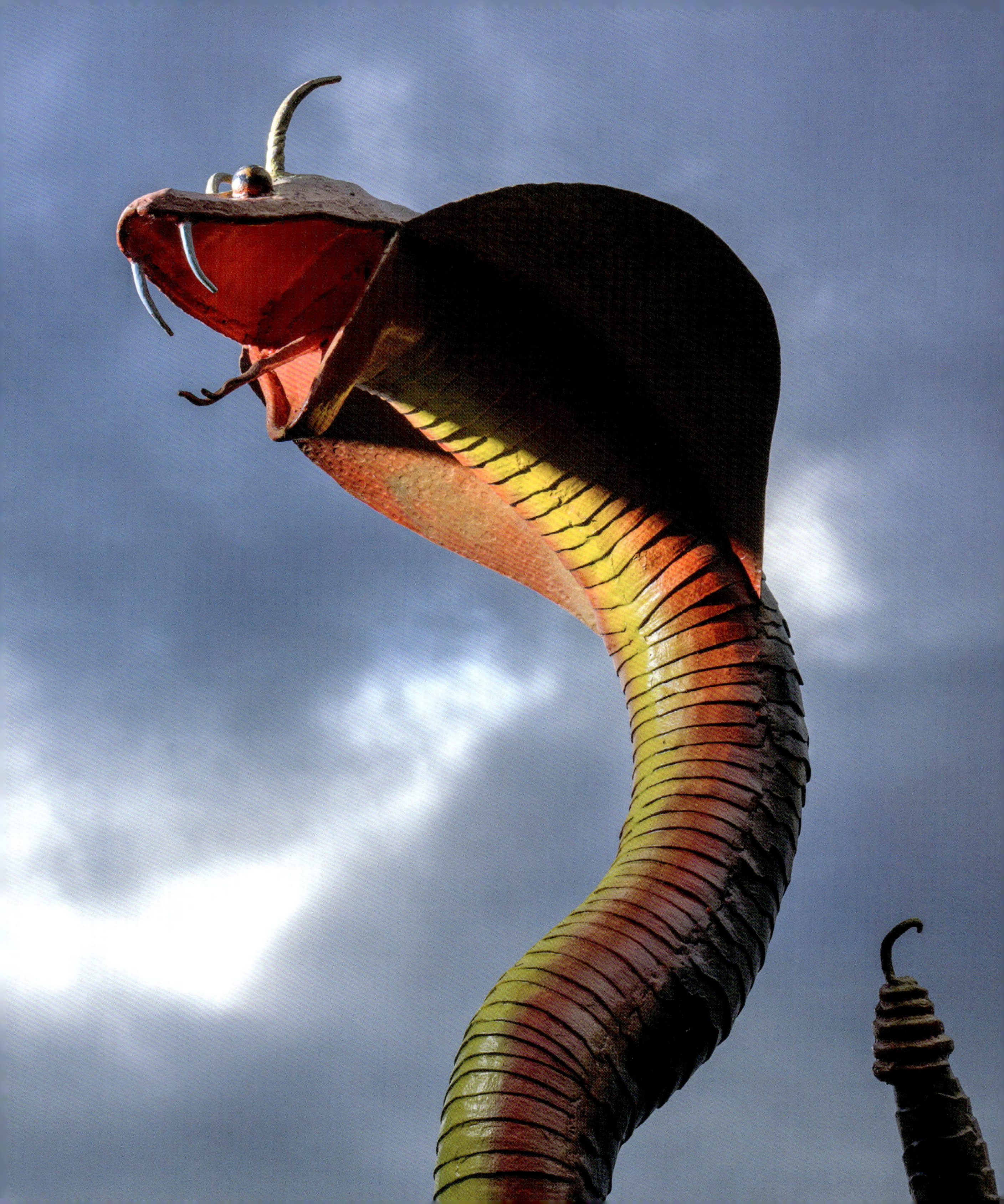

There are three basic components of a flash: a power source, a capacitor, and an airtight chamber filled with xenon gas to generate the light. The power source (typically two or four batteries) charges up the capacitor so that the flash is ready for use. The length of time it takes to fully charge the capacitor is known as the recycling time (this extends as the battery becomes depleted, so a lengthy recycling time is a good indication that the batteries are close to exhaustion).

When the flash is fired, the capacitor is discharged, pulsing an electrical charge into the xenon gas-filled chamber, which causes the molecules of gas to release energy in the form of light.

When the flash is fired at full power, the capacitor is fully discharged and it has to be fully recharged before the flash can be fired again. If the flash is fired at ½ power only half the capacitor's charge is used and so the flash will be able to fire twice before it needs to recharge. At ¼ power the flash will be able to fire four times before needing to recharge, and so on.

The power control of a flash lets you adjust the amount of light that falls on your subject. However— slightly counter intuitively—the brightness of the light emitted by the flash remains constant. What changes as you alter the power is the *duration* of the flash. At full power a relatively long flash of light is produced as the capacitor is exhausted, resulting in a flash lasting approximately 1/800 sec. At ½ power the flash lasts half as long (approximately 1/1600 sec.), which results in a halving of the light emitted. At ¼ power the flash duration is halved again (1/3200 sec.) and the amount of light emitted is reduced still further and so on.

This reduction in the flash duration makes a lower power flash setting ideal for freezing movement. The downside is that you either have to use a higher ISO, wider aperture, or move closer to your subject to compensate for the reduction in light.

A "guide number" or "GN" indicates the power or maximum amount of light a flash can produce. The GN determines the effective range of the flash in either feet or meters. If you increase the ISO on your Leica M10, the GN also increases—by a factor of 1.4x every time the ISO is doubled. Therefore, to avoid confusion, camera and flash manufacturers use ISO 100 as the standard reference when quoting a GN.

If you know the GN of a flash, you can use this to determine either the required aperture value for a subject at a given distance or the effective range of the flash at a specified aperture. The formula to calculate both is respectively:

Aperture=GN/distance
Distance=GN/aperture

Let's take the Leica SF 26 flash as an example. As the name suggests, this flash has a GN of 26 meters (85 feet), so at an aperture of f/8 and ISO 100 we can determine that the effective flash distance will be 3.25m (10½ft).

If the ISO on the camera is doubled, the effective flash distance is multiplied by a factor of 1.4, so at ISO 200 (and maintaining an aperture of f/8) the effective flash distance would increase to approximately 4.55m (almost 15ft).

⌄ MOTION BLUR
Flash is usually fast enough to "freeze" movement when it fires. If you or your subject moves during the exposure, the subject will be sharp, but the background—unlit by flash—may be blurred.

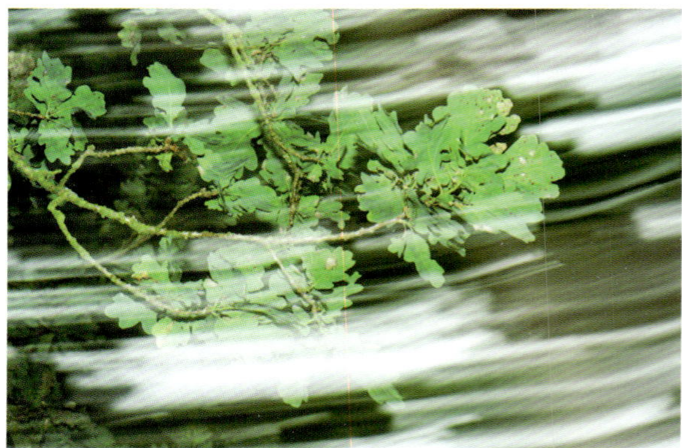

» FLASH BASICS

› Sync speed

The fastest shutter speed that can be used when shooting with flash is known as the synchronization (or sync) speed; the Leica M10's sync speed is 1/180 sec., which is indicated by the red ⚡ symbol on the shutter speed dial. If you attempt to use a shutter speed faster than this, the attached flash will not fire (see page 127 for an exception to this).

However, while this is the maximum shutter speed you can use with flash, there is no reason not to use a slower shutter speed for creative effect. Although this will have no effect on the flash exposure, a slower shutter speed *will* let you control the exposure for areas of the scene that are *not* illuminated by the flash (i.e. those areas illuminated by the ambient light).

› Full-power flash

The aperture setting can control the flash exposure when you are using a flash that is set manually at full power. The smaller the aperture used, the shorter the effective distance of the flash. If your subject is further than the effective flash distance for the aperture, the subject will be underexposed. Using a wider aperture setting can cure this.

If the subject is closer than the effective flash distance there is a risk of overexposure, so you will either need to reduce the flash output or set a smaller aperture to reduce the effective flash distance.

Use the grids on the following page to calculate the flash working distance for specific ISO and aperture combinations when using Leica's SF 26, SF 40, and SF 64 flash units.

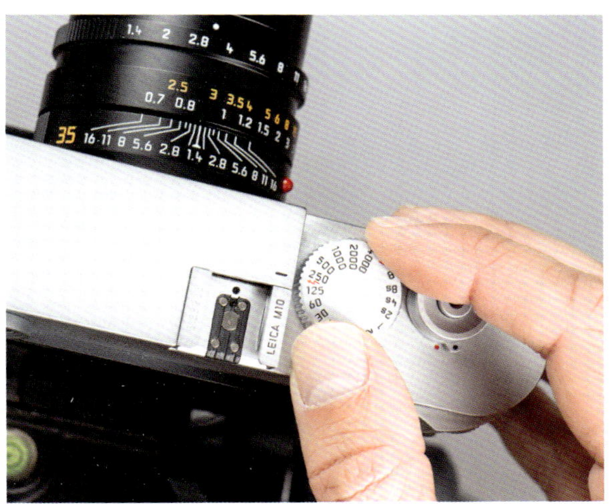

⌃ **SETTING THE FLASH SYNC SPEED**

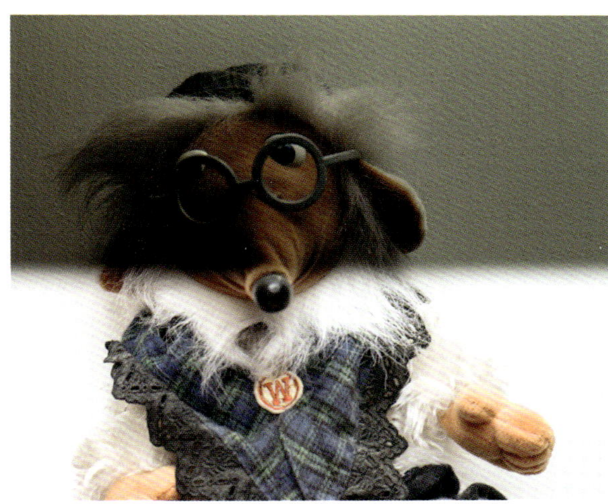

⌃ **TOO FAST**
If you use a shutter speed faster than the sync speed, the flash cannot illuminate the entire frame. This will result in a dark band across the image.

Leica SF 26

ISO/Aperture	f/2.0	f/2.8	f/4	f/5.6	f/8	f/11	f/16
100	13m/43ft	9m/29ft	6m/20ft	4.5m/14ft	3.2m/10ft	2.3m/7.5ft	1.6m/5ft
200	18m/60ft	13m/43ft	9m/29ft	6m/20ft	4.5m/14ft	3.2m/10ft	2.3m/7.5ft
400	26m/85ft	18m/60ft	13m/43ft	9m/29ft	6m/20ft	4.5m/14ft	3.2m/10ft
800	37m/121ft	26m/85ft	18m/60ft	13m/43ft	9m/29ft	6m/20ft	4.5m/14ft
1600	52m/170ft	37m/121ft	26m/85ft	18m/60ft	13m/43ft	9m/29ft	6m/20ft
3200	74m/242ft	52m/170ft	37m/121ft	26m/85ft	18m/60ft	13m/43ft	9m/29ft
6400	104m/340ft	74m/242ft	52m/170ft	37m/121ft	26m/85ft	18m/60ft	13m/43ft

Leica SF 40

ISO/Aperture	f/2.0	f/2.8	f/4	f/5.6	f/8	f/11	f/16
100	20m/65ft	14m/46ft	10m/33ft	7m/23ft	5m/16.4ft	3.6m/12ft	2.5m/8.2ft
200	28.3m/93ft	20m/65ft	14m/46ft	10m/33ft	7m/23ft	5m/16.4ft	3.6m/12ft
400	40m/132ft	28.3m/93ft	20m/65ft	14m/46ft	10m/33ft	7m/23ft	5m/16.4ft
800	56.6m/186ft	40m/132ft	28.3m/93ft	20m/65ft	14m/46ft	10m/33ft	7m/23ft
1600	80m/262ft	56.6m/186ft	40m/132ft	28.3m/93ft	20m/65ft	14m/46ft	10m/33ft
3200	114m/374ft	80m/262ft	56.6m/186ft	40m/132ft	28.3m/93ft	20m/65ft	14m/46ft
6400	160m/524ft	114m/374ft	80m/262ft	56.6m/186ft	40m/132ft	28.3m/93ft	20m/65ft

Leica SF 64

ISO/Aperture	f/2.0	f/2.8	f/4	f/5.6	f/8	f/11	f/16
100	32m/105ft	23m/75ft	16m/53ft	11m/37ft	8m/26ft	5.8m/19ft	4m/13ft
200	45m/148ft	32m/105ft	23m/75ft	16m/53ft	11m/37ft	8m/26ft	5.8m/19ft
400	64m/210ft	45m/148ft	32m/105ft	23m/75ft	16m/53ft	11m/37ft	8m/26ft
800	90m/295ft	64m/210ft	45m/148ft	32m/105ft	23m/75ft	16m/53ft	11m/37ft
1600	128m/420ft	90m/295ft	64m/210ft	45m/148ft	32m/105ft	23m/75ft	16m/53ft
3200	181m/594ft	128m/420ft	90m/295ft	64m/210ft	45m/148ft	32m/105ft	23m/75ft
6400	256m/840ft	181m/594ft	128m/420ft	90m/295ft	64m/210ft	45m/148ft	32m/105ft

› Fitting a flash

The M10 has a built-in hotshoe for attaching external flashes. To fit a flash, turn off both the Leica M10 and the flash. Remove the hotshoe cover (if fitted) and slide the foot of the flash into the hotshoe. Do not try to force the flash if resistance is high; remove the flash and realign if necessary. Once the flash is fully on the camera, tighten the clamping ring on the flash (if one is fitted). Turn on the Leica M10 followed by the flash.

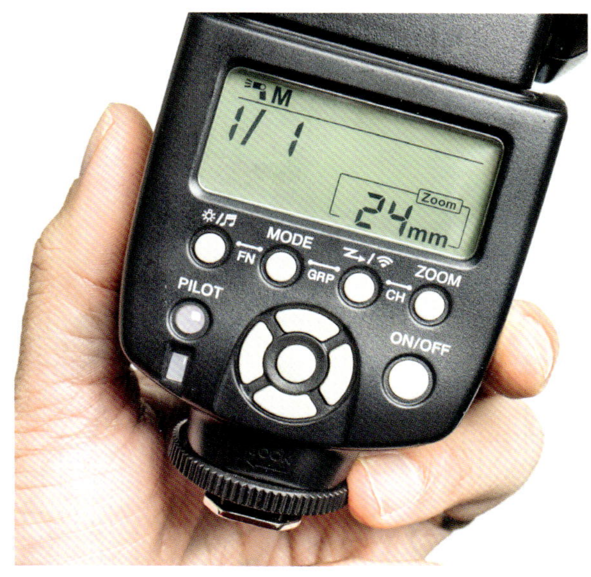

⌄ FLASH

You do not need to use Leica flash units exclusively. You can use any third-party flash that fits to a standard hotshoe fitting and has a single, positive center pin to fire the flash. However, do not use proprietary flashes made for other camera systems. These often have extra pins around the center pin and these may damage your camera if they align with one of the other contacts on the Leica M10's hotshoe.

⌃ MANUAL

Using a third-party flash with one firing pin means losing any sort of automation with flash exposure, such as TTL. Flash exposure will have to be calculated manually and you will need to set the flash zoom manually as well. The zoom should be set to the same focal length as the lens fitted to your Leica M10 (or as close as possible if the exact value is not available).

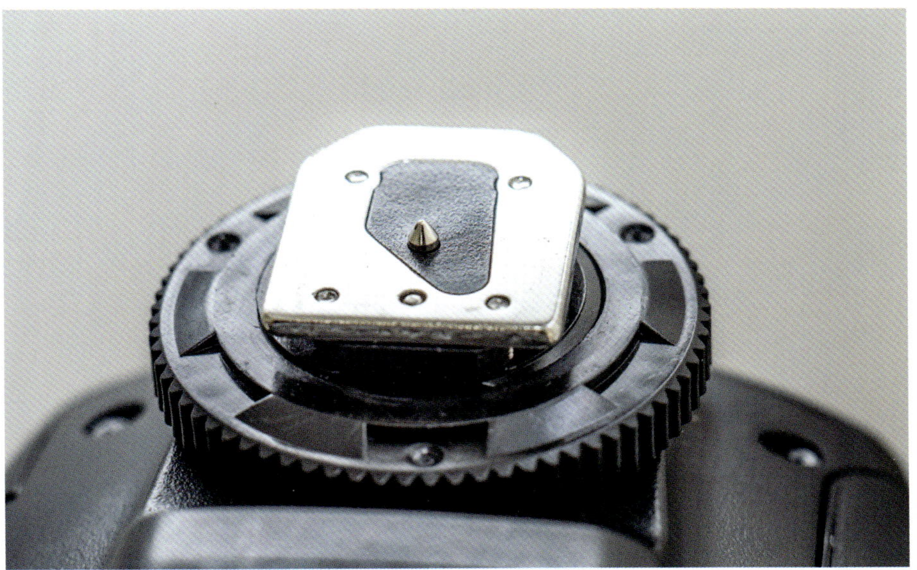

Note
- You can clean the flash contacts with a pencil eraser. This will remove any grease on the contacts that might cause a signal failure between the flash and the camera.

» FLASH FUNCTIONS

› Automated flash

When you fit a compatible flash to your Leica M1, the power output of the flash will be calculated automatically by the camera, which will attempt to balance the flash with the ambient lighting. If the ambient light levels are high, flash output will be reduced by up to 1⅔ stops to maintain this balance. If the ambient brightness is so high that the required shutter speed exceeds the flash sync speed, the flash will not fire.

Setting automated flash

1) Attach the flash and make sure both the flash and camera are turned on.

2) Set the flash to TTL or GNC (Guide Number Control) mode.

3) Set the Leica M10 to the desired shutter speed (1/180 sec. or slower) or to Aperture Priority.

4) Set the required aperture. This should be large enough so the effective flash distance is equal to, or greater than the subject distance. If the aperture is too small, your subject may not be illuminated correctly.

5) Lightly press down on the shutter-release button to switch on the Leica M10's exposure metering. If you press down on the shutter-release button missing out this step the flash may not fire.

Note
- When a compatible flash is attached to the Leica M10, ⚡ will be displayed in the viewfinder.

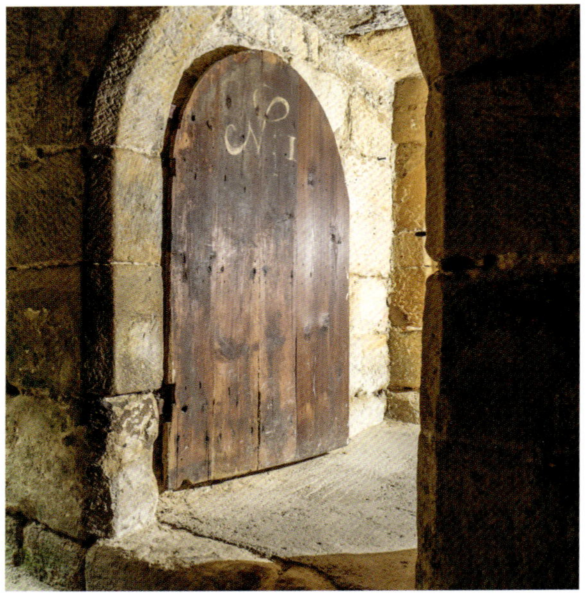

⌃ OFF-CAMERA FLASH
Flash is ideal for adding light when the ambient light level is low or simply not esthetically pleasing. In this photograph a flash was used to illuminate the interior beyond the doorway. This added visual interest to what was an otherwise dark and dingy scene.

› Flash troubleshooting

If the ⚡ symbol does not appear in the viewfinder after the flash has been fitted and turned on, this indicates there is a problem. Usually this is because the shutter speed dial is set at a shutter speed faster than the sync speed of 1/180 sec. (although some flashes have an HSS or High Speed Sync mode that allows the use of faster shutter speeds; see page 127). If this is not the reason, check that the flash is properly seated in the hotshoe.

When the ⚡ symbol flashes slowly in the viewfinder the flash is still charging. Once the flash has charged ⚡ will remain lit. As the flash batteries run down, the time it takes the flash to recharge will increase.

If ⚡ disappears from the viewfinder after a flash exposure, this indicates potential underexposure. Check the power output of the flash and that your subject is within the effective flash distance for the aperture you have set.

› Fill-in flash

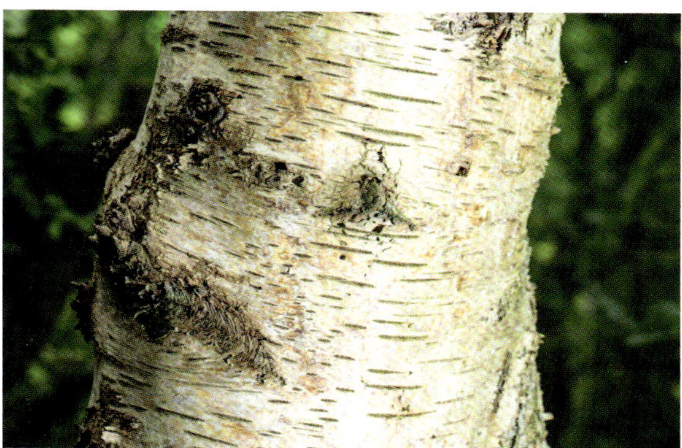

⌃ FILL-IN FLASH
I often use fill-in flash to balance exposure and reduce contrast. This birch tree was relatively dark compared to the background. Fill-in flash helped to reduce the difference in exposure to produce a more pleasing shot.

Fill-in flash is a particularly useful technique when shooting a backlit subject, as it helps to reduce contrast and even out the exposure across the scene. However, fill-in flash must be used with care. If the flash output is too strong, the subject will look over-lit compared to the background. To avoid this, adjust the power output of your flash. How much adjustment you need to make will depend on how dark your subject is in comparison to the background, but typically ½–1½ stops is a good starting point.

› 1ˢᵗ-curtain and 2ⁿᵈ-curtain sync

The Leica M10 has a focal-plane shutter that comprises two light-tight metal "curtains," one in front of the other. At the start of an exposure the 1ˢᵗ (or front) curtain rises, exposing the sensor to light. After a delay the 2ⁿᵈ (or rear) curtain follows on, stopping light from reaching the sensor. The time between the two curtains starting to rise is the selected shutter speed.

Normally this is irrelevant, but in certain situations when using flash you have an interesting choice to make: you can either set your flash to fire when the 1ˢᵗ curtain rises (**Start of Exp.**) or when the 2ⁿᵈ curtain follows (**End of Exp.**). This is important when shooting subjects that will move across the frame during a relatively long exposure.

If the flash fires at the start of the exposure your subject will be "frozen" by the light from the flash immediately. Any movement after this will be recorded as a blur that appears *in front* of the subject in the final image.

However, if the flash fires at the end of the exposure your subject will be "frozen" by the flash after a delay. Therefore any movement up to this point will be recorded as a blur *behind* the subject. Of the two, **End of Exp.** usually looks more natural, although it can be fun to experiment with the effect.

Setting flash curtain synchronization
1) In shooting mode press MENU.

2) Select **Flash Settings** from the Main Menu (page 1).

3) On the **Flash Settings** sub-menu page highlight **Flash Sync Mode** and press ● to toggle between **Start of Exp.** and **End of Exp.**.

4) Press the shutter-release button down lightly to return to shooting mode.

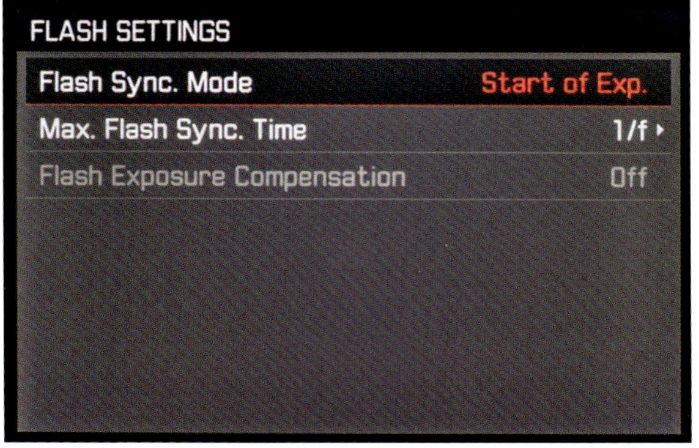

› Slow synchronization

A flash is useful for adding light to your subject, but even the most powerful flashes have a limited range; although your subject may be correctly exposed you may find the background is underexposed. The solution is to use a relatively slow shutter speed so the exposure is correct for the ambient light levels. This technique is known as slow synchronization.

Slow synchronization is particularly effective outside at dusk. At this time of day there is generally sufficient ambient light so the shutter speed doesn't exceed the Leica M10's 125 second limit. Once night has fallen and the sky is black there may be little or no ambient light to light the scene.

Shoot in Aperture Priority and you can choose how your Leica M10 behaves when selecting a shutter speed. The shutter speed can be biased so that the risk of camera shake is reduced depending on the focal length of the lens fitted (**1/f**, **1/[2f]**, or **1/[4f]**) or you can specify the fastest shutter speed the Leica M10 will use when a flash is fitted (between **1/125s–1/2s**). The longer the maximum shutter speed, the more likely the background will be correctly exposed, particularly when shooting in low ambient light.

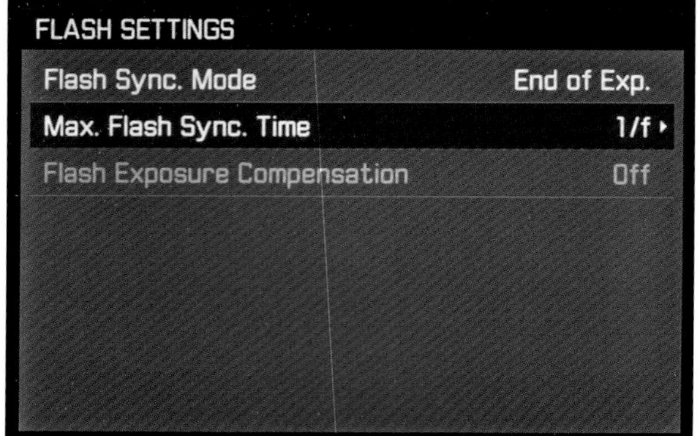

Notes
- Deliberately moving your camera during a long exposure combined with flash can be used creatively: anything lit by the flash will be pin sharp, everything else in the image will be rendered as a streaked blur. The longer the shutter speed, the more pronounced the effect.

- Shoot in Manual mode and you can select the required shutter speed—between 1/180 sec. and 8 seconds—using the shutter speed dial.

Setting slow synchronization

1) Set the shutter speed dial to A and press MENU.

2) Select **Flash Settings** from the Main Menu (page 1).

3) On the **Flash Settings** sub-menu page select **Max. Flash Sync Time**.

4) Select **1/f**, **1/[2f]**, or **1/[4f]** if you want your Leica M10 to alter the shutter speed (up to a maximum of 1/125 sec.) depending on the focal length of the attached lens. To avoid camera shake the shutter speed will be set at a higher value the longer the lens used.

5) Choose a shutter speed from the list to determine the fastest shutter speed that will be used for slow sync shooting. The options cover the range 1/125 sec.–1/2 sec., which is the *maximum* shutter speed that will be selected automatically by the Leica M10. Note that the *ambient light levels will determine the actual shutter speed selected*.

6) Press lightly down on the shutter-release button to go directly to shooting mode.

Note
- The **1/f**, **1/[2f]**, and **1/[4f]** settings require a lens with 6-bit coding.

MAX. FLASH SYNC. TIME
1/f
1/(2f)
1/(4f)
1/125 s
1/60 s
1/30 s
1/15 s
1/8 s

› High Speed Sync

The Leica M10's 1/180 sec. sync speed can be limiting when the ambient light level is high, especially if you want to use a large aperture to restrict depth of field. Fortunately, there is a solution. Both the Leica SF 40 and SF 64 flash units have a High Speed Sync (HSS) mode. This allows the use of flash with shutter speeds up to 1/4000 sec.

High-speed sync works by rapidly pulsing the output of the flash, effectively turning the flash into a constant light source during an exposure. Unfortunately, there is one big drawback to using HSS: the power of the flash—and therefore its effective distance—is reduced considerably (largely because the flash discharges many times rather than once). However, as long as you understand this limitation and keep your subject close to the camera, HSS offers another creative flash option.

With HSS you can use flash more effectively as a fill-in light when shooting backlit subjects. You can also use HSS as a way to overpower the ambient light of a scene by setting a shutter speed fast enough to underexpose the background (essentially the exact opposite of using slow sync flash). This technique is commonly used to shoot fashion or editorial subjects as it helps the subject to stand out more from its background.

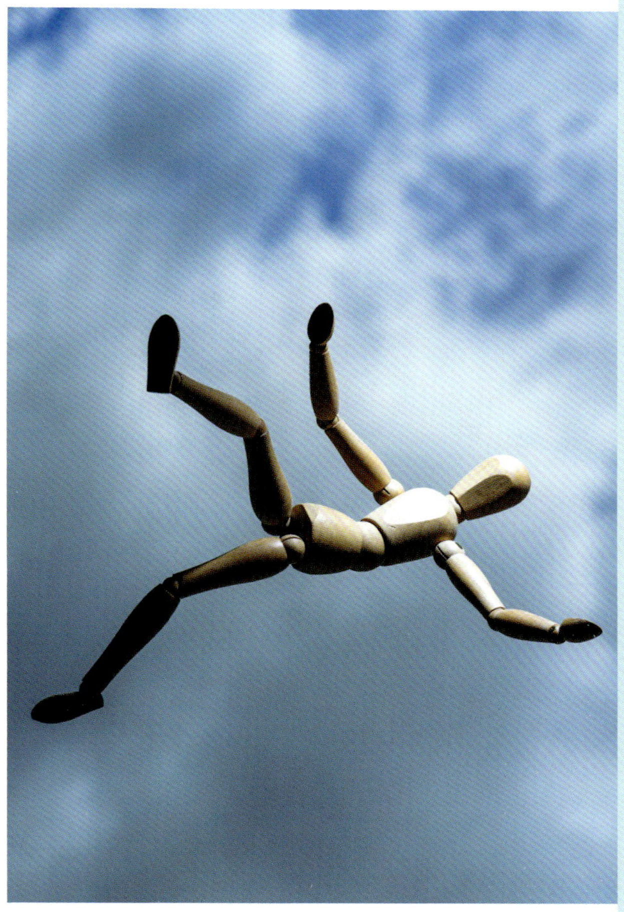

⌃ HSS
High-speed sync is particularly useful when you want to underexpose a brightly lit background. For this shot I used a shutter speed of 1/500 sec. to deliberately underexpose the background, knowing that the flash exposure would be unaffected.

» MODIFYING FLASH LIGHT

› Bounce flash

Light from a camera-mounted flash typically illuminates your subject frontally. This is not particularly flattering, especially as flash is a "hard" light source that casts deep, sharp-edged shadows. A very simple technique to soften and re-direct the light from a flash is to bounce the light off another surface before it illuminates your subject. The technique requires a flash with an adjustable head, which is something that all three of Leica's flash units feature.

Low ceilings are ideal for the bounce flash technique, but a nearby wall or reflector is equally useful. The key attribute of the surface is that it is neutral in color—a surface that has a color tint will add an unwelcome colorcast to the light from the flash.

⌄ BOUNCED
Bounced flash can make a huge difference to the esthetic qualities of a flash shot. Compare here the direct flash image (left) with the image (right) shot with the flash light bounced off a reflector held over the subject. One thing to note— particularly when using manual flash—is that the technique increases the flash-to-subject distance. You therefore need to ensure that the flash output, selected aperture, and/or ISO are set to take this into account.

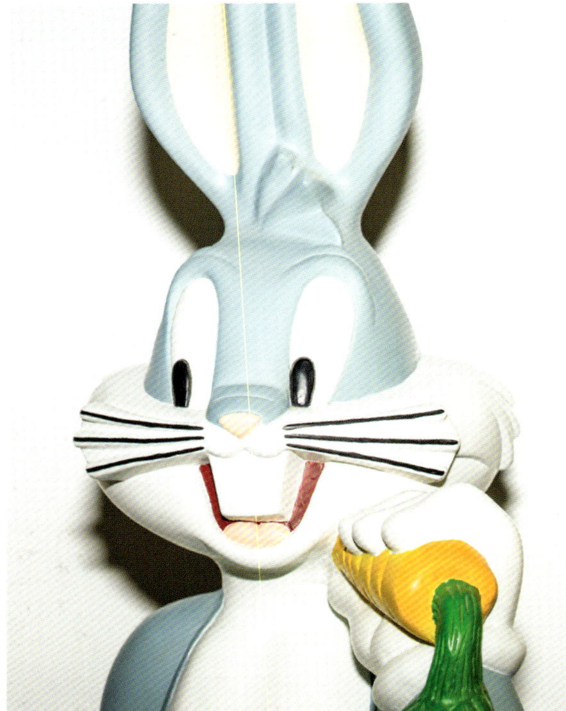
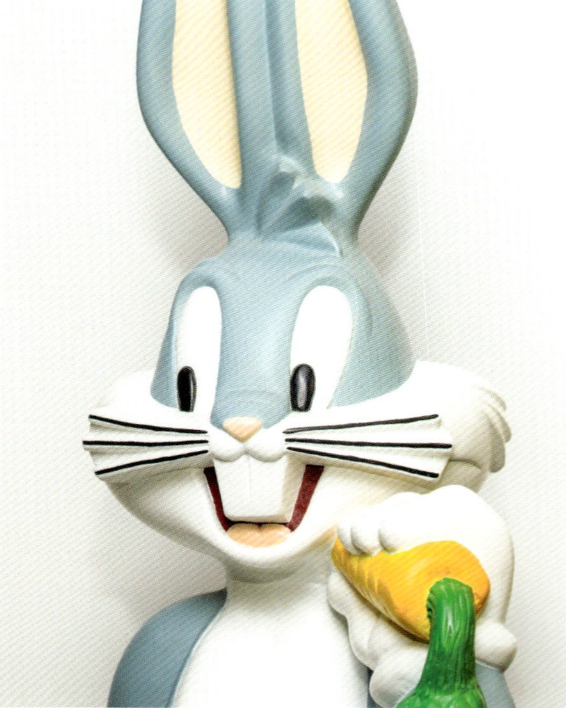

› Diffusers and reflectors

A flash diffuser is a translucent box that attaches to the flash head. They are used to soften the light by scattering ("diffusing") the light from the flash, making it appear to emanate from a larger area. Although a diffuser does not stop flash from lighting your subject frontally, it will reduce the heavy, hard-edged shadows, albeit with a slight reduction in the power output of the flash.

Another flash-fitted accessory is a reflector (the SF 64 has one built into the head). Reflectors soften light in much the same way as bouncing the light from a flash, but without the need for a convenient ceiling or wall. Some of the flash output is absorbed up by the reflector's surface, reducing the illuminating power of the flash, but the flash-to-subject distance is reduced less than it would be if you used a wall or ceiling to bounce the light off.

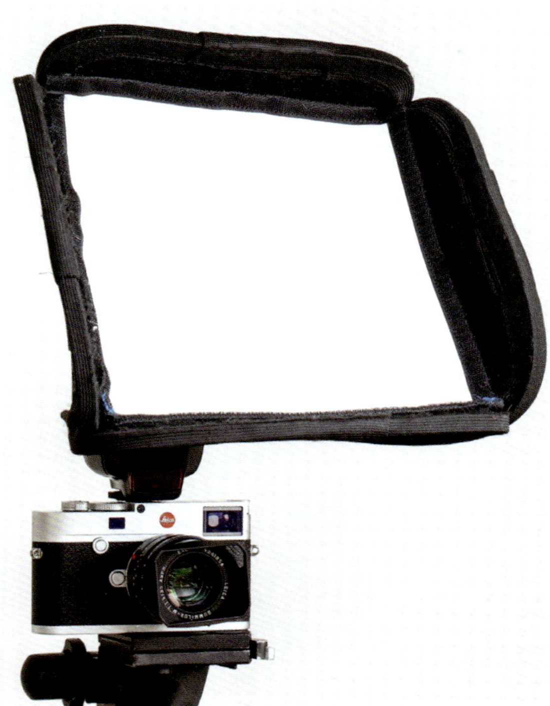

« BOXED

Diffusers come in different shapes and sizes. The smallest fit snuggly over the head of a flash, and because of their size are ideal for keeping in a camera bag. However, their small size means the diffusion effect is limited. Larger diffusers (known as "box diffusers") are bulkier, but soften the light more dramatically. The diffuser shown here is approximately 8 x 8in (20 x 20cm)—larger diffusers can be up to 32 x 32in (80 x 80cm) in size, but are only usable with off-camera flash.

» LEICA SF 26

The SF 26 is the smallest and lightest of Leica's three flash units. It is also the least well specified in terms of power and specifications. However, this does not mean that it is not a capable piece of equipment: the SF 26 can be used as a slave for off-camera flash, and the inclusion of two diffusion screens allows it to be used with lenses between 24mm and 85mm in focal length.

Guide number:
79ft/24m @ ISO 100 (increases to 85ft/26m with telephoto adaptor fitted)

Flash head adjustment:
Vertical (90°); Horizontal (N/A)

Color temperature:
5600K

Flash modes:
Wireless flash (slave mode only); LED video light

Flash head zoom range:
24–85mm

Approximate recycling time:
1–4 seconds

Batteries:
2 x AA

Dimensions:
(W x H x D): 2.48 x 3.35 x 3.35in/63 x 85 x 85mm

Weight:
4oz/115g (without batteries)

Included accessories:
Instruction manual, protective bag, pedestal, slip-on diffusion attachment

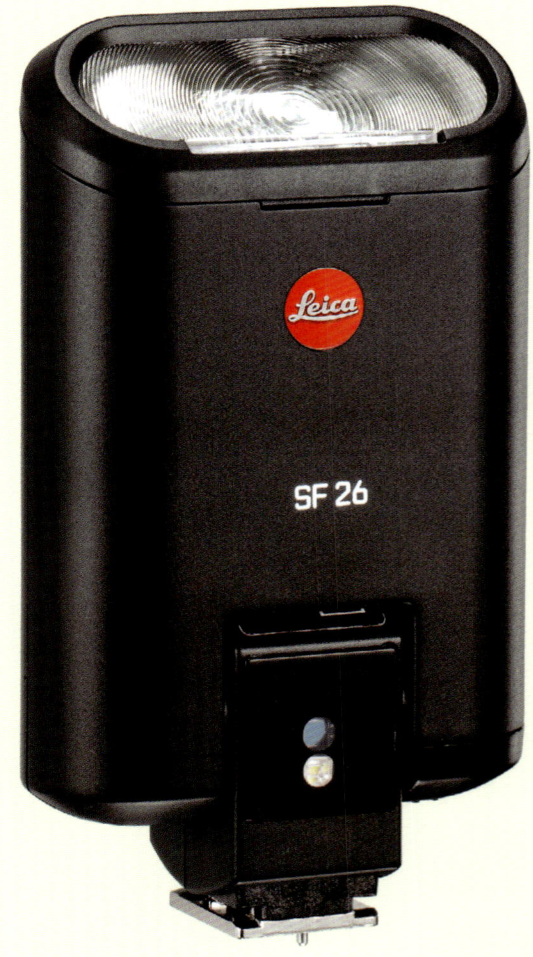

© Leica

» LEICA SF 40

The SF 40 is Leica's mid-range flash and is fully compatible with all of Leica's digital cameras. It includes a facility for optical wireless shooting, an LED video light (which is largely irrelevant when shooting with a Leica M10, but is useful for Leica cameras such as the M Typ 240), and a diffusion attachment. With compatible lenses the flash can use the focal length information to optimize the flash output for each lens.

Guide number:
130ft/40m @ ISO 100

Flash head adjustment:
Vertical (45°, 60°, 75°, 90°);
Horizontal (30°, 60°, 90°, 120°, 150°, 180°)

Color temperature:
5600K

Flash modes:
HSS; 1st/2nd-curtain sync; red-eye reduction;
slow sync; wireless flash (slave mode only);
flash exposure compensation (±2 stops in ½-stop
increments); Manual output 1/1–1/256 power

Flash head zoom range:
24–105mm

Approximate recycling time:
1–4 seconds

Batteries:
4 x AA

Dimensions:
(W x H x D): 2.4 x 3.35 x 3.35in/61 x 85 x 85mm
(with flash head angled to the front)

Weight:
7oz/200g (without batteries)

Included accessories:
Instruction manual, protective bag, pedestal,
slip-on diffusion attachment

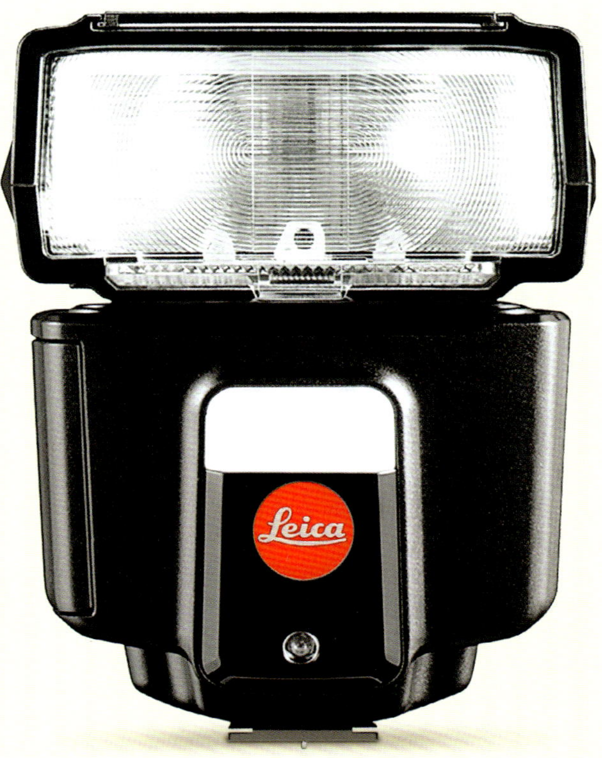

© Leica

» LEICA SF 64

The SF 64 is Leica's flagship flash and one of the world's most powerful accessory flash units for any 35mm camera system. The SF 64 sports an integrated USB port to allow firmware updates as needed. With compatible lenses the SF 64 can use the focal length information to optimize the flash output for each lens.

Guide number:
210ft/64m @ ISO 100

Flash head adjustment:
Vertical (-9°, 45°, 60°, 75°, 90°); Horizontal, clockwise (60°, 90°, 120); Horizontal, counterclockwise (60°, 90°, 120°, 150°, 180°)

Color temperature:
5600K

Flash modes:
HSS; 1st/2nd-curtain sync; slow sync; red-eye reduction; wireless flash (slave mode only); flash exposure compensation (±2 stops in ½-stop increments); Manual output 1/1–1/256 power; stroboscopic mode; AF assist light

Flash head zoom range:
24–200mm (12mm possible when integrated wide-angle fresnel adaptor is used)

Approximate recycling time:
0.1–4.4 seconds

Batteries:
4 x AA

Dimensions:
(W x H x D): 3 x 5.8 x 4.4in/78 x 148 x 112mm (with flash head angled upward)

Weight:
15oz/422g (without batteries)

Included accessories:
Instruction manual, protective bag, pedestal, integrated reflector card and wide-angle fresnel adaptor

» REMOTE FLASH

Flash sync cables let you shoot with the flash at a distance from the camera (the distance will be determined by the length of the sync cable). Shooting with flash off-camera lets you position your flash so you can take a more creative approach.

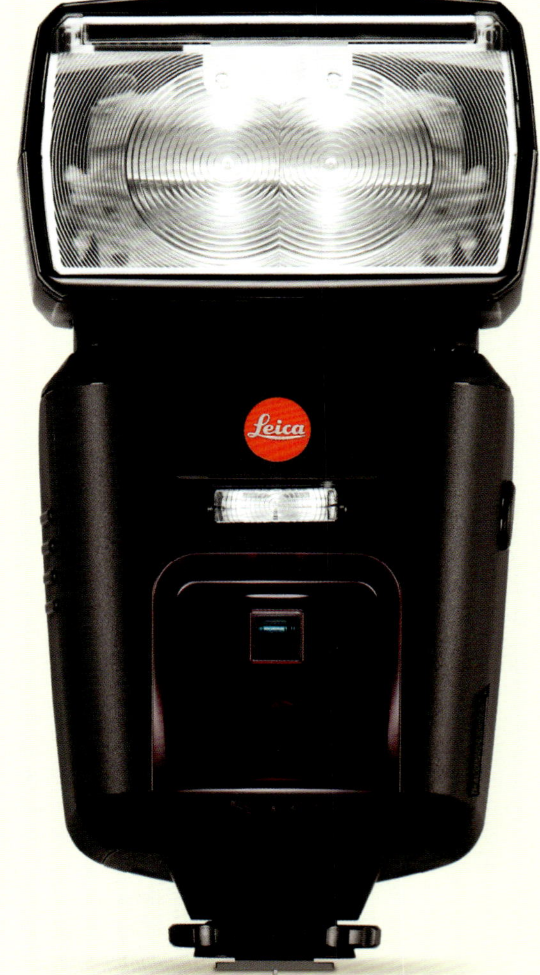

© Leica

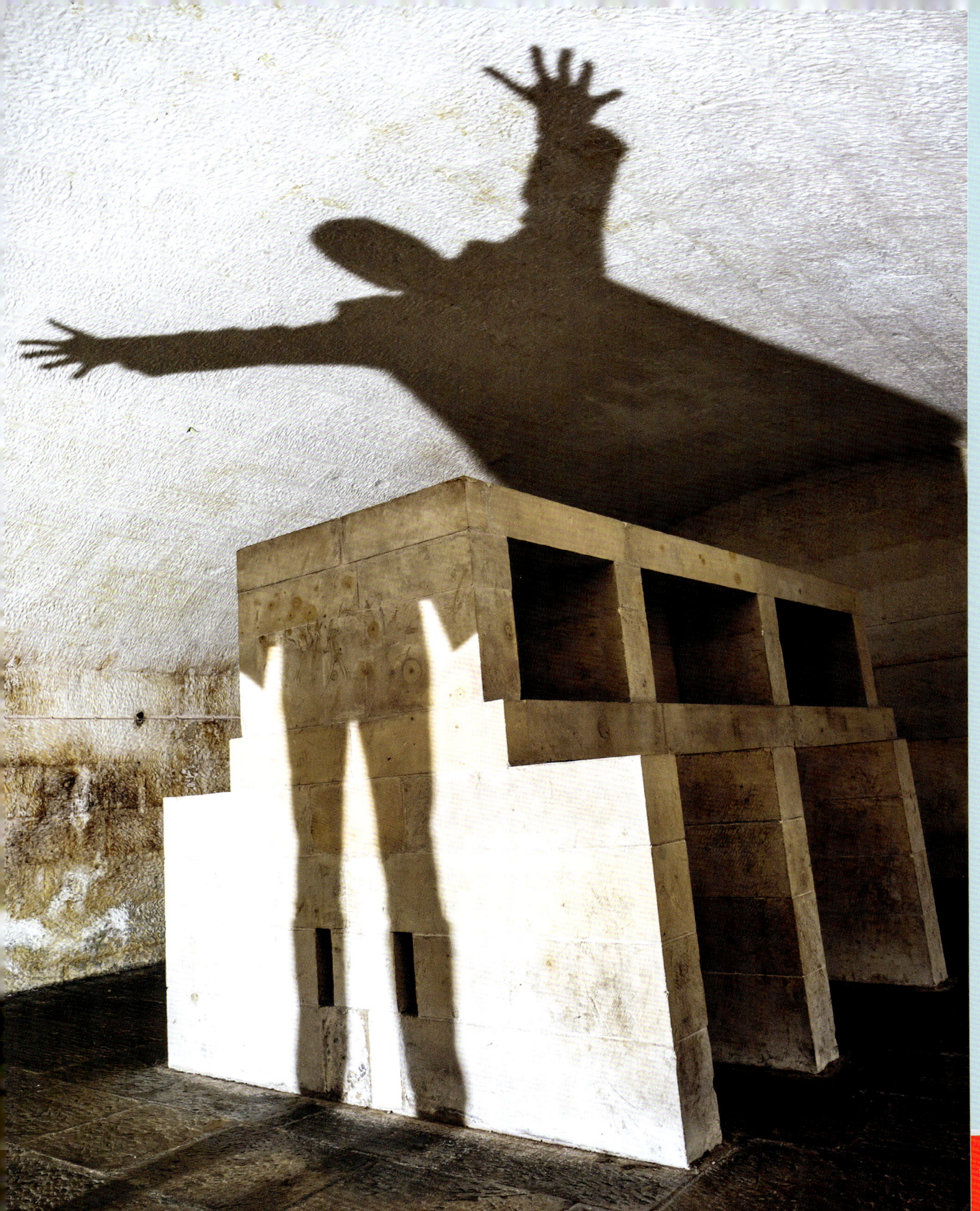

CHAPTER 6
ACCESSORIES

Photographers are often infected with a strange affliction: the need to constantly add shiny new equipment to their collection. Thankfully, this can be cured with willpower and careful thought...

The range of accessories made for the M10 by Leica and third parties can seem bewildering at first. However, before buying an optional accessory it is worth thinking hard about how—if at all—it will improve your photography. Many accessories that seemed a good idea at the time can end up at the back of a cupboard gathering dust.

Accessories fall into two broad categories: those that make the use of your camera easier by improving its ergonomics (optional grips, for example), and those that extend the capabilities of the camera in some way (such as filters). The key to choosing a new piece of equipment is to consider how you use your camera and what you like to photograph. Some equipment is for quite specific purposes: if you are a portrait photographer, for example, you may never need to own a polarizing filter, but for landscape photography it is almost essential.

›› FILTERED
Filters are essential accessories for landscape photographers, but less important for portraits.

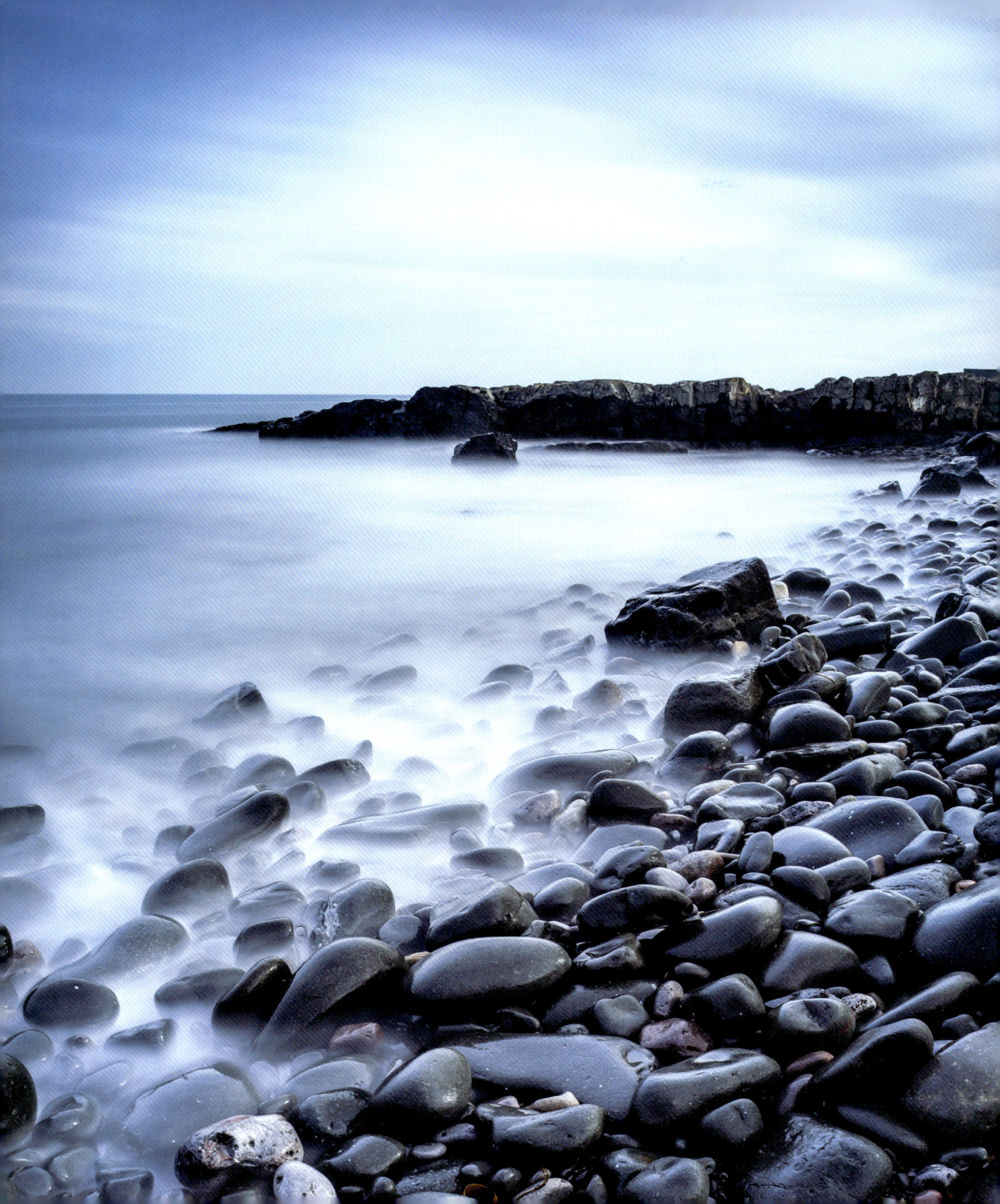

Leica produces a number of accessories for the M10 (and other M-series cameras) that aid the photographic process or protect the camera. Each accessory is made to the same high standard as the cameras themselves.

Camera protector

It is all too easy to bash your Leica M10 so Leica has designed a soft-leather protector—available in red, brown, or black—that wraps around the base and sides of the camera. The various camera controls are all still accessible.

Diopter correction lenses

It can be slightly tricky to see around the edges of the viewfinder if you wear eyeglasses. Fitting a correction lens to the viewfinder ocular means you will be able to see clearly through the viewfinder without them. Correction lenses are available in ±0.5, 1, 1.5, 2, and 3 diopters. As standard, the M10's viewfinder is set at -0.5 diopters, which you need to take into account when you determine which diopter you need (if your eyeglass prescription is +1.5 you would need a +2.0 correction lens, for example).

Leica Visoflex (Type 020) EVF

This 2.4MP electronic viewfinder fits into the hotshoe of the Leica M10. A live feed from the sensor is then sent to the viewfinder, allowing you to compose in Live View without using the rear LCD. The viewfinder also features a GPS receiver that can be used to tag geographical coordinates to images.

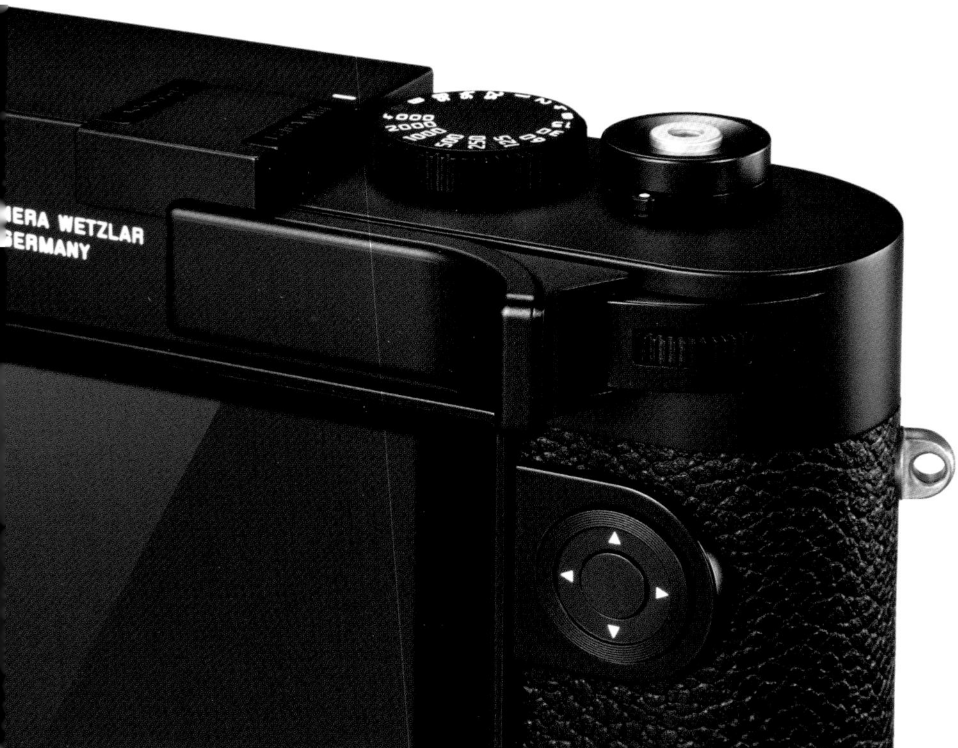

« THUMB SUPPORT
A thumb support is an ergonomic accessory that clips into the hotshoe. Your thumb rests in the curve of the support, giving you a better grip on the camera. This can help to reduce camera shake and make the Leica M10 easier to handle.
© Leica

» FILTERS

A filter is a piece of glass, gelatin, or optical resin designed to alter the light that passes through it in a very specific way. You can buy filters in one of two forms: round and threaded, enabling them to be screwed to the front of a lens, or square/rectangular, to be slotted into a holder attached to the lens.

Round filters are generally made of high-quality optical glass with a metal or heavy-duty plastic surround. They are ideal if you only have one lens or have several lenses with the same sized filter thread. However, when you own two or more lenses with different filter thread sizes you would need to buy another filter of the same type in a different size or buy a step-up or step-down adaptor ring to use the same filter on your various lenses.

Filter holder systems are more easily adapted to different sizes of lens as they are fitted to lenses via low-cost adaptor rings. There are a number of different filter holder systems to choose from. Cokin produces a popular series of holder systems: the A-system, which takes 67mm filters; the 84/85mm P-system; the 100mm Z-Pro system; and the 120mm X-Pro system. Other manufacturers of filter holder systems include LEE Filters (with 75mm and 100mm systems), Formatt, Hitech, and NiSi.

Filters can be stacked together, but even adding one filter can have a detrimental effect on an image. Generally the price you pay for a filter is reflected in its optical quality; expensive filters are expensive because their production is overseen to ensure consistency and filters that fail tests for quality are rejected.

› UV and skylight filters

UV and skylight filters absorb ultraviolet light, typically found at high altitude and on hazy days. UV light can cause a distinctive blue cast in an image. Skylight filters have a slightly pink tint to them, helping to warm up the image. UV filters are more neutral. Neither filter affects exposure.

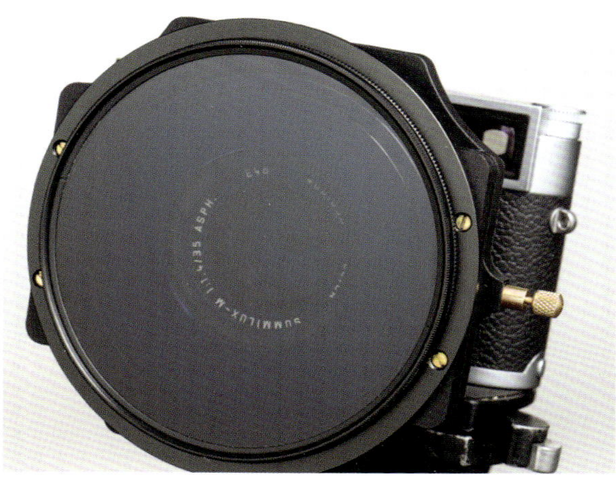

⌃ FILTER SYSTEM
A Leica M10 and Lee 100mm filter holder. One big drawback to using a filter holder (particularly one of the larger types) is that the viewfinder is obscured. One solution is to use Live View, the other is to fit your camera to a tripod and compose without the filter holder in place. It is only when you have composed the shot that you would fit the filter holder.

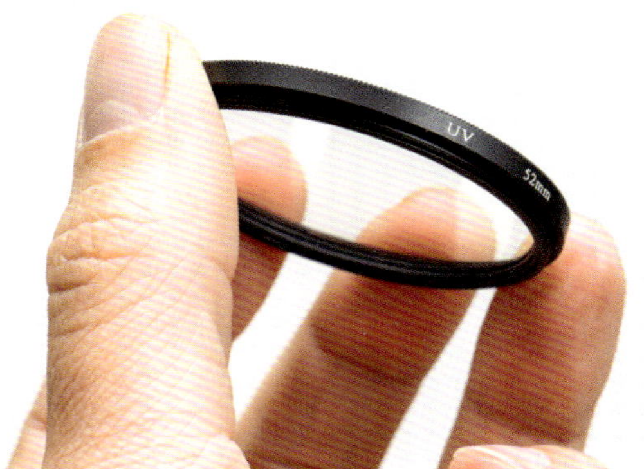

« PROTECTION
Many photographers like to have a skylight, UV, or dedicated "protection" filter attached to their lenses at all times. The theory is that if the lens is dropped, the filter will protect the front lens element from being smashed—at the cost of an easily replaceable filter. However, placing any filter between the scene and the camera's sensor may have a slightly detrimental effect on the final image quality.

The lowest native ISO setting on the Leica M10 is ISO 100. Although this is relatively low, it can still be difficult to select a slow shutter speed for creative effect in bright conditions, especially if a large aperture has been selected.

The solution is to fit a neutral density (ND) filter. An ND filter reduces the amount of light that passes through it in an analogous way to sunglasses, which opens up the creative possibilities of using a wider range of shutter speeds and apertures. ND filters come in a variety of strengths, which indicates how much light is "blocked" by the filter. Strengths range from 1 stop to 15 stops, and are available as both screw-in and square filters.

Note
- When using an ND filter the ISO should be set at 100: using a higher ISO or even Auto ISO negates the effect of the filter.

❯ EXTENDED
A 10-stop ND filter can turn an exposure of 1/30 sec. into 30 seconds, making tidal water blur into near mist.

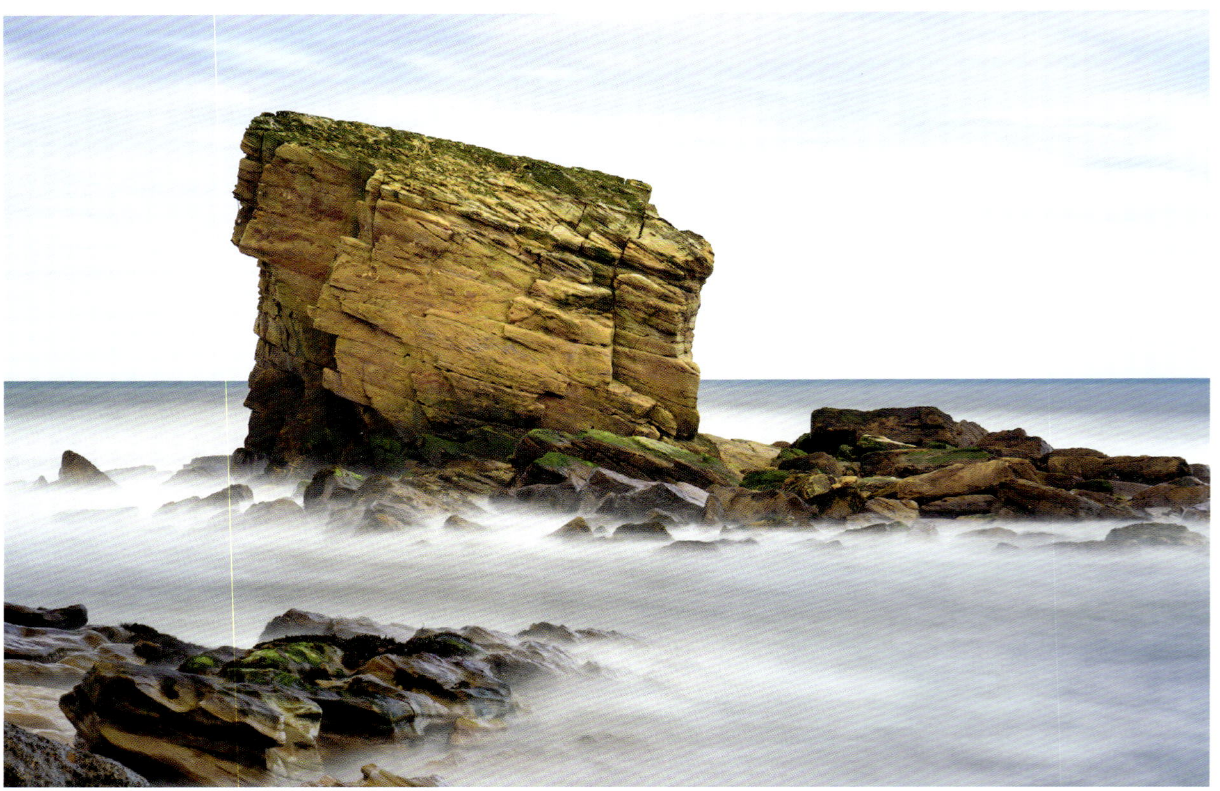

› Polarizing filters

When light hits the surface of a non-metallic subject the rays of light are scattered randomly. The visual effect of this is a sheen or glare on the surface of the subject, which reduces the apparent color saturation of the surface. Light scattered in this way is said to have been polarized.

This sheen can be removed by using a polarizing filter (or polarizer). Non-metallic surfaces that are affected by polarizers include water, shiny paint, and even wet or glossy leaves on trees. The only restriction is that the effect only works when the camera/polarizer combination is at roughly 35° to the surface.

Polarizers are made of glass mounted in a holder that can be rotated through 360° to control the strength of the polarizing effect. A polarizer is slightly opaque and will reduce the amount of light reaching the sensor. The exposure meter in the Leica M10 should automatically compensate for this when a polarizer is fitted, but if you are shooting in Manual exposure mode and using a handheld lightmeter you will need to adjust the exposure manually. The amount of adjustment required is typically 2 stops.

⌄ CLOUDS

A polarizing filter can also be used to deepen the color of a blue sky. This effect is strongest when the polarizer is aimed toward the sky at 90° to the sun, with the effect diminishing noticeably away from this angle. The height of the sun also affects how strongly the polarizing filter appears to work.

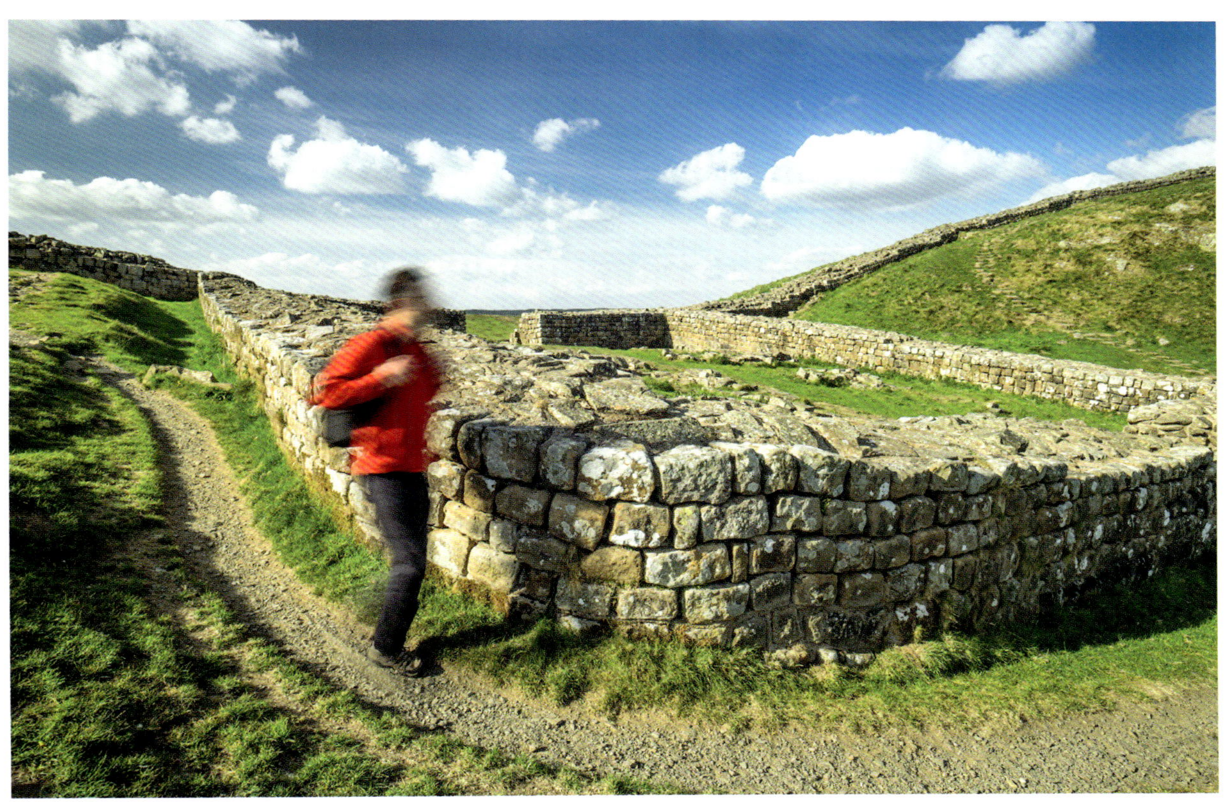

Landscape scenes often benefit from the use of a graduated ND ("ND grad") filter. ND grads have a semi-opaque top half and a clear bottom half, so are typically used to balance the exposure between an area of a scene that is more brightly lit than another area (a bright sky and darker foreground, for example).

Just like regular ND filters, ND grads are available in different strengths; typically 1, 2, or 3 stops. The greater the brightness difference across the image, the stronger the ND graduate filter needs to be. Generally, skies look most natural when they are exposed 1 stop brighter than the foreground. Therefore, if the difference between the sky and the foreground is 3 stops, a 2-stop ND grad would usually be the "correct" option. However, this is very much about personal preference and using a stronger filter can add drama to a sky (although the effect can be easily overdone if you are not careful).

ND grads are most useful in square or rectangular form, fitted to a filter holder than in screw-in form. This allows the transition zone of the filter to be placed where the lighter part of the scene blends to the darker. This flexibility is not possible when using a screw-in ND grad, as the transition zone is usually fixed centrally.

⌄ LIGHT
ND grad filters are typically used when the foreground of a scene is lit only by ambient light and the sky lit by direct sunlight. The key is not to use too dense a filter, as this can make a sky appear unnaturally dark.

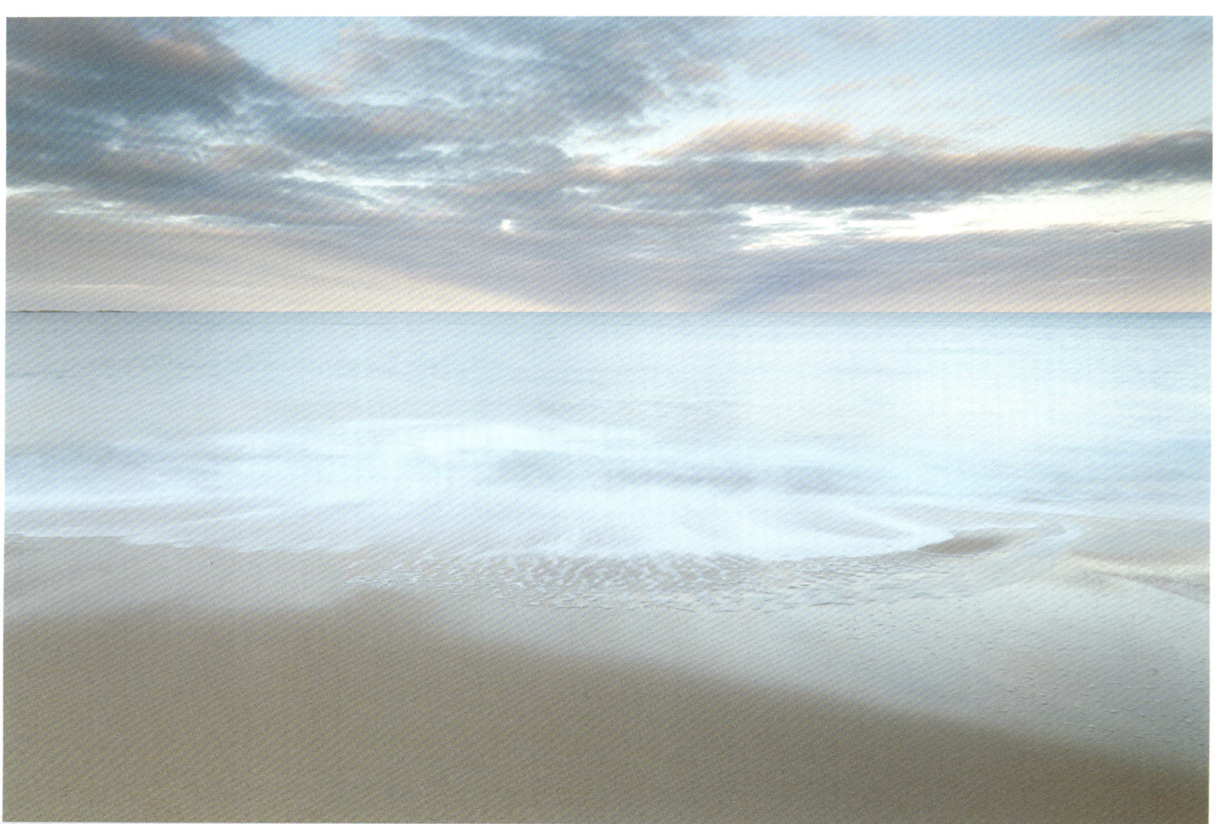

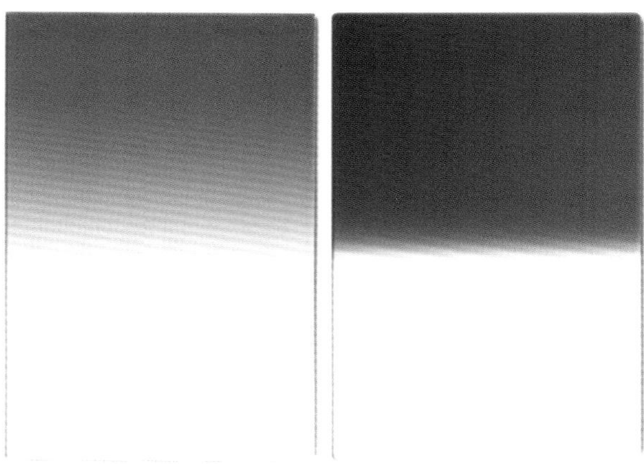

« TYPES
ND grads can be either "hard" or "soft," which refers to how sudden the transition from clear to opaque is: hard filters have a relatively sharp transition, while soft filters are subtler. Which you choose is also very much a personal choice. As a general rule, a soft ND grad (far left) is useful where the line between light and dark in a scene is irregular (a horizon broken by trees or buildings, for example), while a hard ND grad (left) is better suited to clearly defined transitions (such as the horizon in a seascape). Hard ND grads are also easier to position, as the transition is much more obvious.

› Using filters with a rangefinder

Filters such as ND grads and polarizers need to be precisely aligned or rotated to control their effect. This makes them hard to use when looking through the M10's rangefinder, simply because you cannot see the effect they are having. The problem can be resolved by using Live View (or the optional EVF), but if you are determined to use the direct viewfinder the following tips may help:

Polarizer

If you use a screw-in polarizer, carefully mark one part of the turning ring with a hardwearing spot of paint. Look through the polarizer and turn it until you've achieved the required degree of polarization. Note where the paint spot is and then screw the polarizer to the lens. Rotate the ring until the paint spot is at the same angle.

If your polarizer is mounted to a filter holder, take the holder off the lens and adjust the polarizer with it held up to one of your eyes. Once you've achieved the correct amount of polarization, replace the filter holder on the lens in exactly the same orientation, without adjusting the polarizer further.

ND grads

Mark the exact center of your filter holder on both sides with a hardwearing spot of paint. Place the filter holder on your lens and make marks on both sides of the holder, both top and bottom, to show where the glass of your lens comes to on the holder. If you have several lenses use different colors for each lens.

Look through the viewfinder of your Leica M10 and judge where the transition zone should be. With the filter holder in your hands, use the marks you made to position the ND grad.

CHAPTER 7
CAMERA CARE

The Leica M10 is a well-built camera that should last a lifetime, as long as it is not abused. You should not be complacent, though: the world can throw atmospheric conditions at you that will challenge both you and your camera in different ways.

In common with all digital cameras, the Leica M10 should be used, but not abused. Dust, moisture, and extreme temperatures can all have a detrimental effect on the camera's operation. However, by taking a few simple precautions you should receive optimum performance from the camera and prolong its useful life.

One simple way to keep your Leica safe is to keep it in a bag until it is needed. This can be as simple as a small holster-style bag attached to a belt buckle or shoulder strap, or a full-size rucksack that would allow you to carry extra lenses and other accessories: the former is ideal for spontaneous shooting, while the latter is better when you need to carry more equipment (both photographic and non-photographic).

›› SNOW
Landscape photography invariably means waiting for the right lighting conditions. Wearing lots of layers helps to trap heat close to your body and keep you warm.

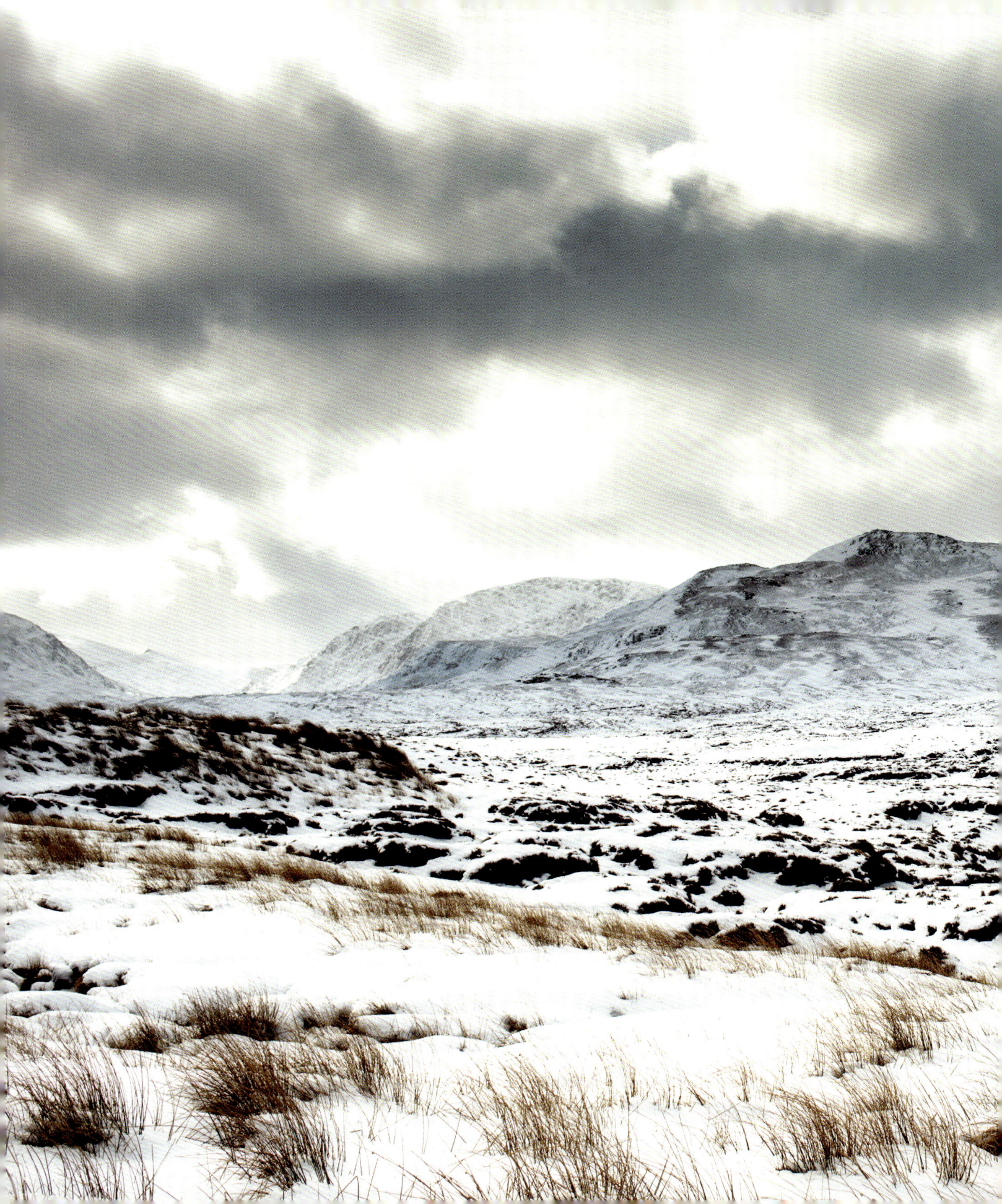

» LEICA SUPPORT

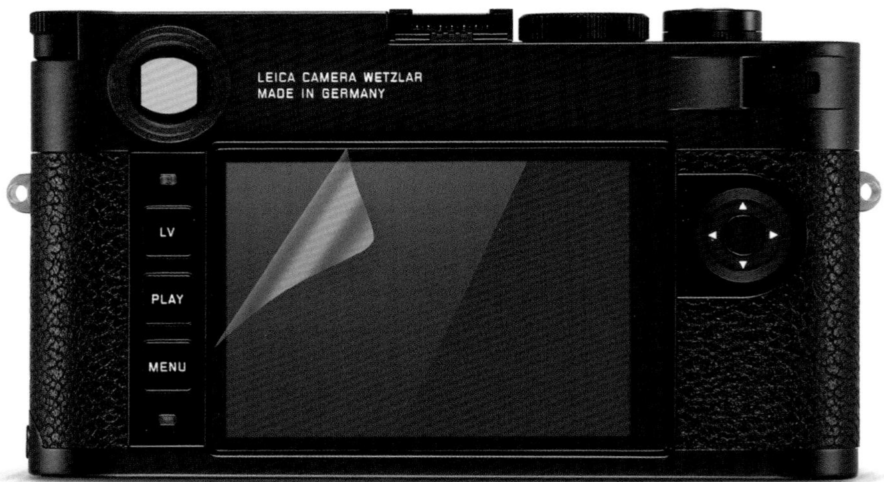

Should the worst happen and your M10 stops functioning it should only be sent to an authorized repair center: the Leica warranty will be immediately invalidated if you use an unofficial repair service. Choose your region from the list below:

⌃ PROTECTION
Leica sells a number of accessories that help protect your camera, including protective film that can be placed over the M10's LCD.
© Leica

United States of America & Canada

Leica Camera Inc.
1 Pearl Ct, Unit A
Allendale, New Jersey 07401
repair@leicacamerausa.com

United Kingdom

Leica Camera Ltd.
34 Bruton Place
London
W1J 6NR
owner@leica-camera.co.uk

Germany

Leica Camera AG
Leica Customer Service
Solmser Gewerbepark 8
35606 Solms
cs@leica-camera.com

France

Leica Camera Sarl
310 impasse de la Tuilerie
74410 Saint Jorioz
support@leica-camera.fr

» ATMOSPHERIC CONDITIONS

› Dust and sand

Of all the conditions you can shoot in, airborne dust and sand pose the greatest risk to you camera. Water is almost as bad, but dust and sand can be less noticeable, meaning they can find their way undetected into the nooks and crannies of your camera, scratching sensitive surfaces such as the sensor or gumming up moving parts. This can lead to irreparable damage.

When working in dusty or sandy conditions it is therefore a good idea to keep your camera in your camera bag until you actually need to use it. Your Leica M10 is particularly vulnerable when you change lenses, as dust or sand can enter the interior of the camera through the open lens mounting. The risk is highest when there is also wind. Therefore, when changing lenses in these conditions, try to do it in a sheltered spot to limit the camera's exposure to any wind-borne particles. Even using your body to shield your camera is better then nothing.

Dust or sand can also lead to scratched lens elements. If your glass elements are covered with sand or dust, *do not* wipe them clean; use a blower to remove the sand or dust.

When not using the camera, it is a good habit to always attach a lens or body cap, but when attaching the body cap, you should remove any dust from it first.

⌄ SAND
A breeze on a beach can whip small particles of fine sand into the air. Changing lenses is not recommended during these conditions.

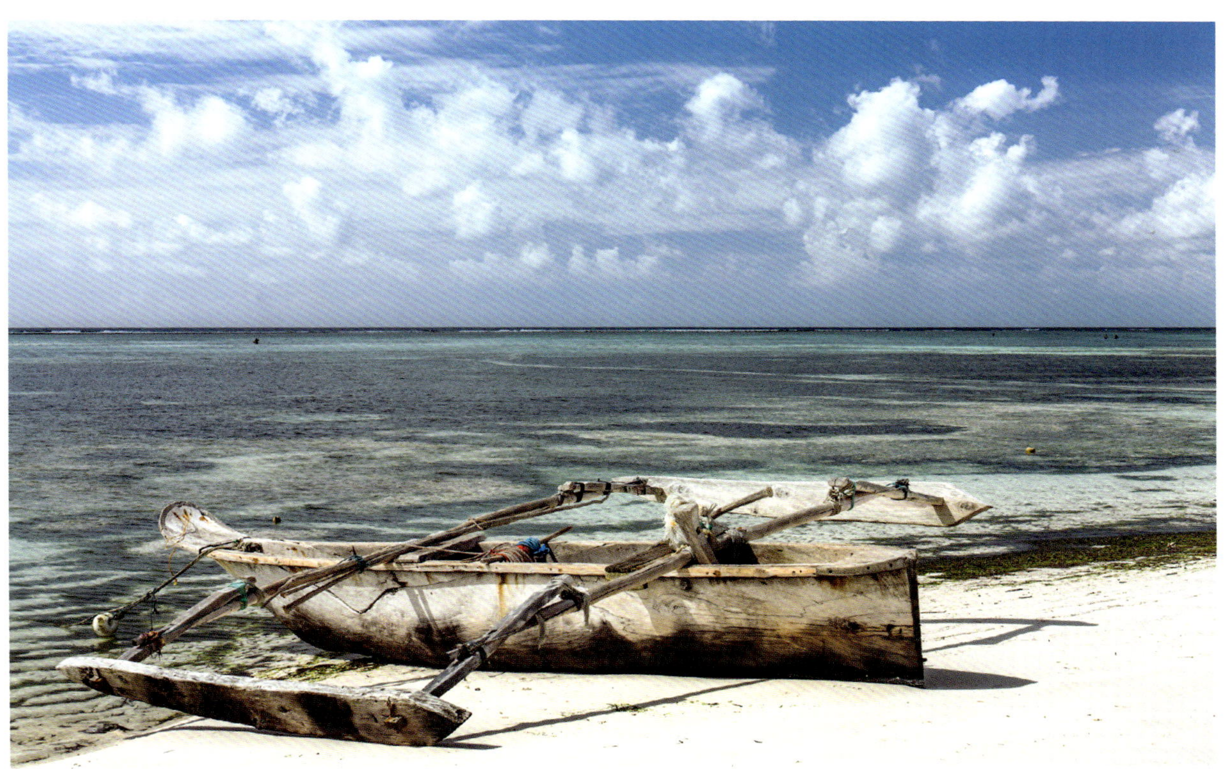

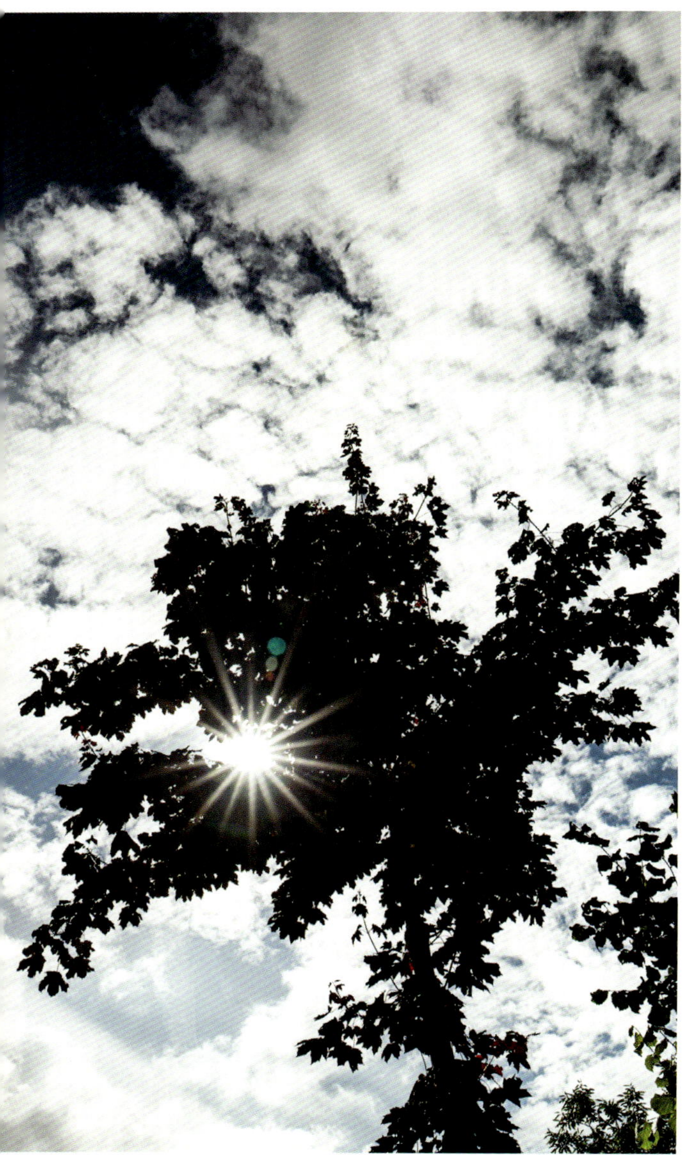

SUN
Be careful never to leave your camera lying in direct sunlight without the protection of a lens cap. If the lens points directly at the sun for extended periods the effect of heat—magnified by the lens—can cause the shutter blades inside the camera to warp.

› Heat

Exposure to extreme levels of heat can damage your Leica M10 in a number of ways. The most disastrous is camera body warping. The Leica M10 is a precision instrument and anything that is slightly out of "true" will potentially result in malfunction or an inability to achieve fine focus. Heat can also affect the lubricating oils that enable the camera to operate smoothly.

To avoid heat damage do not leave the camera for long periods in a hot place, such as a car on a sunny day. If you need to keep a camera in a warm place then use an insulated camera bag or even a food cool box if you have one. Although less effective, wrapping the camera in a light-colored fabric will also offer some protection.

› Humidity

Humid conditions come with their own risks. Condensation, if it is allowed to build up on the Leica M10, can have a detrimental effect on the camera. If you find that condensation has formed on the camera (or lens), switch the camera off and leave it to stand at room temperature for at least one hour. The condensation should gradually evaporate over that time.

Storing your camera in an airtight container or plastic bag—with a sachet of silica gel—is strongly recommended in humid conditions. The silica gel will absorb any moisture and prevent condensation building up on the camera itself. Note that if you regularly work in humid conditions you will need to frequently replace the packet of silica gel.

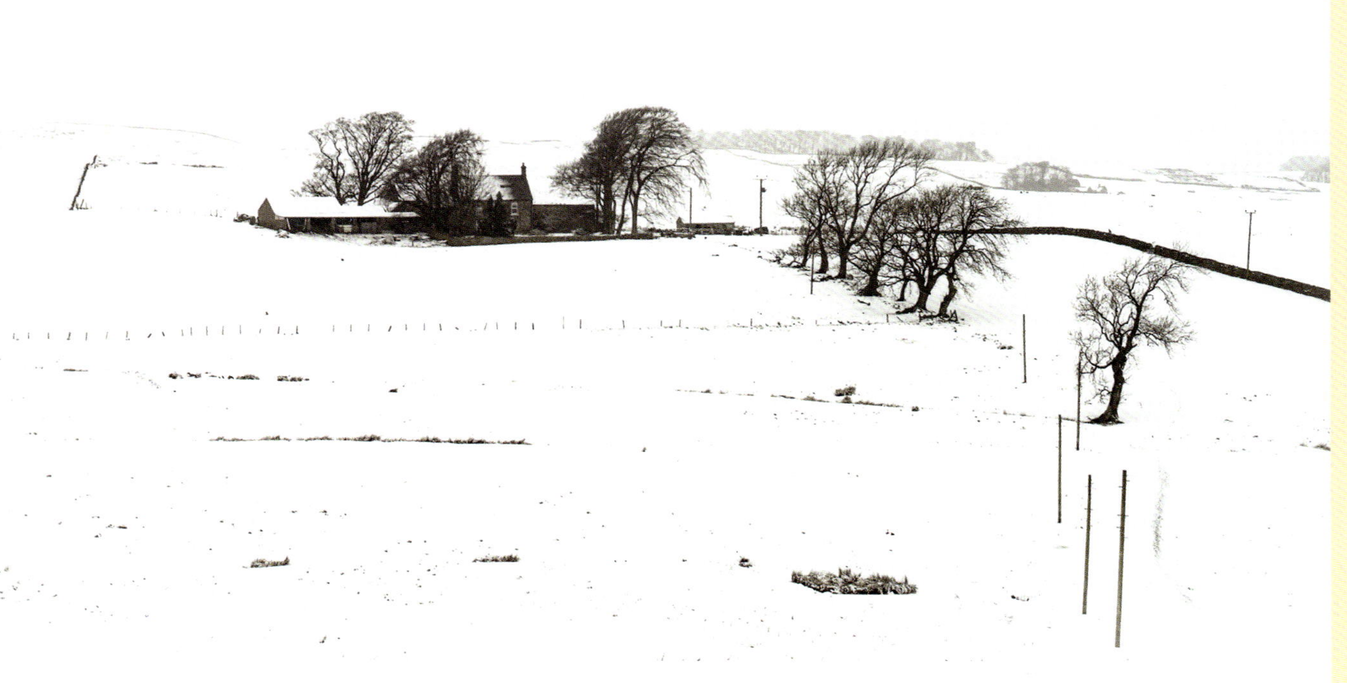

› Cold

Extreme cold can have an effect on the performance of your Leica M10, and the most vulnerable part is the battery. In low temperatures (below 32°F/0°C), battery performance will fall off noticeably. It is a good idea to keep one or two fully charged spare batteries with you as a backup if you plan to be out in cold conditions for a lengthy period. Carry the batteries where they will be kept as warm as possible until needed, such as your jacket's inside pocket.

The performance of the Leica M10 in low temperatures will also be improved if you are able to keep it warm between shots. When you are not using it, store it in your camera bag, rather than carrying it exposed to the elements. If you need to keep it handy, temporarily wrap it in a layer of insulation, such as a spare hat or scarf.

Apart from poor battery performance, other symptoms that indicate the camera is too cold include a darkening of the monitor and a general slowing down of its operation.

⌃ WINTER

Wind chill can make a big difference to how cold you feel on a winter's day. Wearing fleecy layers that trap heat under a windproof jacket is a simple way to keep comfortably warm.

Water can cause any camera to malfunction temporarily and in some cases may even result in permanent damage to the camera, battery, or memory card (although memory cards are surprisingly tough).

As with dust and sand, if you need to change lenses while photographing in rain or snowy weather, shield the camera to prevent water from getting inside the camera or onto the inner lens elements.

Keeping your Leica M10 inside a bag until needed is also sensible and some makes of camera bag have rain covers that offer extra protection to the bag's contents. Rain covers can also be useful for keeping your camera bag and its contents dry if you wish to put it down on damp ground.

⌄ WET
Light can be at its most dramatic between two weather systems, so being prepared to be out in all weathers is a useful trait for a landscape photographer. One of the most useful items in my kit bag is a small umbrella, which can be set up quickly to protect the camera and myself during rain showers.

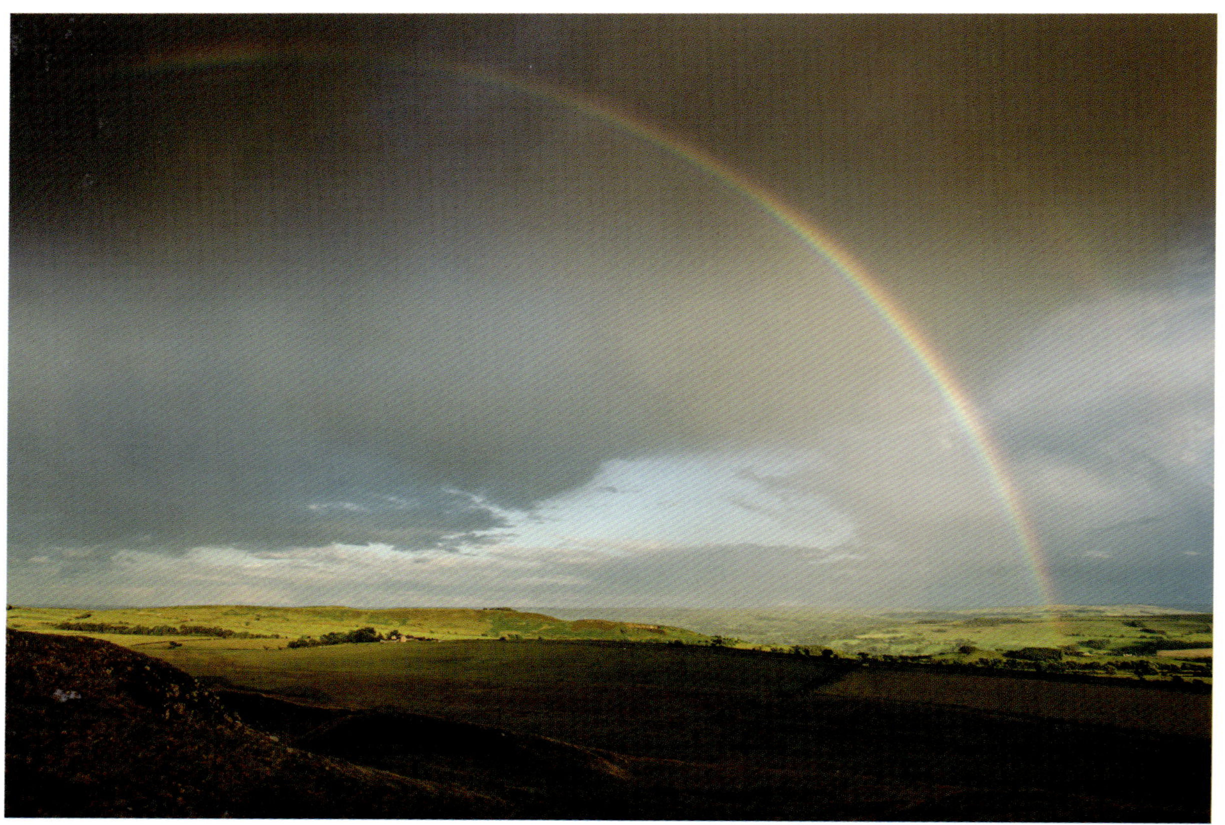

› Water damage

Water in its many forms is a favored subject for a lot of photographers. However, getting your camera soaking wet is not recommended.

If your Leica M10 is dropped in salt water, remove the battery and memory card immediately. Dry the camera—as well as the battery and memory card—as best you can with an absorbent cloth and contact your local Leica repair center for advice as soon as possible: salt is highly corrosive and will permanently damage your camera without immediate attention.

A fresh water soaking is still far from ideal, but less damaging. As with salt water, dry the camera, memory card, and battery with an absorbent cloth and contact your local Leica repair center for advice. To help dry the camera

further get a large bowl and place your camera in it with the body cap or lens fitted. Fill the bowl with rice so the camera is entirely covered. The rice will start to absorb any water from the camera (it may take a day or so to dry it fully). When it is done, clean up your camera, replace the battery, and switch on to test.

⌄ SEASIDE
Salt water spray can be particularly damaging to a camera. If you are taking photographs on the beach and your camera gets wet, clean it with a soft cloth, dampened with fresh water. Then dry it thoroughly with a soft, dry cloth.

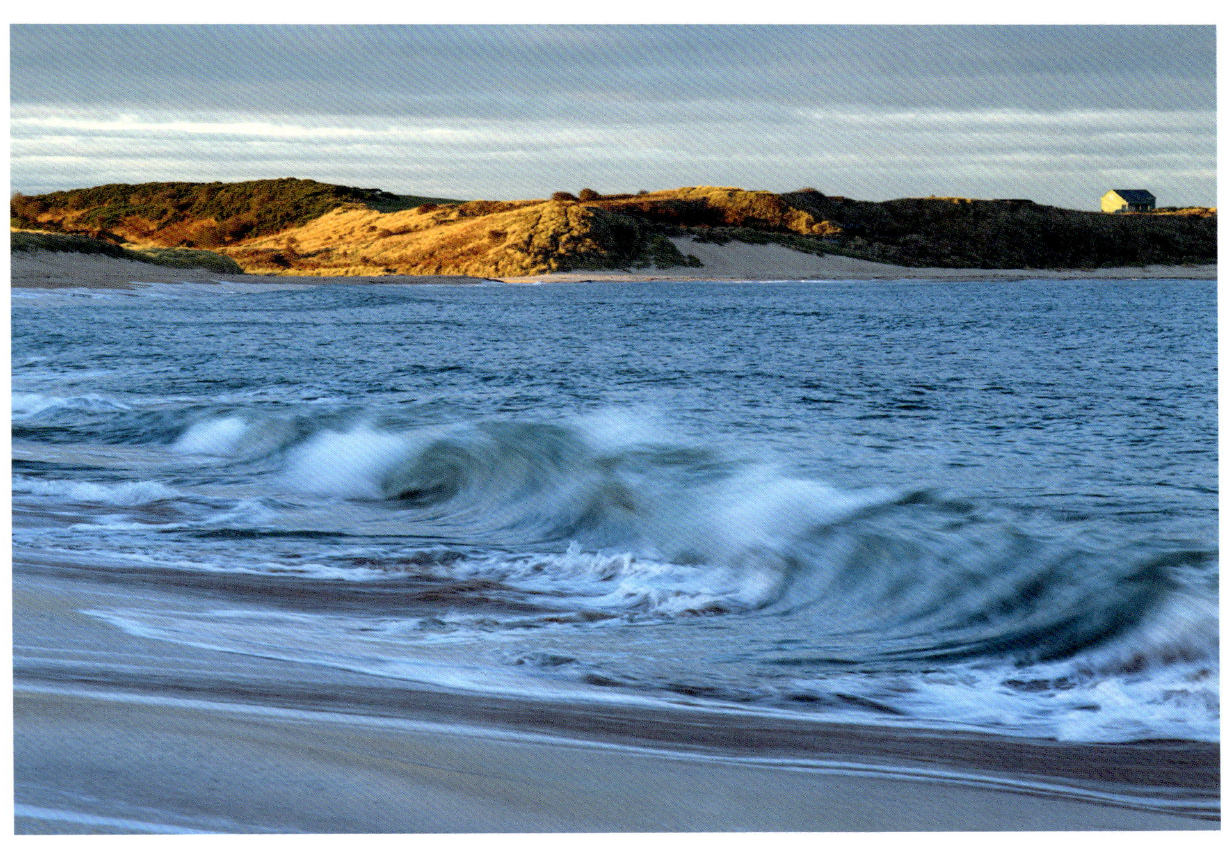

» TAKING CARE OF YOUR CAMERA

› Caring for lenses

Leica lenses are robust and should last a lifetime. However, you still need to take as much care of them as possible to protect your investment. The most vulnerable parts of a lens are the exposed surfaces of the front and rear glass elements. These can be scratched, so care must be taken when cleaning them.

Do not use cleaning cloths that have been kept loose in pockets; dedicated lens cleaning cloths should be kept in a packet until needed. Ideally you should use a lint-free microfiber cloth as this will minimize the risk that the cloth will add fluff and other fibers to the surface of the lens. If possible, blow any loose dust off with a blower before cleaning the lens.

⌄ SPOTS

Rain spots, fingerprints, or other grease marks can increase the likelihood of flare occurring. These should be cleaned off carefully with your lens cloth. Without pressing too hard, move the cloth in a circular motion around the lens surface. If a mark is particularly stubborn use a lens-cleaning fluid or distilled water.

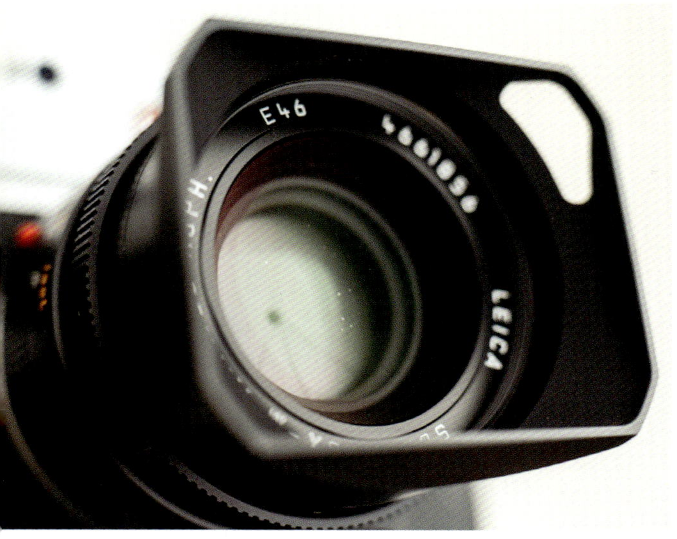

› Cleaning the sensor

By far the simplest way to clean the Leica M10's sensor is to use a low-pressure air blower to blow dust particles from the sensor surface. However, a blower is only effective on dry particles such as dust. Wet particles, such as rain and pollen, will adhere to the sensor and cannot be removed by blowing. This type of mark must be removed using a wet-cleaning process, such as a swab impregnated with sensor-cleaning fluid wiped carefully across the sensor. Swabs should only be used once and then discarded. If you're nervous about this, your local Leica service center will do it for you (for a fee).

Assessing the problem

1) Press MENU and select **Sensor Cleaning** from the Main Menu (page 4).

2) Select **Dust Detection**.

3) Set the aperture on your lens to its minimum value.

4) Aim your camera toward a white or light gray surface, such as a sheet of paper or blank wall. The surface should be even in tone. You don't need to focus, but ensure that the surface fills the frame.

5) Press down on the shutter-release button to expose an image.

6) Once the image has been processed, your Leica M10 will display a high-contrast version of the image showing the dust particles on the sensor.

7) Switch off your camera.

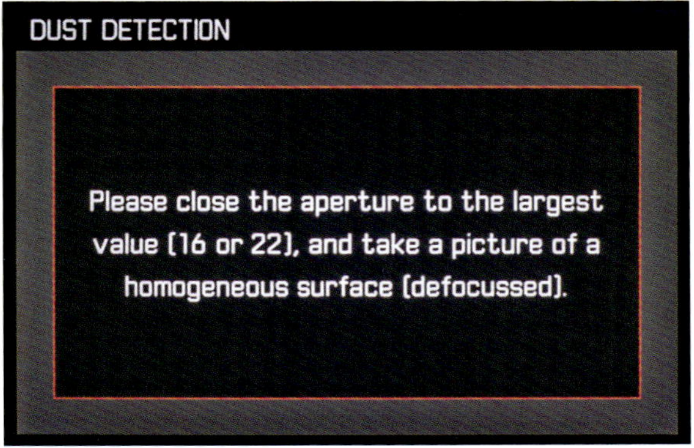

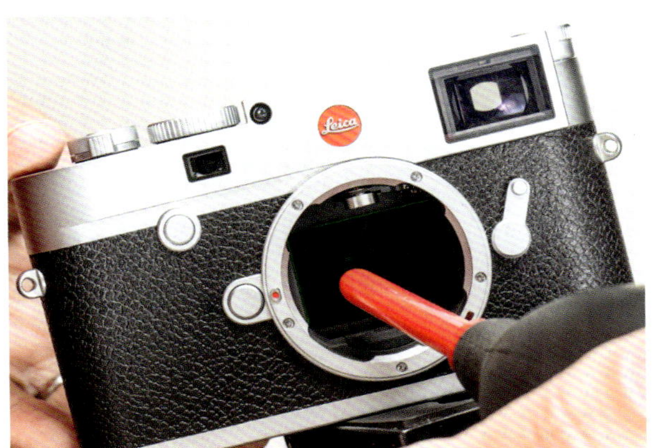

Sensor cleaning

1) Sensor cleaning can only be done when the shutter blades are open, revealing the sensor behind. To do this, press MENU and select **Sensor Cleaning** from the Main Menu (page 4).

2) Select **Open Shutter**.

3) On the sub-menu select **Yes** to continue.

4) Remove the lens or body cap.

5) Hold your Leica M10 upside down with the lens mount facing downward.

6) Insert the tip of an air blower carefully into the sensor chamber without touching the sensor itself. Blow air over the sensor until you think the dust has been removed. Remove the tip of the blower from the sensor chamber.

7) Replace the lens/body cap and switch off your M10.

Notes

- If the battery charge is less than 60% you won't be able to activate sensor cleaning and the message **Attention Battery too low for sensor cleaning** will be displayed on the LCD.

- If the battery charge drops below 40% during the cleaning process the message **Attention Please stop sensor cleaning immediately** will be displayed on the LCD and a continuous tone will be played. Remove the blower from the sensor chamber and switch off your camera.

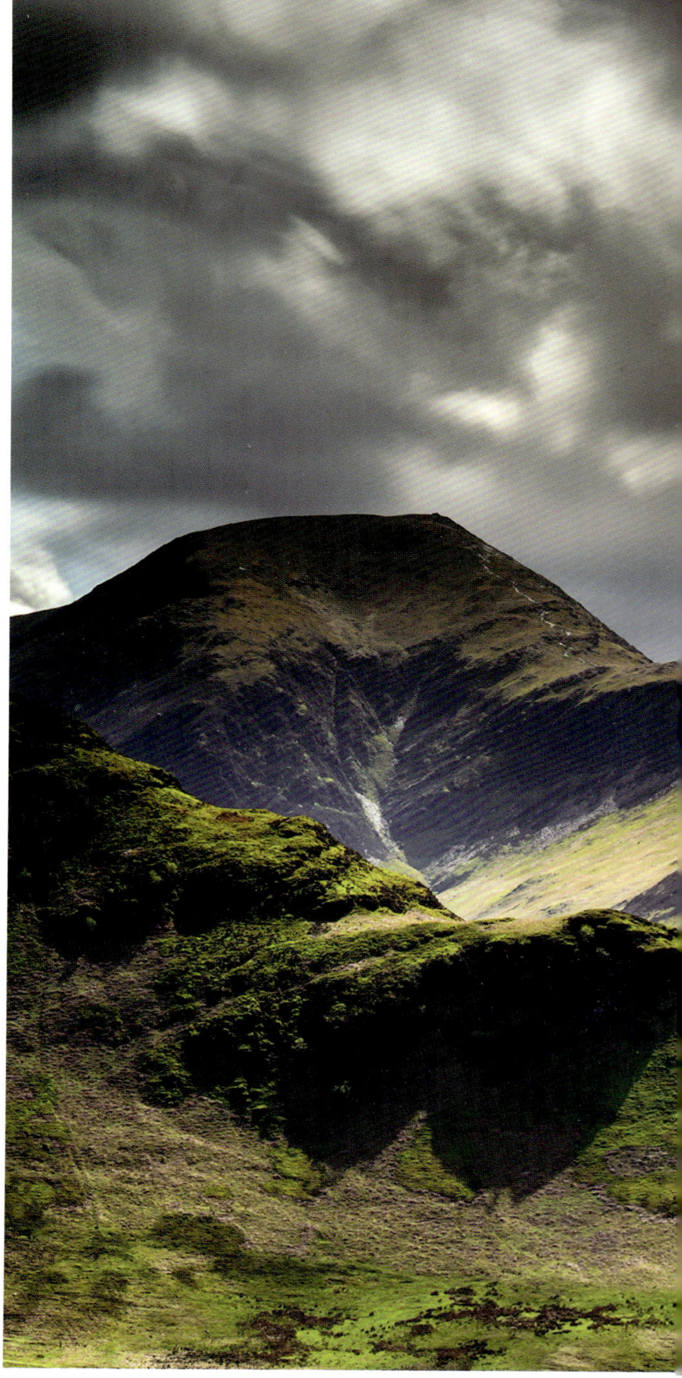

» OTHER WEATHER

Strong wind can affect your photography in a number of
ways. It can cause camera shake even when your camera
is mounted on a tripod (particularly if you have raised the
center column). In very strong wind it can even blow your
tripod over, with potentially disastrous results. To shoot
this long exposure image in high wind I set the camera
on a tripod low to the ground. I also sheltered it as best
I could with my body during the exposure.

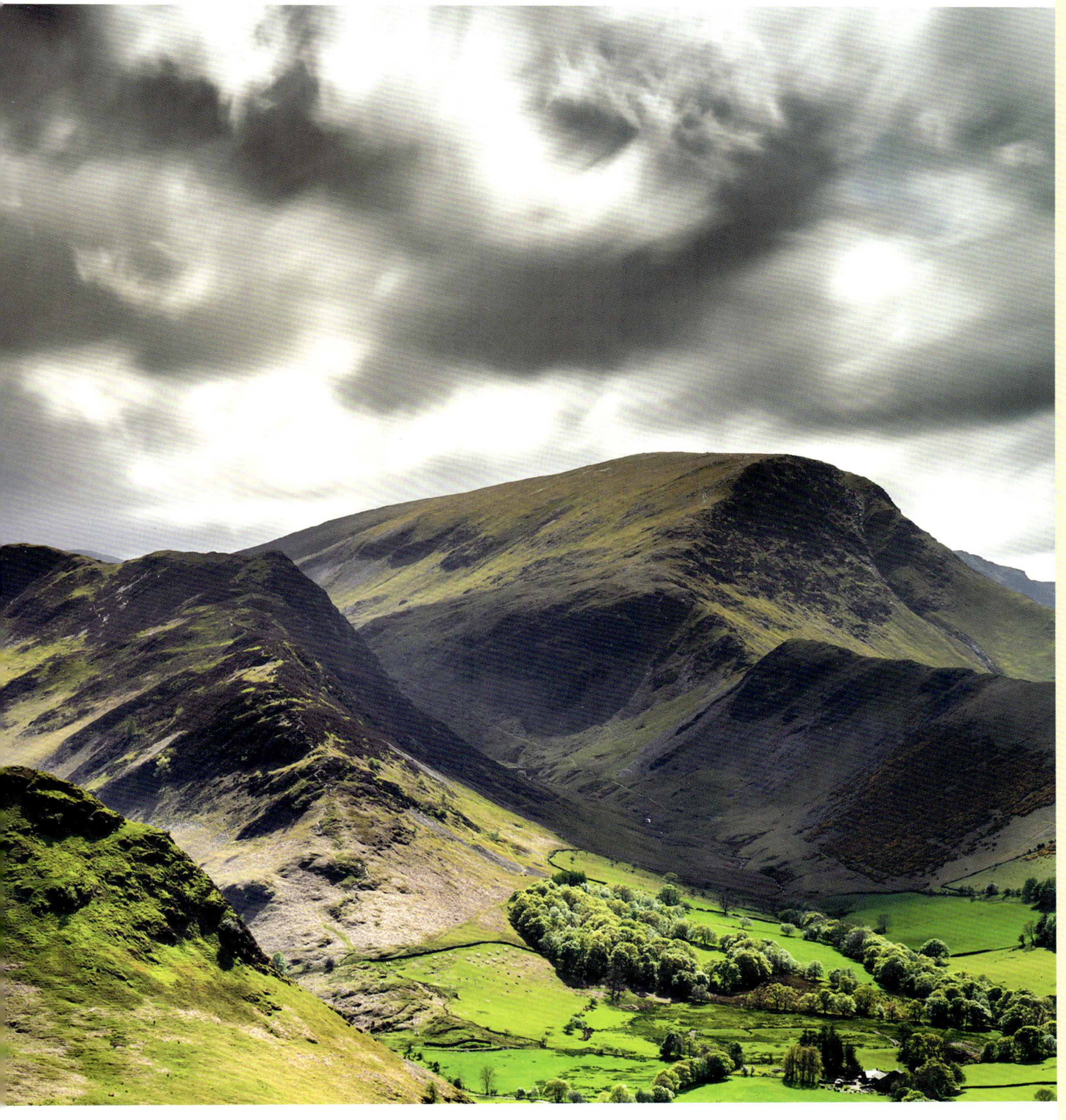

CHAPTER 8
IN THE FIELD

Once you have charged the battery, installed a memory card, and fitted a lens you can start shooting with your Leica M10. However, there is more to making successful images than pressing the shutter-release button down.

Photography can be neatly divided into two halves, and mastering both is the only way to improve and produce pleasing images. The first half is a technical understanding of photography. This can be daunting when you start out, particularly if you are not comfortable with numbers (the seemingly eccentric sequence of aperture values gives many new photographers pause for thought).

The second half of photography—producing esthetically pleasing images—is harder to learn. This area of photography involves learning about multiple elements that include (but are not limited to) an understanding of how light affects an image; the art of composition; when to use color; and when to think in black and white. It is simply impossible to cover everything you need to know about the esthetic side of photography here, but this chapter will give you a taste of some of those things.

» CASTLE
The joy of photography for a lot of people is its variability. One day you can be shooting spontaneously using fast primes at maximum aperture, while the next day you could be shooting relatively formal compositions using long exposures with your camera mounted on a tripod.

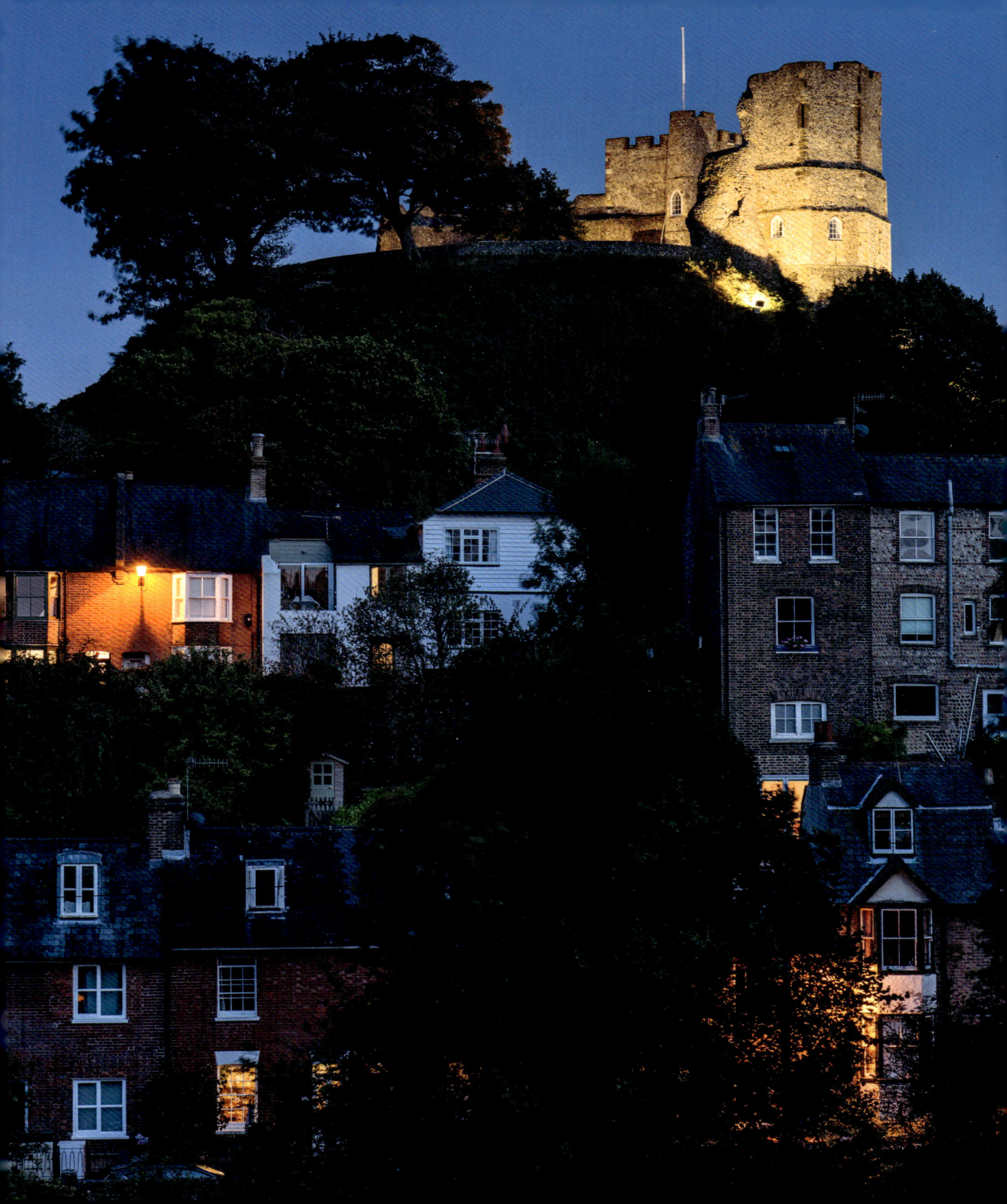

» UNDERSTANDING EXPOSURE

There are three elements that must be considered in order to make a "good" exposure: the shutter speed, lens aperture, and ISO setting. The first two control the amount of light reaching the sensor, while the third determines how much light actually needs to reach the sensor to make an image to start with.

› Shutter speed

The shutter speed is a unit of time measured in fractions of a second. On the Leica M10 you can manually select shutter speeds from 1/4000 sec. (the fastest shutter speed) to 8 seconds (the slowest). This range increases when you use Aperture Priority, as the Leica M10 can automatically select a shutter speed of up to 125 seconds. This is also the longest time the shutter can be held open for when using Bulb mode.

A typical range of shutter speeds is 1/1000 sec., 1/500 sec., 1/250 sec., 1/125 sec., and so on. The difference between each of these values is 1 stop, with each 1-stop difference representing either a halving of the amount of light reaching the sensor (as the shutter speed increases) or a doubling (as it decreases). For example, a shutter speed of 1/500 sec. lets twice as much light reach the sensor as a shutter speed of 1/1000 sec., but half as much as 1/250 sec.

› Aperture

The aperture is an iris in the lens that can be varied in size to allow more or less light to pass through. The size of the aperture is measured in units called f/stops, represented by f/ and a suffix number. A typical range of f/stops on a Leica lens is f/2.8, f/4, f/5.6, f/8, and so on. As this is essentially expressing a fraction, the larger the suffix number, the smaller the aperture is.

As with shutter speed, each f/stop value on a lens represents either a doubling or halving of the amount of light let through; f/4 will allow in half as much light as f/2.8, but twice that of f/5.6, for example.

To make a photographer's life slightly more complicated there is no "standard" aperture range in the Leica lens line-up; different lenses have different maximum and minimum apertures (as shown in the lens charts on pages 114–117).

> **Note**
> - Shutter speed can be adjusted in ½-stop increments on the Leica M10, so 1/750 sec. would be the ½-stop step between 1/1000 sec. and 1/500 sec.

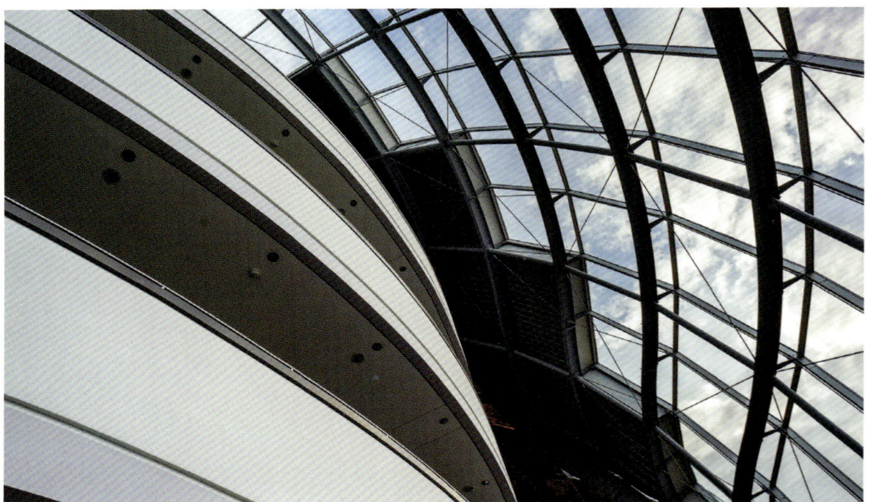

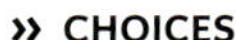
» CHOICES
This image was shot at f/11 with a shutter speed of 1/60 sec. The aperture was chosen to ensure sharpness throughout the frame, while ensuring a shutter speed that was fast enough to avoid camera shake with a 24mm lens. However, I could have used f/8 at 1/125 sec. or f/16 at 1/30 sec. (and many other combinations) to maintain the same level of exposure overall.

› Reciprocity

Shutter speed, aperture, and ISO have a reciprocal relationship, so if you change one, you must change at least one of the others to maintain the same level of exposure overall. For example, if you increase the shutter speed by 1 stop, the aperture must be made 1-stop wider (to let more light through to the sensor) or the ISO should be increased by 1 stop (making the sensor more "sensitive" to light) to deliver the same overall exposure.

Selecting a particular combination of aperture and shutter speed is one of the fundamental creative decisions you need to make as a photographer, as each control has a visual effect on the resulting image.

The aperture setting is one of the factors that determines the depth of field of an image, which we will look at in greater detail on the following pages. The smaller the aperture used, the greater the extent of depth of field (which increases overall image sharpness).

However, you will need to use increasingly longer shutter speeds as the aperture closes. Longer shutter speeds means that any movement in your image will be blurred.

Conversely, a wide aperture will minimize depth of field but will allow a fast shutter speed enabling you "freeze" movement more effectively.

⌄ LANDSCAPE

My particular photographic interests are landscape and architecture. This means that I typically prioritize aperture—with its control over depth of field—over shutter speed. If I need to adjust the shutter speed without affecting the aperture I either increase the ISO, or more commonly, use an ND filter to lengthen shutter speed, as I did with this image.

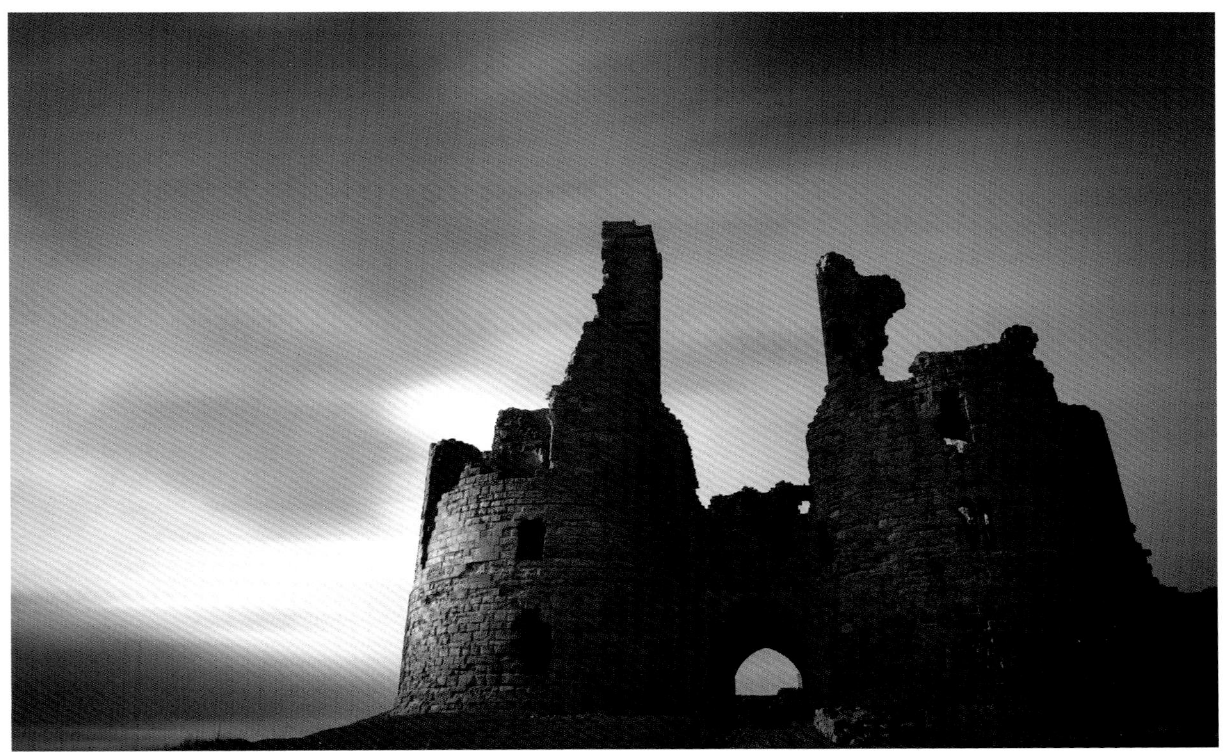

» DEPTH OF FIELD

Technically, the sharpest part of an image is always the point at which the lens is focused, but there is a zone of sharpness that extends out from the focus point. This is known as "depth of field" and extends twice as far away from the camera position than toward it (so ⅔ of the depth of field lies beyond the focus point; ⅓ lies in front of it). Three factors affect the depth of field in an image:

- The aperture setting: the smaller the aperture, the greater the depth of field (f/11 delivers more depth of field than f/5.6, for example).

- The focal length of the lens: the wider the focal length, the greater the depth of field at any given aperture (a 28mm lens delivers more depth of field than a 135mm lens, for example).

- Camera-to-subject distance: the greater the distance between the camera and the point of focus, the greater the depth of field will be at any given aperture (so depth of field is larger when you focus on a distant subject).

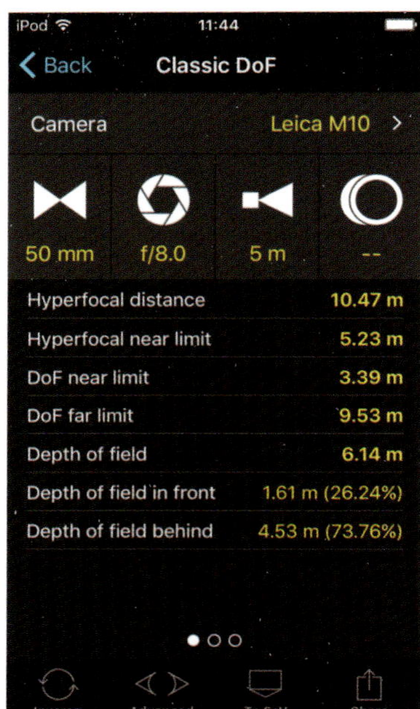

« **CALCULATION**
Apps such as PhotoPills can be used to calculate hyperfocal distance.

› Hyperfocal distance

Given all of the previous notes you might think that maximum sharpness would always be achieved by shooting at a lens' smallest aperture setting. Unfortunately this assumption runs foul of the laws of physics: when smaller apertures are used, lenses can suffer from an effect known as diffraction. When light enters a lens it is randomly scattered, or "diffracted," as it strikes the edges of the aperture blades. This causes a noticeable softening of an image; the smaller the aperture, the greater the softening is, despite an overall increase in the depth of field. Therefore it is generally preferable to avoid using a lens' minimum aperture if possible.

The optimum optical quality of a lens is generally found when the aperture is set 2 or 3 f/stops down than maximum (this is f/8–f/11 on most lenses), although this means you may need to deal with a smaller than desirable depth of field. Fortunately, there is a technique that helps you make most efficient use of depth of field at a given aperture. This is achieved by focusing the lens at a distance known as the "hyperfocal distance."

There are numerous smartphone apps that you can use to calculate the hyperfocal distance, but these are largely unnecessary when using Leica lenses. This is because Leica lenses feature a depth of field scale that can be used to set the hyperfocal distance, as outlined opposite.

Note
- The slightly disconcerting aspect of setting the hyperfocal distance is that it often means you do not focus where your subject is positioned—you will need to ignore the split-image in the viewfinder as it will not be aligned correctly.

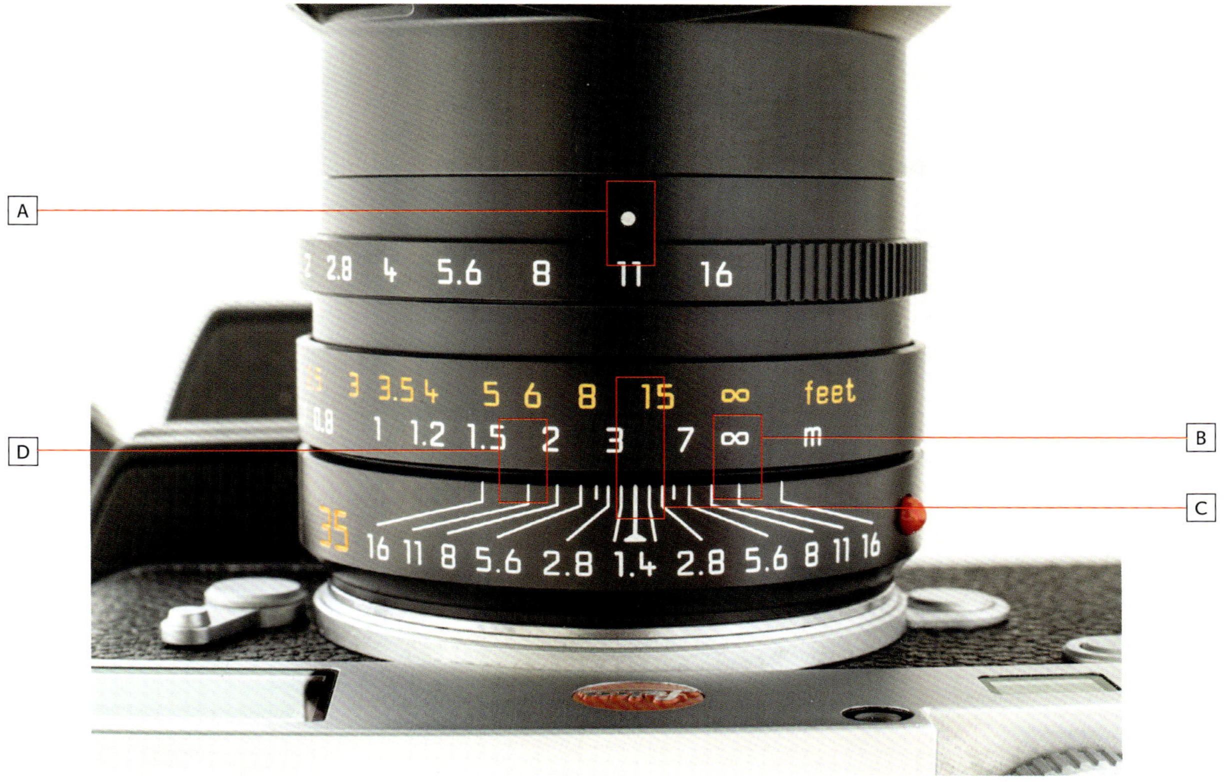

SETTING THE HYPERFOCAL DISTANCE

A To focus at the hyperfocal distance, first set the desired aperture (A); in this example f/11.

B Then, move the focus ring so that the furthest point you want sharp—in this case ∞—is aligned with the appropriate aperture mark at the right side of the depth of field scale (B). The focus is now set at the hyperfocal distance!

C In this example, the hyperfocal distance is approximately 12ft/3.6m (C).

D The closest distance of the depth of field can be seen by looking at the focus distance next to the aperture mark at the left side of the lens (here 6ft/1.8m) (D).

Here, the depth of field extends from 6ft (1.8m) to infinity, and everything within that range will appear acceptably sharp.

» SHUTTER SPEED

The invention of photography opened up a visual world that was previously unseen. The use of the appropriate shutter speed can either reveal hidden detail in a fast-moving subject, or blur movement for artistic effect.

› Long shutter speeds

Long shutter speeds blur movement, and the longer the shutter speed or the faster the movement, the greater the degree of blurring will be. It is often tempting to shoot moving subjects with a fast shutter speed to "freeze" movement, but this can produce strangely static and lifeless results, whereas blurring movement helps to convey a sense of speed.

The degree of blur in an image is entirely an esthetic choice; there is no right or wrong answer. Use too long a shutter speed, though, and your moving subject may vanish entirely from the resulting image! Although using a longer shutter speed can create an impressionistic effect it can be worth incorporating static elements into the image too, as these can help "ground" an image in reality and add visual contrast.

› Fast shutter speeds

When you select a fast shutter speed you can record a small slice of time (this can also be achieved with flash, as the duration of flash light is measured in extremely small fractions of a second). The fastest shutter speed available on the Leica M10 is 1/4000 sec., which is fast enough to freeze all but the swiftest movement.

To achieve a fast shutter speed you will need to use a lens with a large maximum aperture and/or set a high ISO. As the Leica M10 doesn't have autofocus it is a good idea to pre-focus at the distance that your subject will be from your camera.

Shooting a fast-moving subject also requires a certain amount of anticipation; shoot too early or too late and you may miss the optimum (or "decisive") moment. In these situations, using your M10's Continuous drive mode gives you a safety net as you can shoot first and then review the sequence later to find the most pleasing image.

» FROZEN
A shutter speed of 1/360 sec. was fast enough to freeze these runners—if they were larger in the frame I would have needed to use a faster shutter speed.

⌄ ARCHITECTURE
Darkened interiors are ideally shot with a tripod-mounted camera. However, without a tripod I had to shoot this using the largest possible aperture setting and a high ISO (ISO 800). The resulting shutter speed of 1/20 sec. was still slow enough to run the risk of camera shake with a 24mm lens, but good handholding technique meant I got a shake-free image.

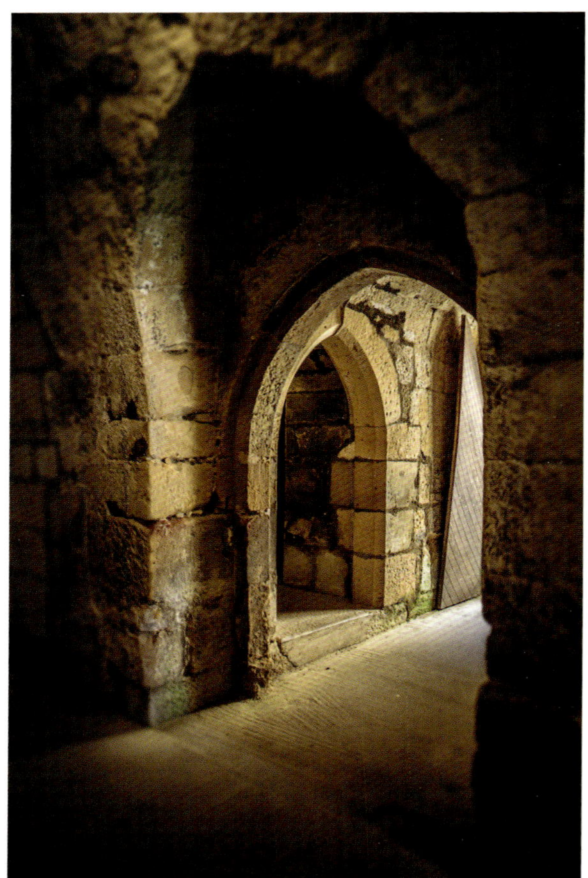

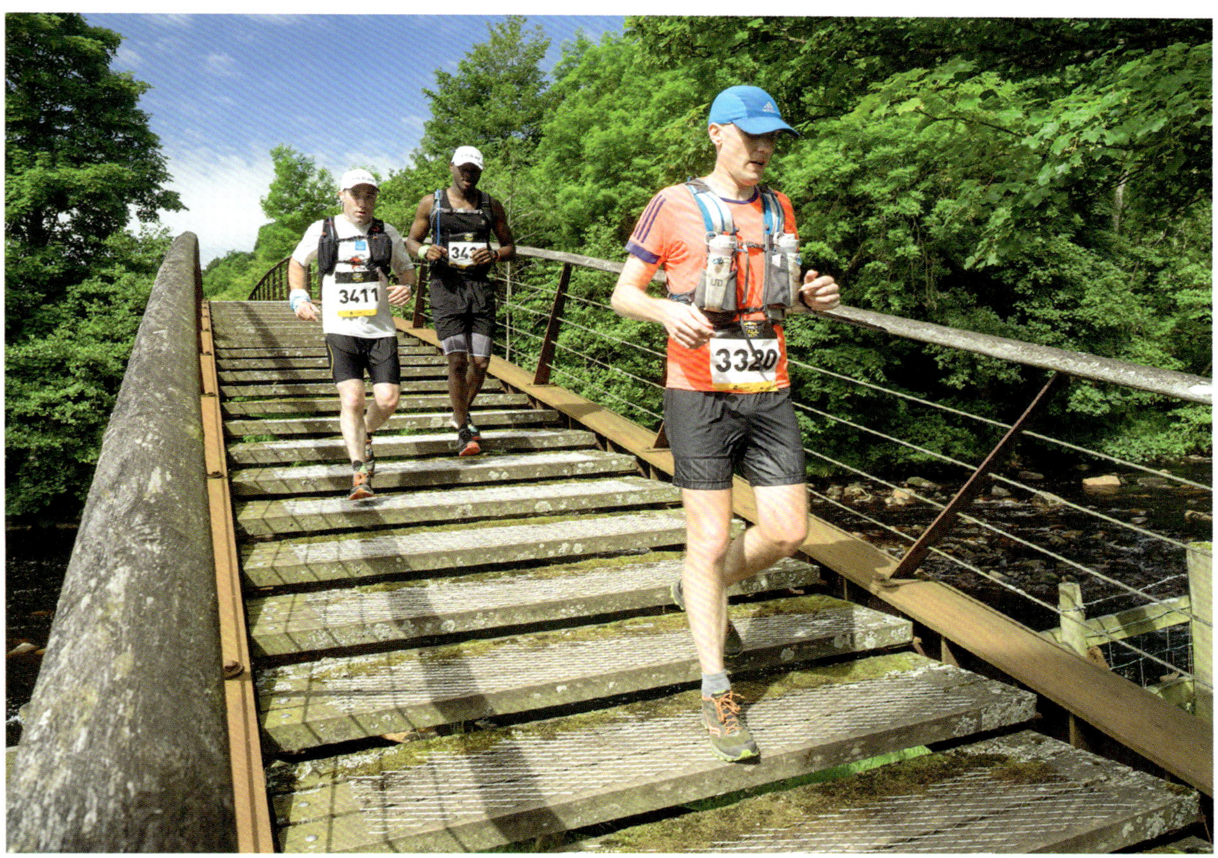

› Avoiding camera shake

Camera shake is caused when the camera moves during an exposure. Typically this happens when a relatively long exposure is used. It is relative because it is affected by a number of factors. How steady you are is one of the most important factors and this not only varies from person to person, but also across a person's lifetime.

The focal length of a lens is another factor. Generally, the longer the focal length of a lens, the faster the shutter speed will need to be to avoid the effects of camera shake. Shooting on a tripod is the best way to avoid camera shake, but there are techniques to minimize the risks when handholding your M10:

- Stand in as relaxed a position as possible, with your feet approximately shoulder-width apart.

- Tuck your elbows lightly against your body. If you are shooting from a kneeling position, steady your upper body by resting your elbow on one knee.

- With your right hand, hold the camera firmly with your index finger resting lightly on the shutter-release button. Use your left hand to support the base of the camera and the lens.

- Breathe in and out. Before you breathe in again gently push the shutter-release button down smoothly to take the shot.

With a few exceptions, the Leica M10 can be used for almost any type of photography.

› Street and documentary photography

Leica M cameras were once the first choice of street and documentary photographers in the days before SLR cameras. In many ways they are still very relevant to this type of photography as the M10's shutter mechanism is quiet—particularly compared to a DSLR—and the camera is also visually unobtrusive, which means you are less likely to be noticed when shooting.

Although the difficultly of using lenses longer than 135mm could be seen as detrimental to street and documentary photography, it encourages a more intimate—and rewarding—engagement with your subject (there is no shooting from a safe distance with a Leica camera!).

Suggested lenses
35mm; 50mm; 135mm

› Portraiture

Until the digital era, the role of the studio camera was largely taken by medium- and large-format cameras. However, this does not mean that the Leica M10 cannot be used in the studio as a portrait camera.

Portraits are generally intended to be flattering, so wide-angle lenses—with their spatial distortions—are not necessarily the best option unless you're shooting environmental portraits and want to show your subject in the context of their surroundings.

For tighter portraits, longer lenses are a better choice, as you typically stand further back from your subject, producing a flatter—and more flattering—perspective. A 50mm lens is a good option for a looser, less intimate composition, while a 90mm lens is excellent for head-and-shoulder shots.

Suggested lenses
50mm; 90mm

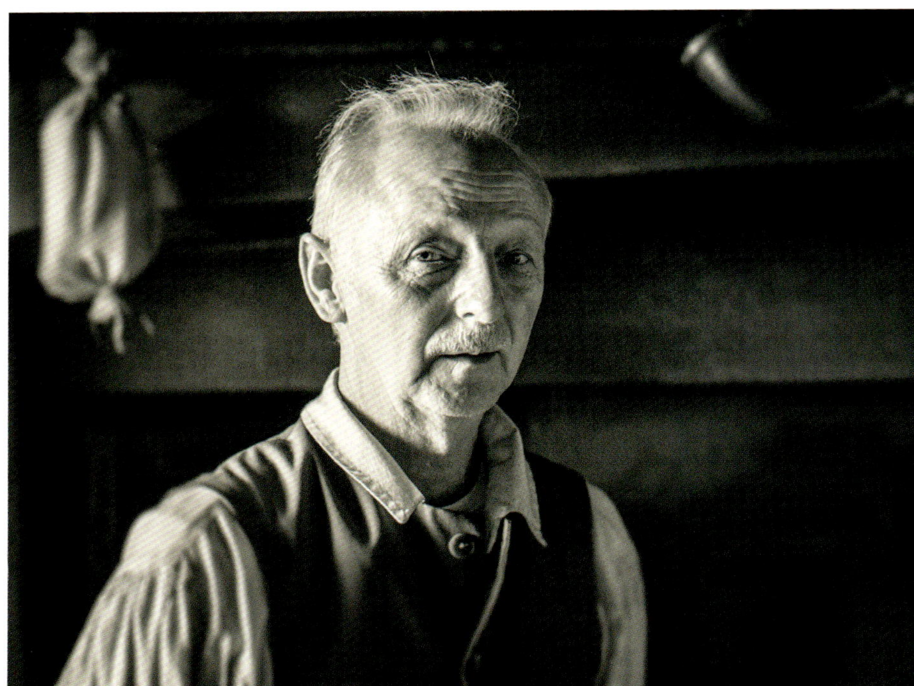

‹‹ PORTRAIT
Shooting a portrait means engaging with your subject on some level. A simple way to achieve this is to have a short conversation before shooting.

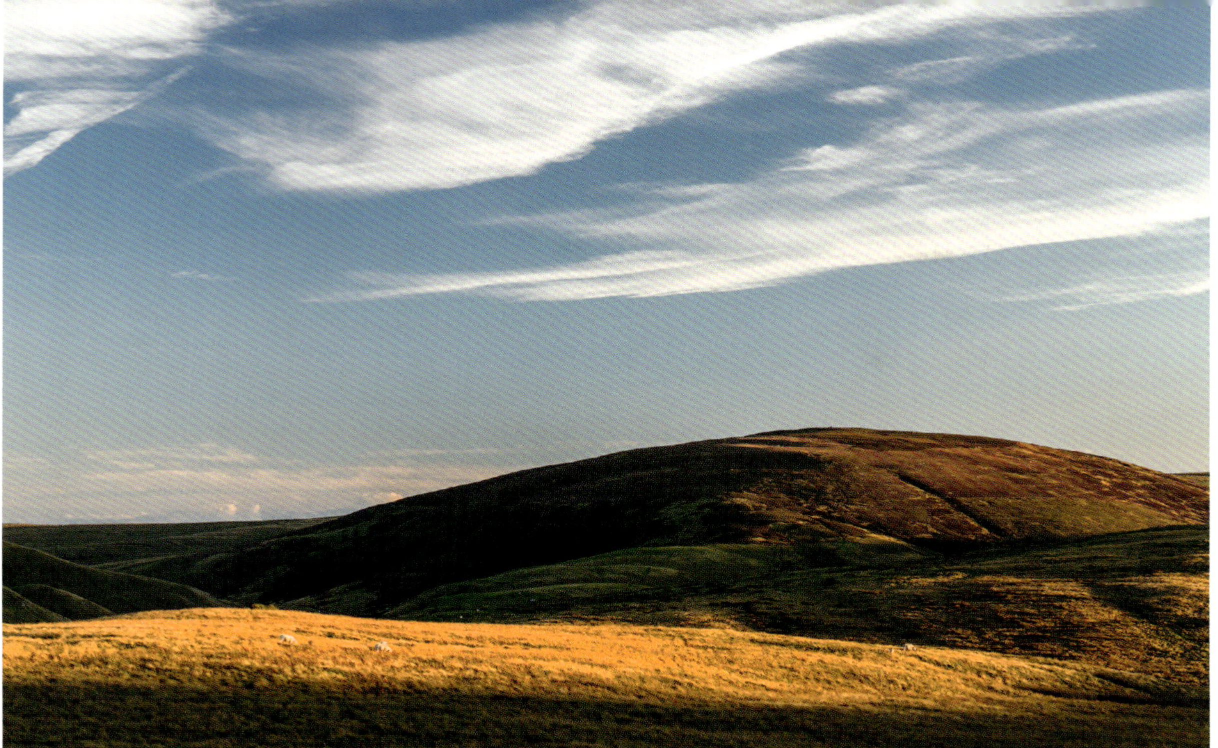

› Landscape

Landscape photography covers a wide range of subjects, from seascapes to desert wastes, open moorland to well-kept gardens. One benefit of shooting landscapes with a Leica is that the lenses are often smaller and lighter than comparable lenses for a DSLR. This can make a big difference to the weight of a camera bag, which is welcome when it is necessary to walk some distance to reach a suitable subject.

Weight is also a good reason to consider using Leica lenses with relatively small maximum apertures in preference to their faster—and heavier—siblings. As a general rule, the maximum aperture of a lens is largely irrelevant to landscape photographers, as the aperture is usually stopped down to increase depth of field.

Wide-angle lenses in the region of 21–28mm help to convey a sense of space and are therefore seen as the first choice of the landscape photographer. However, longer lenses should not be dismissed, as these can be used to pick out smaller details within the landscape.

Suggested lenses
21mm; 35mm, 50mm; 75mm

⌃ TELEPHOTO
Telephoto lenses have their place in landscape photography. The narrow angle of view helps to simplify a landscape to its essential elements.

Note
- Subjects that require the use of very long focal lengths—such as wildlife or sports —are not an ideal fit for the Leica M10. This is especially true if your chosen subject is moving, as pre-focusing can be difficult if you are unable to accurately predict the movement of your subject (a common problem with wildlife subjects). You are also less able to rely on depth of field to ensure sharpness, particularly if you prioritize shutter speed over aperture and minimize depth of field.

» METERING BASICS

A camera's built-in exposure meter works by averaging the tones in a scene to a mid-gray. This means it takes all the shadows, all the highlights, and all the tones in between and averages them out to mid-gray. This may sound primitive, but it is surprisingly effective, as the tones in a "normal" scene typically average out to mid-gray.

However, this assumption falls apart when dark or light tones dominate the scene, which is when exposure errors are likely to occur. A good example of a non-average scene is a brightly lit snow scene. A range of light, near-white tones generally results in an underexposed image, because the meter in the camera produces a reading that pulls the light tones down to that mid-gray average. As a result, snow scenes typically require 1½ –2 stops of positive exposure compensation to ensure the whites are white.

The opposite is true of a scene dominated by dark tones: in this situation the exposure meter will tend to overexpose as it lifts the dark tones to a mid-gray average, requiring negative exposure compensation.

One way to assess a potentially problematic exposure is to view the image histogram (see page 52). Alternatively, you can take your exposure reading from a photographer's gray card (available from most good camera stores). These cards reflect 18% of the light that falls on them, which corresponds to the mid-gray average the camera is looking for. Because of this, a gray card can help you determine the correct exposure regardless of the tonal range of the scene you wish to photograph.

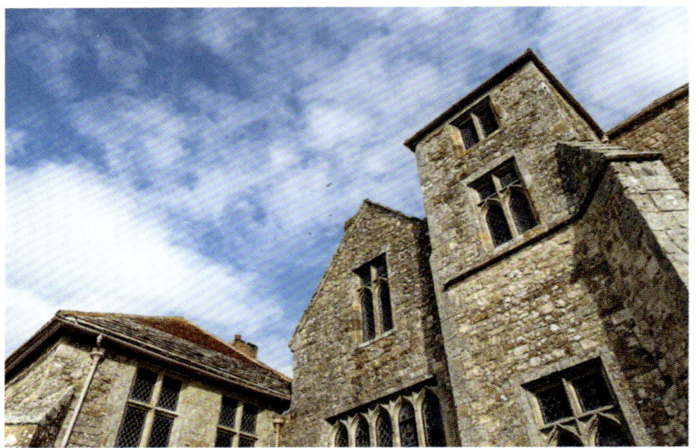

⌃ AVERAGE
This scene of average tonality required no exposure compensation at the time of shooting (or correction in postproduction). This is easy to see by converting the image initially to black and white and then blurring it. The blurred image has some light and dark areas, but it is essentially an average gray throughout.

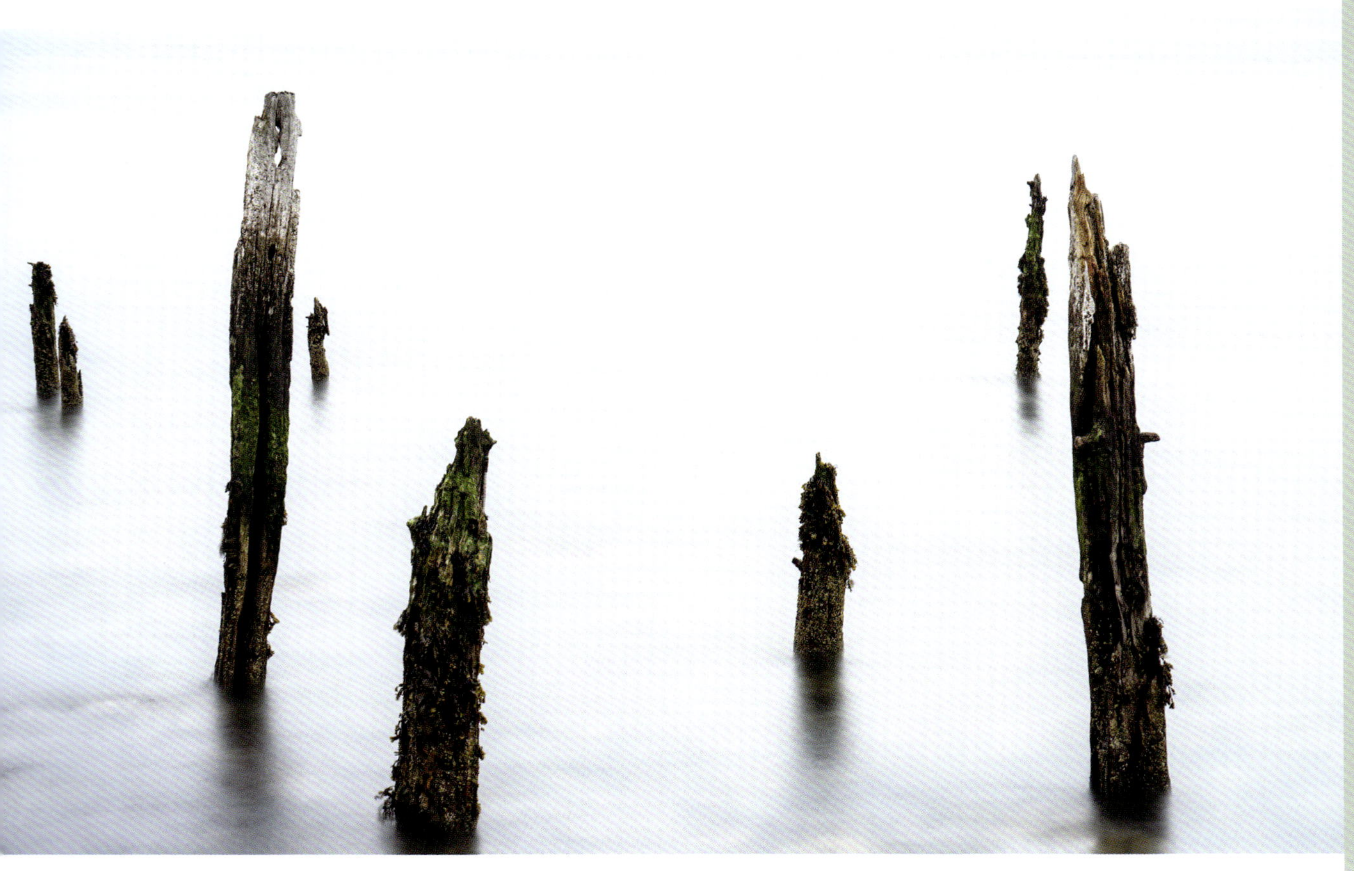

Using a gray card

1) Set your camera to Manual exposure and set either the aperture or shutter speed to the desired value.

2) Hold the card in front of the lens so it fills the frame (the card should be in the same light as the scene you want to photograph). If you set the aperture previously then adjust the shutter speed until the Leica M10 confirms that exposure is correct (if you set the shutter speed first, adjust the aperture instead).

3) Remove the gray card and take the shot.

⌃ HIGH KEY
This lighter-than-average scene required 2 stops of positive exposure compensation to produce the airy, high-key effect I wanted.

» LIGHT

An understanding of light is crucial if you want to progress as a photographer, as the light you use to illuminate your subject will determine—to a large extent—the esthetic success or otherwise of the resulting image. Light has a number of qualities and a good photographer will either use or deliberately alter those qualities to achieve a particular effect.

› Hard and soft

The hardness or softness of a light source determines the level of contrast in a scene and the density and sharpness of the shadows and highlights.

Light that is hard is produced by point light sources, which are light sources that are smaller than the subject being illuminated. Common examples of point light sources are unshaded light bulbs, flash, and the sun in a cloudless sky. Hard light increases contrast and produces hard-edged, dense shadows and bright highlights, which can work well with geometric and inorganic subjects. The effects of hard light can be adjusted by diffusing the light source through a translucent screen or bouncing the light from another surface before it reaches the subject. Both techniques soften the light.

Soft light is produced when a light source is larger than the subject being illuminated. Soft light is low in contrast, and shadows and highlights (if there are any) are diffuse and relatively weak. Overcast daytime skies produce soft lighting, as do photographic accessories such as light boxes. Soft lighting is an excellent lighting scheme for organic subjects and portraiture.

› Lighting direction

The direction the light is coming from also has an effect on how your subject appears.

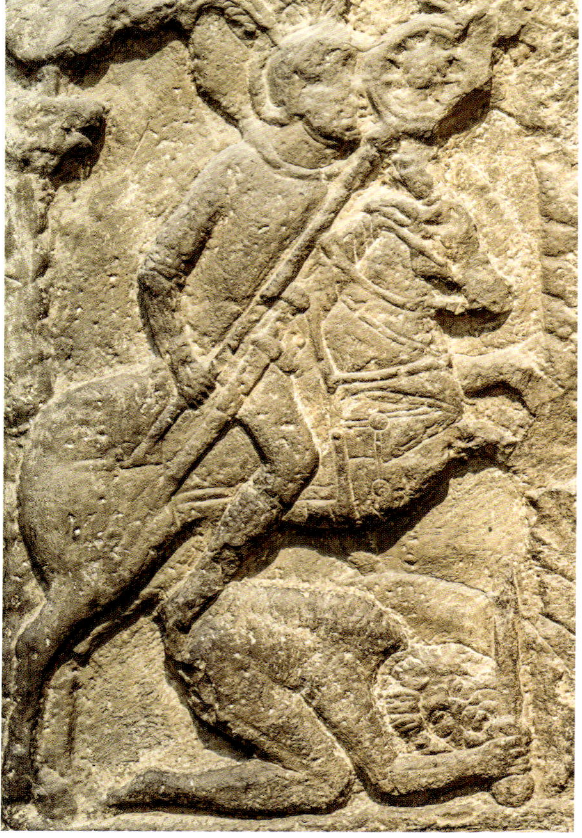

⌃ DEFINITION
Hard lighting can help to define the edges of sculptural subjects.

Frontal lighting

The simplest (and, arguably, least satisfying) lighting direction is frontal lighting. This is light that emanates from or behind the camera position, so it is falling on the front of the subject as the camera sees it. The advantage of frontal lighting is that the subject is usually evenly lit, so it is easy to determine the optimum exposure. However, frontal lighting tends to suppress shadows (shadows are behind the subject, out of sight of the camera), which can result in flat-looking shots that lack depth. Flash fired directly from a camera is frontal lighting.

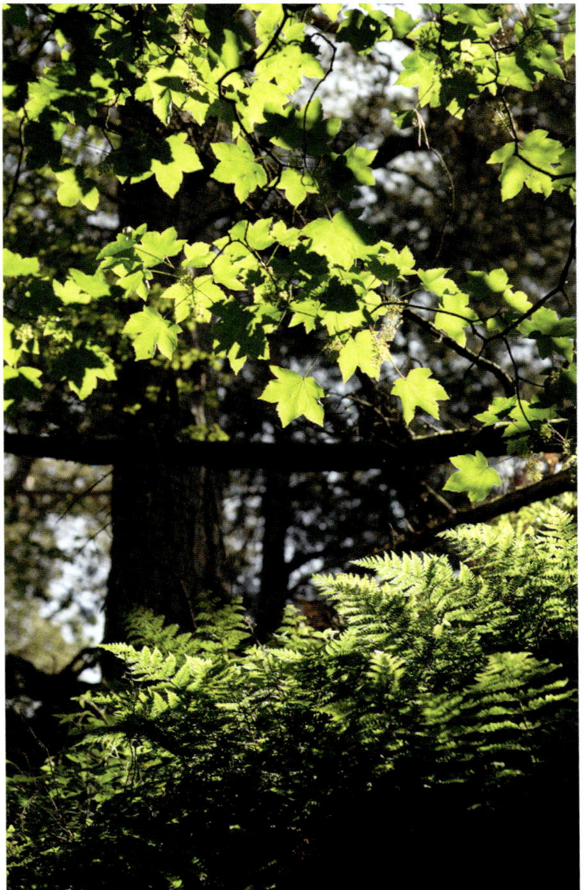

⌃ TRANSLUCENCY
Translucent subjects—such as foliage—can benefit from backlighting; the color of the subject is more intense and any fine detail that is normally hidden will be revealed.

Side lighting

When a light source is placed at roughly 90° to the camera it is known as side lighting. Side lighting helps to emphasize form and texture, making subjects appear more three-dimensional. However, side lighting can result in high contrast, particularly if it is a point light source, so you may need to use a reflector, angled to bounce light back into the shadow areas and reduce contrast. Alternatively, you can use a less intense light source as a fill light to lower contrast. The key is not to overpower the main light source so that the subject looks flat—too much contrast control is almost as bad as too little!

Backlighting

A light source shining toward the camera (usually with the subject in-between) produces backlighting. Contrast is typically very high: if you expose for the light source your subject will be silhouetted, while exposing for your subject will mean the light source is burnt out.

Some sort of contrast control (such as a reflector or fill-flash) is often needed when using a backlighting scheme, although silhouettes can work well if your subject has a distinctive and recognizable shape. With contrast control, backlighting can be a pleasing lighting scheme for portraiture: your subject will not be squinting due to the light being in their eyes, and backlit hair takes on an appealing glow that helps to frame the face.

» TIMELAPSE

A timelapse sequence is a series of individual images—hundreds, even thousands—shot at regularly spaced intervals. The sequence is then either combined into a movie clip that compresses time, or merged into a single still image to produce a composite (this can be used to circumvent the M10's 125 second limit in B mode).

› Shooting

Shooting a timelapse sequence will only be effective if there is constant movement during the shooting period. Subjects that work well as timelapse movies include the natural landscape (tracking the movement of the sun or clouds, for example) and urban environments.

Consistency is the key to shooting successful timelapse sequences so the exposure—particularly the shutter speed—should remain constant. If it does not then the resulting movie can flicker in a visually distracting way. The shutter speed you select will depend on the speed of movement in your chosen scene (use the grid below for pointers), but should always be less than the time selected for the interval.

Note that focus should also stay the same throughout the sequence.

Suggested interval time	Subject
1 second	Traffic; fast-moving clouds
2 seconds	People walking through the scene
3 seconds	Sunrises/sunsets
5 seconds	Clouds
10 seconds	Slow-moving clouds
20–30 seconds	Night sky; natural landscapes

› Creating a movie

Movies are replayed at a particular number of frames per second (fps), which is either 25 fps (in territories such as Europe) or 30 fps (North America and Japan). This means that for each second of footage you must shoot 25/30 individual images. When planning a sequence you should first work out how long the finished movie will run in seconds. You then need to multiply this number by the fps value to calculate the number of individual images you need to shoot. For example, if you want to produce a 10-second movie you would need to shoot 250 or 300 frames depending on your playback speed.

The next calculation you need to make is how long the shooting period needs to be. You can do this by adding the camera's shutter speed to the interval time.

Then, multiply this figure by the number of images required. The resulting figure should far exceed the time you initially worked out for the movie length. If it is not then work back through your calculations to check for errors.

Notes
- You will need to mount your Leica M10 on a tripod to shoot a timelapse sequence. A heavy tripod will be less likely to move during the shooting period.

- Battery life can be an issue when shooting timelapse sequences with the Leica M10. It is a good idea to begin with a freshly charged battery.

- Fast shutter speeds can produce a timelapse sequence that looks too "sharp." Using a longer shutter speed adds a bur that helps the movie to flow in a more visually pleasing way. This technique is known as "dragging the shutter."

- You will need to use movie-editing software, such as Adobe Premiere, to stitch your sequence into a coherent movie.

- Shoot Raw to give yourself more latitude for any exposure correction after shooting (but make sure you have enough memory card space to shoot the planned sequence).

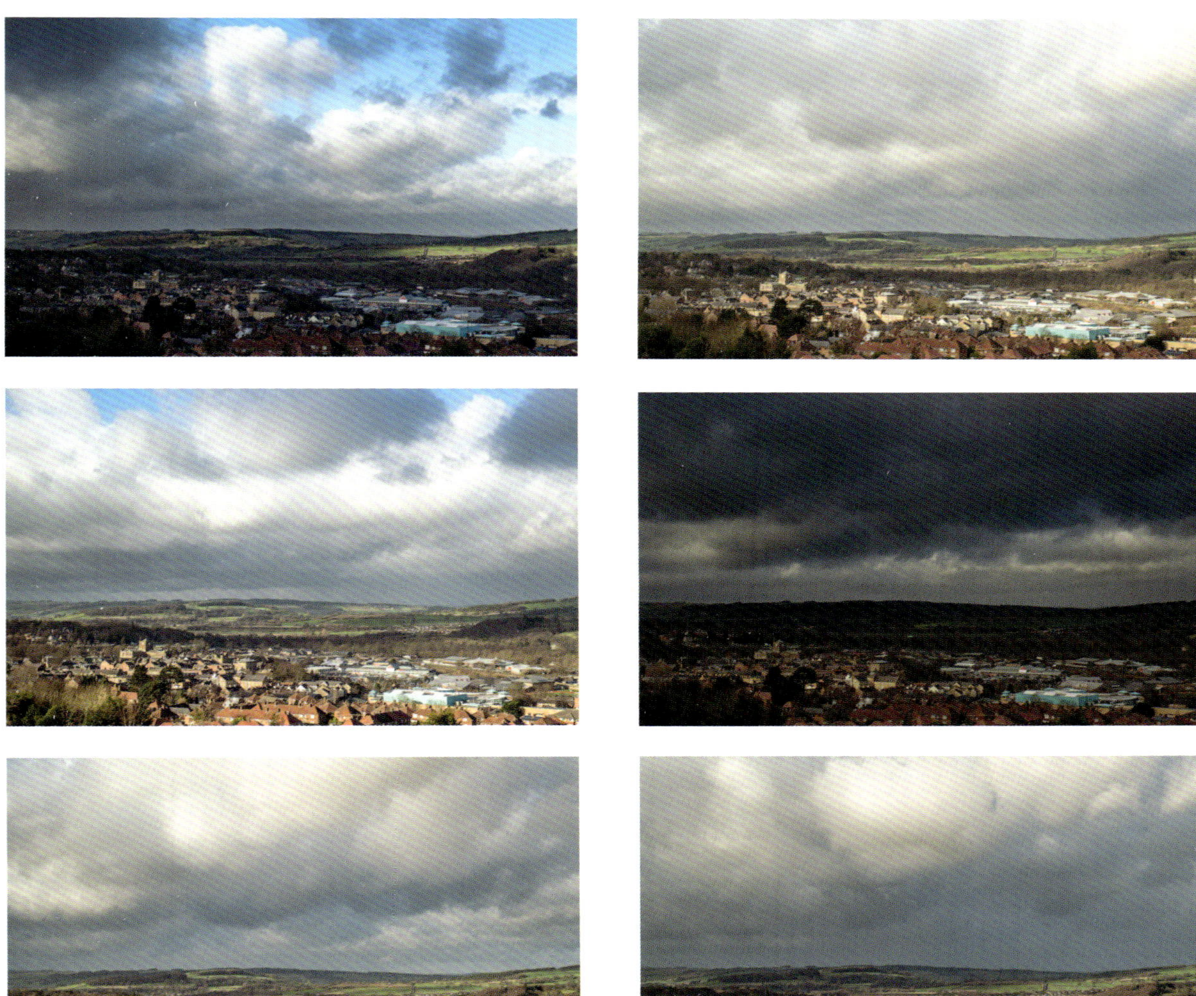

⌃ SEQUENCE

Six frames from a sequence of 320. Shot over an 80-minute period, the resulting movie runs for 12.8 seconds (320/25 fps).

» DIGITAL PROPERTIES

› Clipping

A camera does not work in the same way as the human eye and brain. One important way they differ is the way in which contrast is handled. The human visual system is very adept at handling a wide contrast range, but digital cameras cannot deal with anywhere near the same range. Consequently, when shooting a high-contrast scene there is a risk that the shadows and highlights will clip and detail will be lost in those parts of the image. If you shoot Raw there is some latitude for recovering detail during postproduction, but there are limits.

Photographing a high-contrast scene that exceeds the camera's range in a single exposure can therefore be a compromise: you can retain detail in the shadows or detail in the highlights but not both.

Fortunately, there are several methods to overcome this. One method is to use ND grad filters (see page 140) to "hold back" the exposure of one area of a scene to match that required by another. Another approach is to bracket a series of exposures and blend them together into an HDR (High Dynamic Range) image using software such as Adobe Lightroom.

Note
- Squinting at a scene is a surprisingly useful way to quickly assess the contrast range. If, when you squint, you can't see detail in the shadows, the contrast is high and may exceed the ability of the Leica M10 to retain details in those areas.

⌄ CLIPPED
The Leica M10 and Adobe Lightroom use a similar system to denote when part of an image is close to being clipped: blue for clipped shadows, red for clipped highlights.

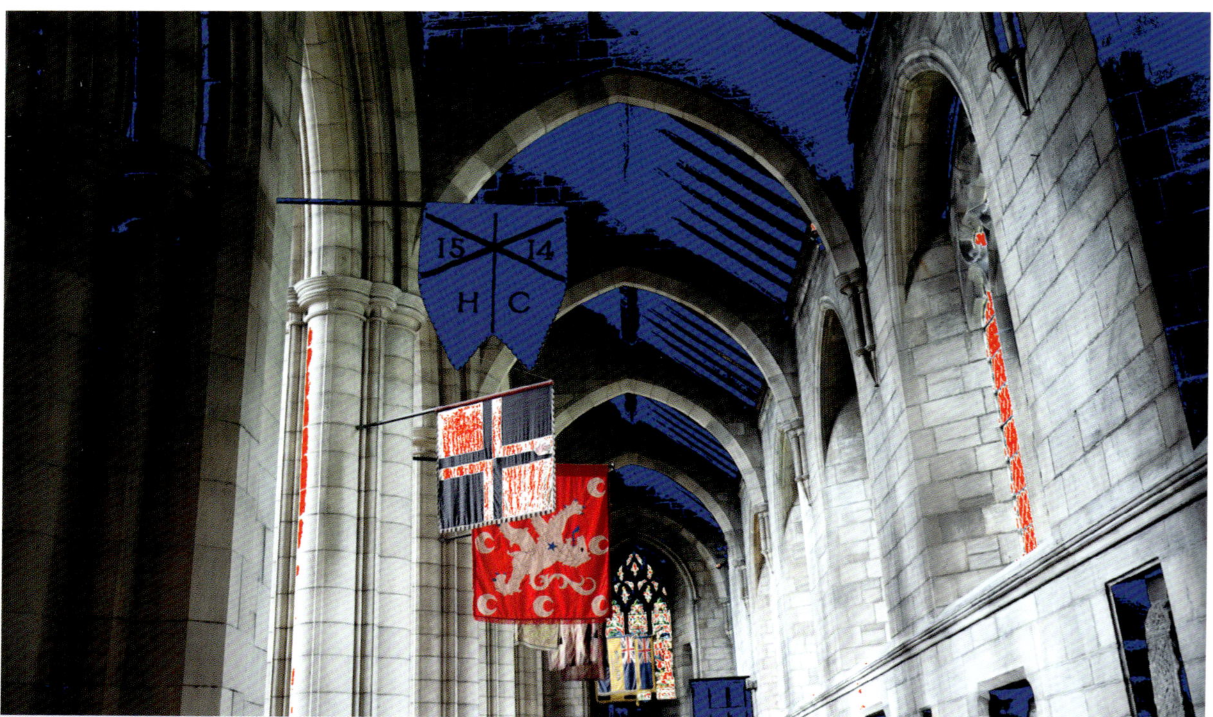

› Sharpness

Moiré is an interference pattern in an image caused by repetitive details—such as the fine weave in fabric—that exceed the resolution of the sensor. To reduce the effects of moiré, most digital cameras have an anti-aliasing (or low-pass) filter over the sensor. Anti-aliasing works by softening the image slightly, which means that some sharpening is required later, either when the camera processes a JPEG or during postproduction.

The Leica M10 is one of few cameras that do not have an anti-aliasing filter on the sensor. This means that correctly focused images are usually acceptably sharp already. However, this does not mean that sharpening should be ignored. It is often necessary for certain tasks, such as preparing an image for printing (the degree of sharpening should be determined by the final size of the image and the distance from which it will be viewed).

Sharpening an image in postproduction is actually a visual cheat achieved by increasing the "acutance," which is the contrast between edges in an image. The higher the acutance, the greater the contrast, and the sharper an image appears.

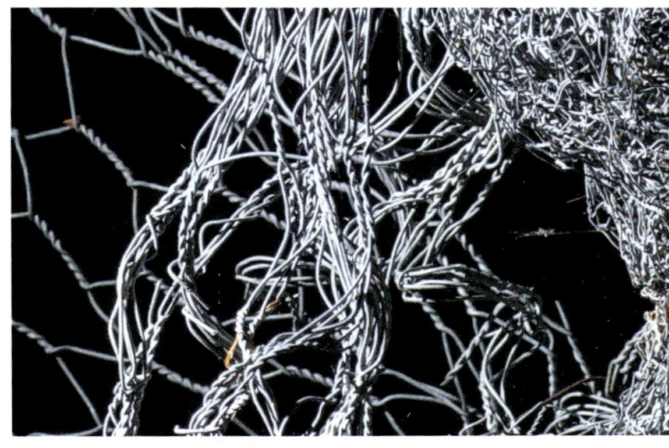

⌄ SHARPENED

Images generally need some sharpening to counteract the slight softening of ink spread across paper. However, if you apply too much sharpening, distinctive and ugly light and dark halos will appear around the high-contrast edges in your images. Compare the unsharpened image above with the over-sharpened image below.

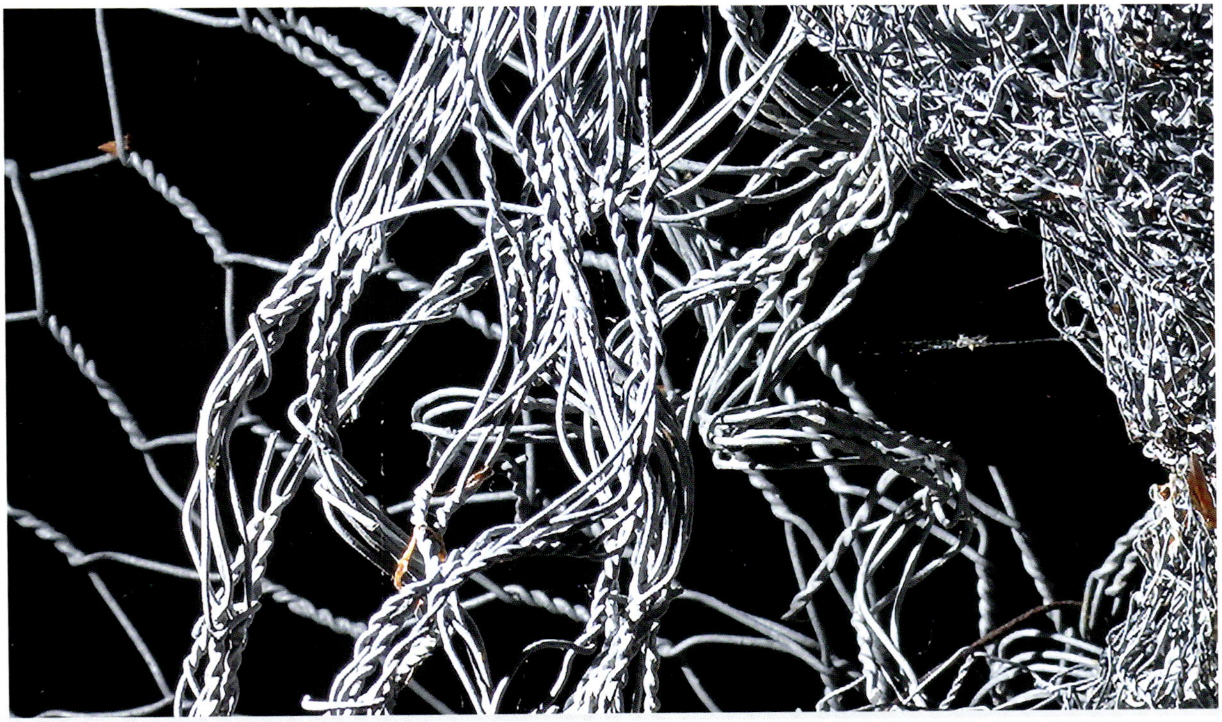

» OPTICAL PROPERTIES

› Flare

Lens flare is commonly seen as colored streaks or circular blobs across a photograph, but it can also result in a lowering of contrast across part or all of an image. It is caused by point light sources—such as the sun or a streetlight—shining directly into the lens or obliquely across the front of the lens without necessarily appearing in the image itself. This non-image-forming light then bounces around the various glass elements in a lens, creating "flare."

Modern lenses have anti-reflective coatings designed to reduce the effects of lens flare, but pre-1970s Leica lenses that were once coated may have gradually had their coating worn away over time. This is worth considering if you intend to buy an older, pre-owned Leica lens, as it may be more prone to flare than its modern equivalent.

Regardless of the age of the lens, there are various techniques that can be employed to reduce the effects of lens flare. The use of a lens hood will stop or reduce light entering the lens obliquely, and all current Leica lenses come with a lens hood—this can be left on permanently unless you intend to fit a third-party filter system.

Keeping the lens glass clean is also important. Greasy fingerprints or dust on the front of a lens increase the risk of flare and can potentially reduce the quality of your images.

› Distortion

Lens distortion is seen as the curving or bending of (what should be) straight lines in an image. There are two main types of distortion created by a lens: pincushion and barrel. Pincushion distortion results in straight lines bowing inward toward the center of an image; barrel distortion causes the bowing of straight lines outward toward the edges of the image. A more complex type of distortion, known as "moustache distortion," is essentially a combination of pincushion and barrel, but this is rarely seen.

Leica lenses are renowned for being relatively distortion free, so distortion will typically not be noticeable on most images. Older or third-party lenses may suffer from more noticeable distortion, but this can usually be eliminated using imaging software such as Adobe Lightroom.

› Chromatic aberration

Also known as achromatism, chromatic aberration (CA) is caused by the inability of a lens to focus all the different wavelengths of light at the same point. This results in colored fringing at high-contrast boundaries in an image (usually where a feature such as the branches of a trees are against a bright sky).

There are two types of chromatic aberration: axial and transverse. Axial CA can be seen across the whole of the image when the aperture is wide open, but is greatly reduced as a lens is stopped down. Transverse CA is seen in the corners of images and is not reduced by stopping a lens down.

› Vignetting

A digital sensor is an array of photodiodes that collect light in order to make an image. These photodiodes are like tiny wells, which means that light ideally needs to fall directly into them to ensure optimal light collection during an exposure. This is generally not a problem when light is focused at the center of a lens, but the light rays entering from the edge of a lens usually hit the sensor at a less-than-ideal angle. The result is that photodiodes at the corners of the sensor receive less light than the center, causing underexposure or vignetting at the edges of images.

The solution used by the Leica M10 is to place tiny micro-lenses over the top of the photodiode well to "bend" light so that it is more perpendicular.

The problem of vignetting is worst when a lens is used at its maximum aperture. Stopping the aperture down usually reduces and even eliminates vignetting. Vignetting can also be removed using image-editing software such as Adobe Lightroom. However, correcting vignetting in postproduction can add noise to the corners of an image. At lower ISO settings this is generally not noticeable, but images shot at high ISOs will be more susceptible to noise when corrected.

»» FLARE

The character of flare is affected by a number of factors, including how dirty the lens is, the number of aperture blades in the lens, and whether the lens is coated or not. Older lenses—such as this adapted lens—are more prone to flare than their modern, coated counterparts.

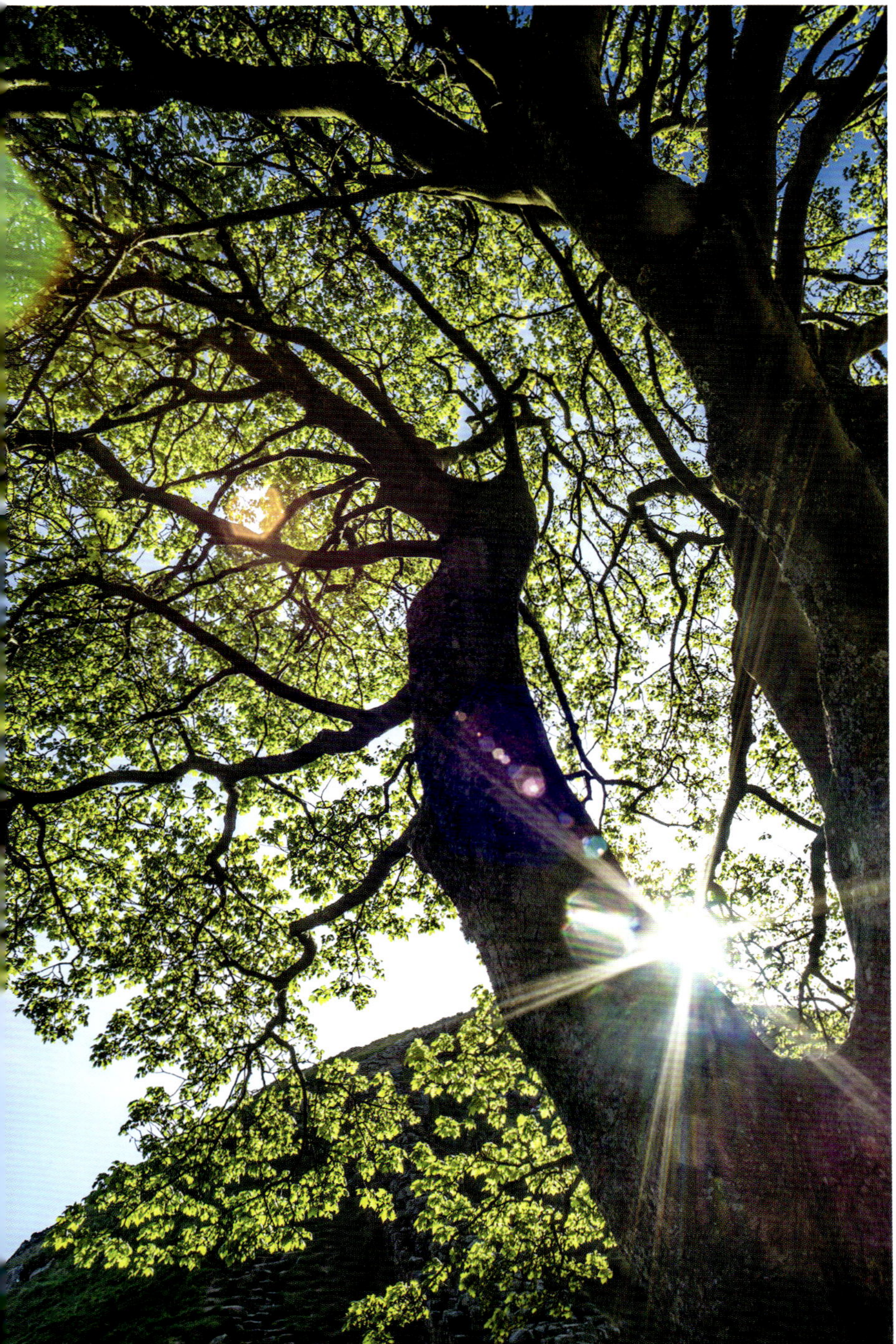

Notes

- Modern lenses are generally designed for digital cameras. Although vignetting is still present, it is typically less of an issue with a modern lens compared to a lens designed in the pre-digital era.

- A different type of vignetting occurs when a lens hood or filter holder appears in the corners of images. Known as "mechanical vignetting," this is most likely to occur when using a wide-angle lens. To avoid this, some filter holder manufacturers make special wide-angle lens adaptors for their systems that bring the filter holder closer to the front of the lens.

CHAPTER 9
CONNECTIONS

One striking feature lacking from the Leica M10 is a USB socket (or indeed, any electronic connections at all, other than the hotshoe). Instead Leica has embraced wireless connectivity with the inclusion of Wi-Fi.

Eventually there will come a time when you will want to export your images to an external device, such as a computer. This will enable you to archive, review, edit, and print your images. Although Wi-Fi is offered, there are several reasons not to use it. The most important is that it will rapidly drain your Leica M10's battery. Another is that—at the time of writing—the implementation of Wi-Fi on the Leica M10 only lets you connect to an Apple iOS device via an app (Windows PCs and Android tablets and phones are not supported).

To copy photos without using Wi-Fi involves removing the memory card from the Leica M10 and plugging it into your computer, either directly or via a USB card reader. Fortunately, card readers are relatively cheap.

The speed at which images can be transferred to your PC will depend on two things: the read/write speed of the memory card and the USB connection. The latest variant of USB is USB 3, which allows for faster data transfer between devices. Older PCs will use either USB 2 (or even USB 1), which has far slower data transfer rates. However, even if your computer only has USB 2 connections, it is still worth considering a USB 3 memory card reader; USB 3 is "backward compatible" with USB 2, so it will make your memory card reader more future proof.

» VIEWING

If you have an iPad, the big benefit of Wi-Fi is that you can show large versions of the images you shoot almost immediately. This is great in portrait situations, as you can get immediate approval from your subject.

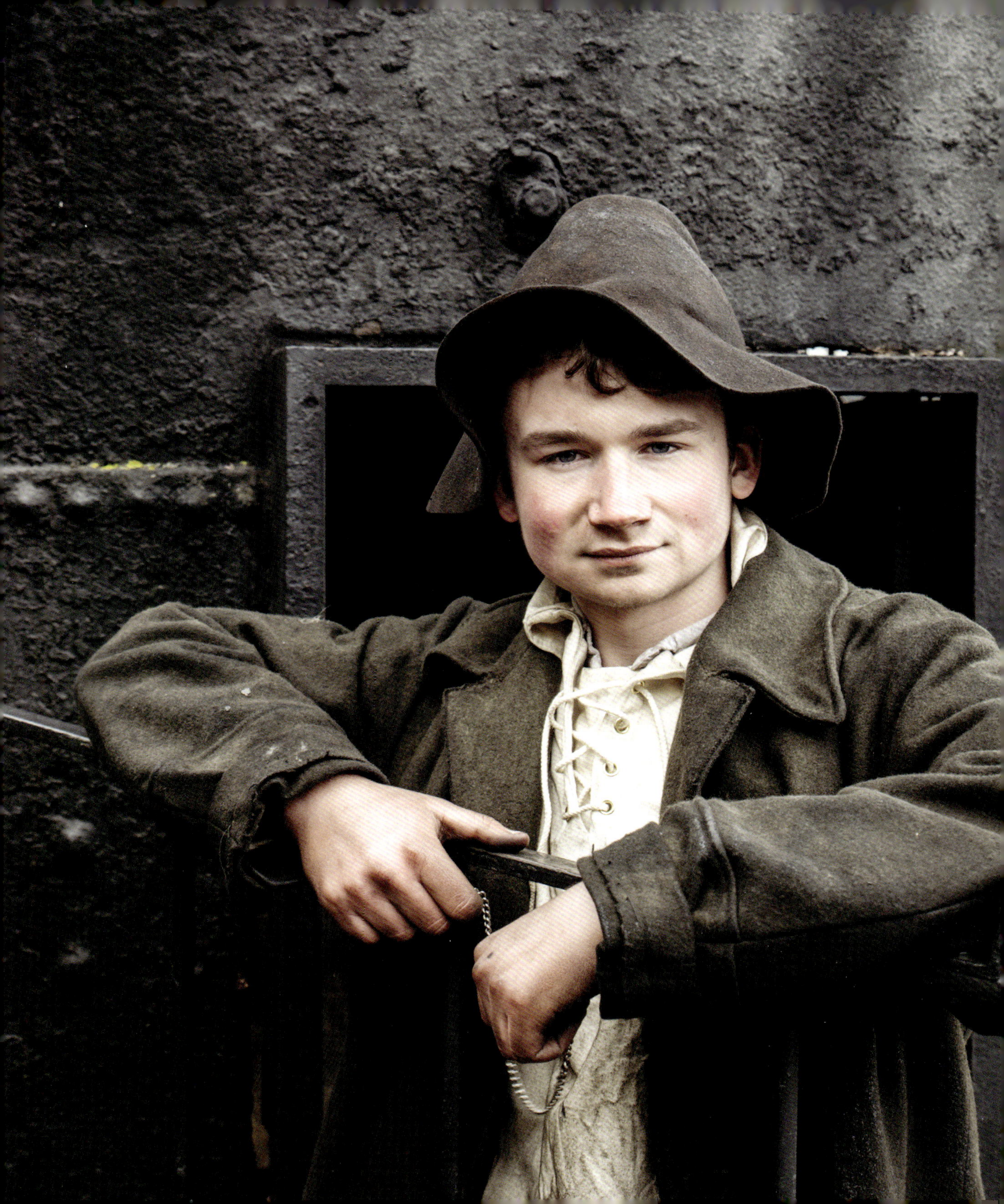

› Wi-Fi

Wi-Fi can be used to connect your M10 to an Apple iOS device such as an iPhone or iPad using the free Leica M app available through Apple's App Store. You can then transfer images, as well as using your tablet or phone to control the camera remotely.

There are two methods of connecting your Leica M10 to a smartphone: making a direct connection between the camera and an iOS device, or via a Wi-Fi router. Both methods have advantages and disadvantages.

Making a direct connection means that you can connect to your Leica M10—as long as it is within range of the iOS device—anywhere, even in the countryside. The downside is that you will need to switch from your standard Wi-Fi connection to the Leica M10 connection every time you want to connect to the camera.

Connecting via a router is more convenient; once the router password has been entered into the Leica M10 you can connect the camera and iOS device virtually instantly. The downside is that you need to be within range of the Wi-Fi router, making it less useful when shooting outdoors.

Making a direct connection

1) Select **WLAN** from the Main Menu (page 3) and set **Function** to **On**.

2) Once Wi-Fi has been activated, highlight **Connection** and set it to **Create WLAN**.

3) Choose **Setup** and select **SSID/Network Name**. Enter a memorable name for your network—this can be anything you like, although most symbols cannot be used.

4) Select **Password** and enter a memorable (and secure) password for your network. The password needs to be between 8–20 characters and can use letters, numbers, and symbols.

5) Turn on your iOS device and select **Settings**, followed by **Wi-Fi**. After a few seconds the Leica network (using the name selected at step 3) should appear in the network list. Select this network, enter the password selected at step 4, and join the network.

6) Launch the Leica M app and follow the on-screen instructions.

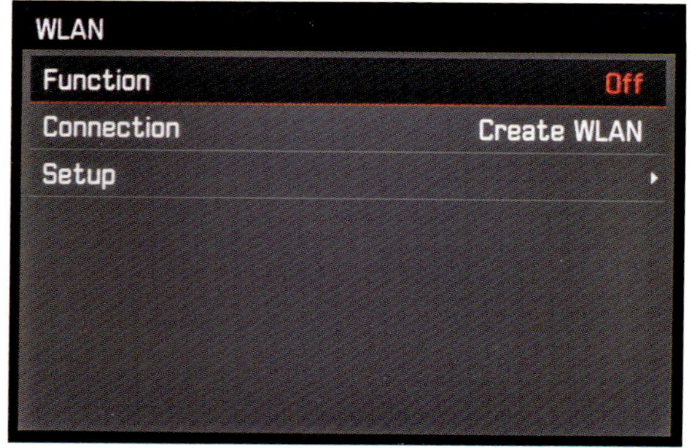

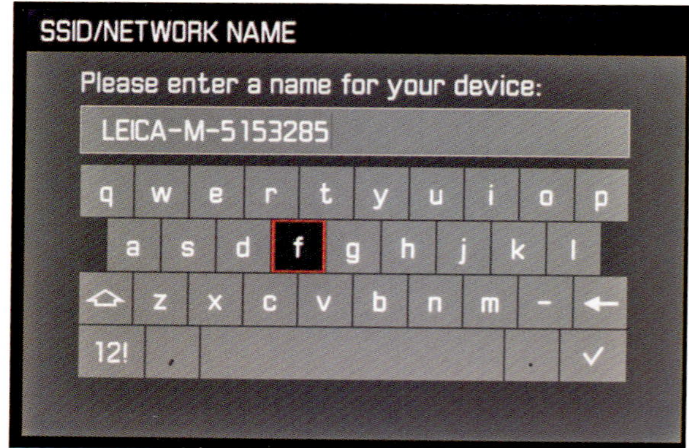

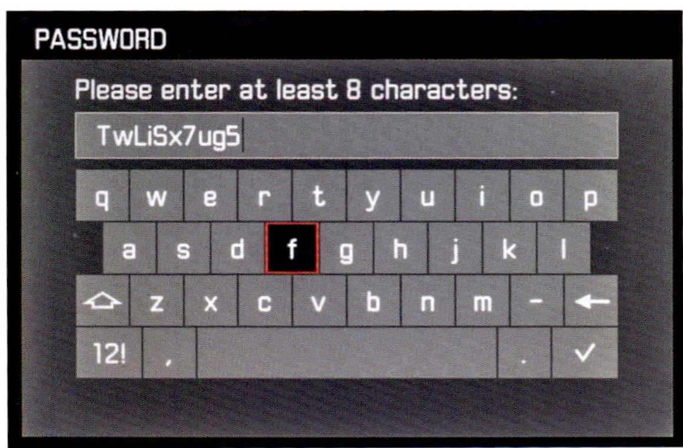

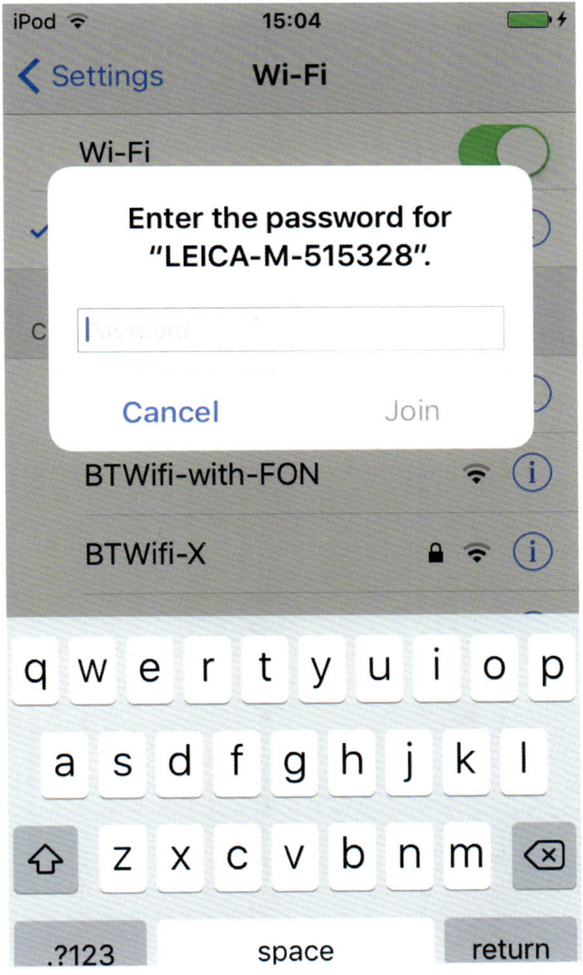

Making a connection via a router

1) Select **WLAN** from the Main Menu (page 3) and set **Function** to **On**.

2) Once Wi-Fi has been activated highlight **Connection** and set to **Join WLAN**.

3) Select **Setup**.

4) A list of Wi-Fi networks should appear on screen. If no list is displayed select **Scan** to force the Leica M10 to search for networks again, or select **Add Network** to enter the network details. For this you will need to know the **SSID/Network Name**, and whether Client Security is **Open** (does not need a password), or **WPA/WPA2** (requires a password). If a password is required, enter it in the **Password** field and then set the **Client IP mode**.

5) Select the network from the list on screen and enter the **Password** (if required), followed by **Connect**.

6) Launch the Leica M app and follow the instructions on screen.

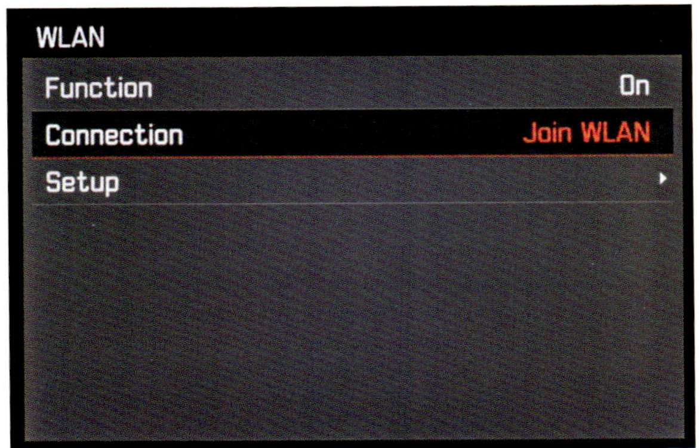

» LEICA M APP

The Leica M app essential replicates the functions of the camera on your iOS device. The app is split into four pages that remotely control different aspects of your M10:

- **Home** controls the connection between your iOS device and the camera.

- The **Camera** screen (shown in detail on the page opposite) allows you to control various aspects of exposure, as well as functions such as white balance. You can see the changes on a Live View image, streamed from the Leica M10 to the iOS device. The one aspect of exposure you cannot control is the aperture setting, which still has to be set manually on the lens.

- **Play** lets you view images stored on the Leica M10's memory card on your iOS device. You can also upload (and download) images to your iOS device and rate your photographs.

- **Menu** displays a cut-down list of Leica M10 menu options, as well as a few unique options, such as the **Camera Roll Resolution**.

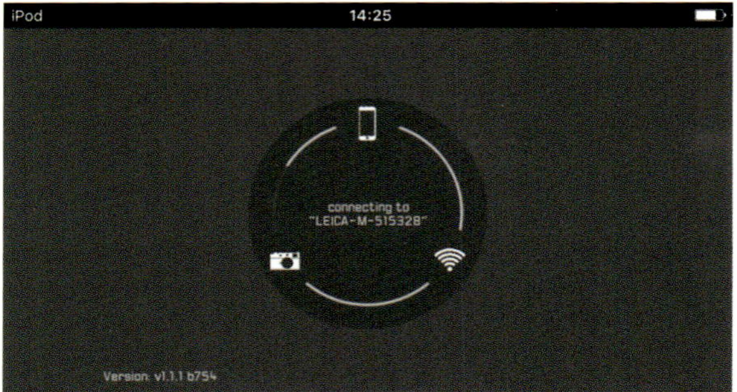

HOME

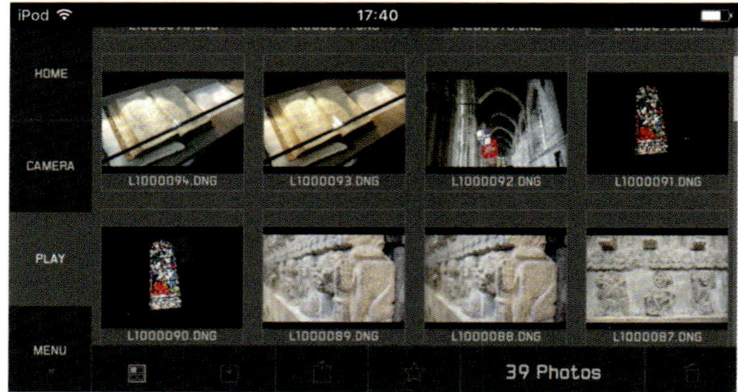

PLAY

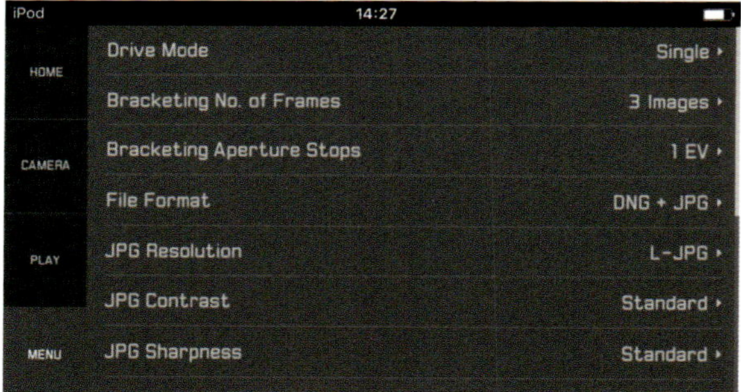

MENU

›› CAMERA SCREEN

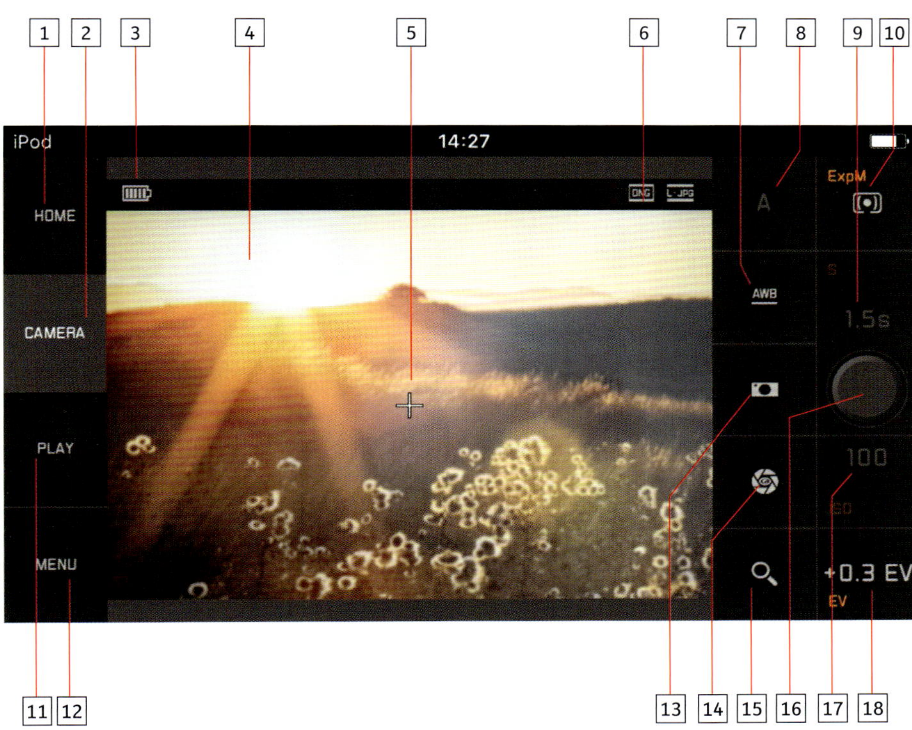

CAMERA SCREEN

1 Home button; connect to iOS device/network	**11** Play; play images on iOS device (with download options)
2 Live View camera mode	**12** Menu; camera functions list
3 Leica M10 battery status	**13** Live view stream on/off button
4 Live View window	**14** Exposure simulation
5 Magnification control point	**15** Live View magnification
6 File type	**16** Shutter-release button
7 White balance setting	**17** ISO setting
8 Shooting mode	**18** Exposure compensation
9 Current shutter speed	
10 Metering mode	

» WORKING WITH DIGITAL IMAGES

Digital photography has one beguiling attribute: you can shoot as many photos as you like once you have bought your camera, at no additional cost. It is therefore extremely tempting to shoot and shoot and shoot in order to achieve some level of photographic success.

In many ways this is no bad thing. The freedom to experiment—even though it will lead to images that do not quite work—will quickly help to improve your photography. The downside is that you will be faced with the time-consuming prospect of looking through hundreds or thousands of images to weed out the good from the bad.

You could of course delete as you shoot, but this is not recommended. Not only can taking time out to review images in the field break your creative flow, but also there is the risk that you may delete an image that—while not immediately attractive—would otherwise grow on you over time.

A better habit to acquire is to think before you shoot. Consider carefully the merits of a photograph before you press the shutter-release button. Ask yourself if you would be happy to spend time editing the image in postproduction. Although digital files are free, time is precious and hours spent looking at a computer screen is time you could be out shooting.

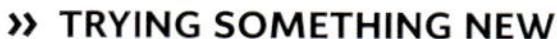

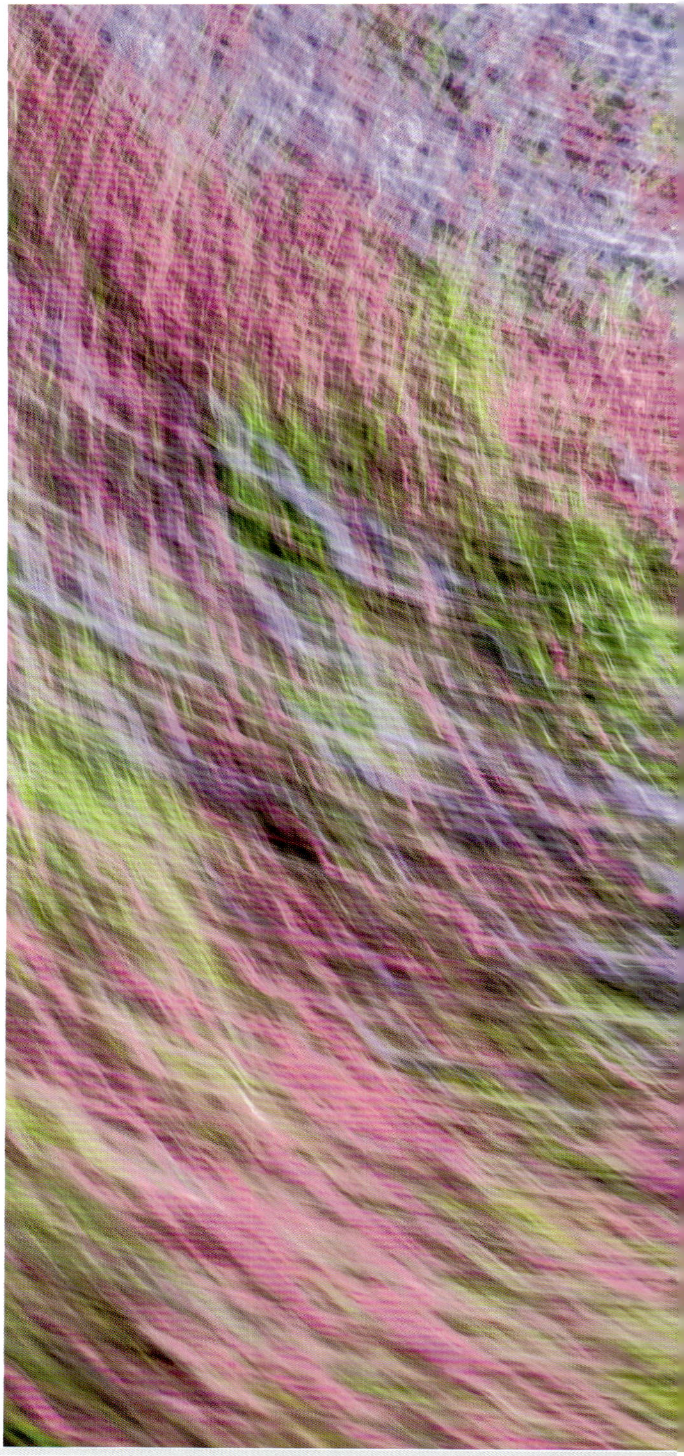

» TRYING SOMETHING NEW
It is often experimental images that take time to grow on you. This "intentional camera movement" shot—created by rotating the camera during a relatively long exposure—has gradually grown on me to the point where it has been added to my image library.

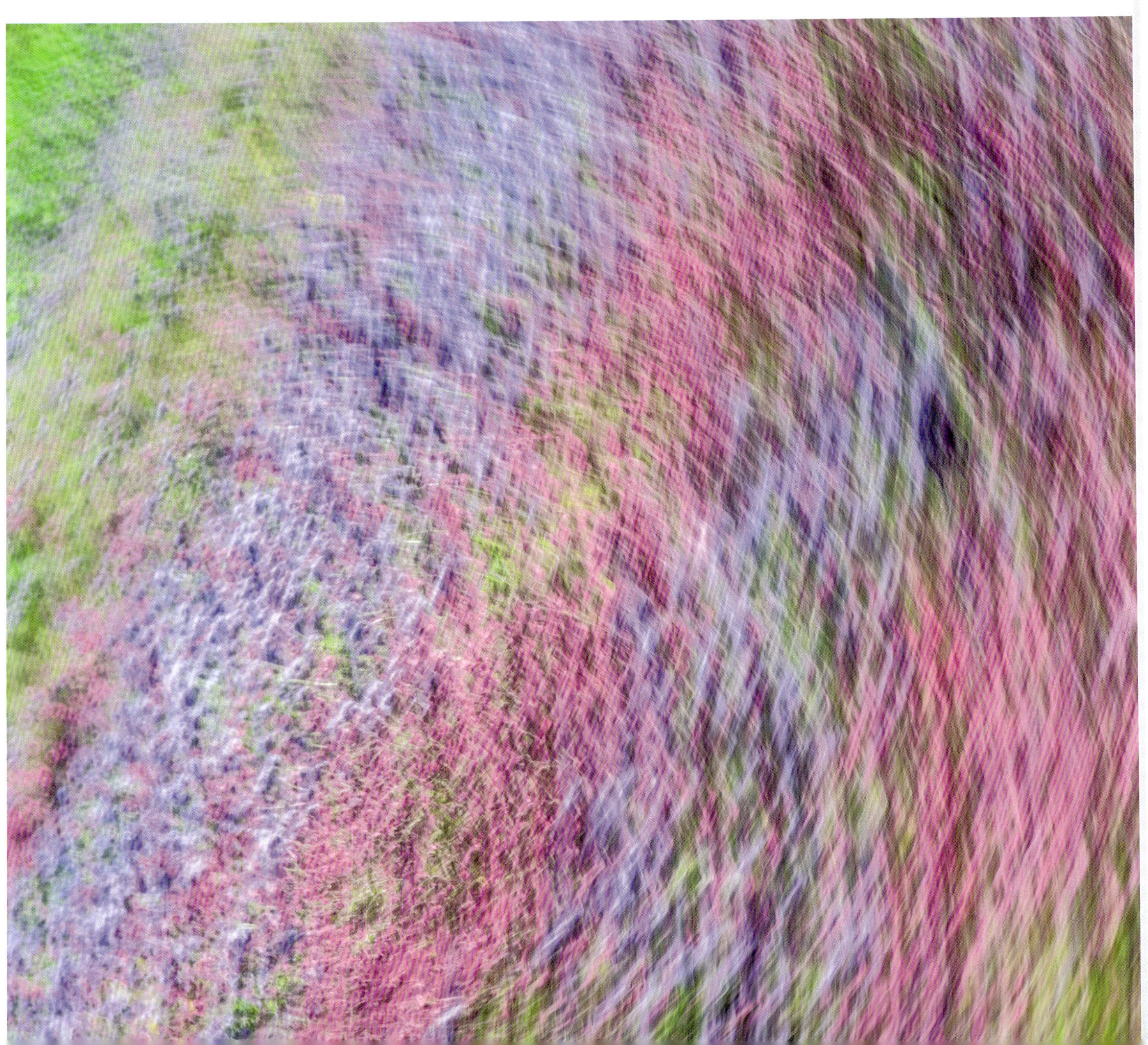

› File naming

Every image you shoot on the Leica M10 has a unique file name. However, the numbers assigned to images are not infinite and, once they reach 9999, they will loop back round to 0001. This means that after 10,000 images you will have image files with the same file name. The other problem with the Leica naming convention is that the file names do not convey much information other than when—numerically—they were shot.

For these reasons it is a good idea to rename your images so they have meaning and you can find a particular image easily. One simple option is to include the month and year in the file name as well as a file number. As an example, a file assigned the name 1712_0025 would be image number 25 created in December 2017. In conjunction with good folder management and the use of keywords, this is a very powerful way to sort and keep track of your images.

⌄ CATALOGUING
I use Phase One's Media Pro digital asset management (DAM) software to organize my images.

› Filing systems

Once you have a filename structure worked out it is a good idea to create a logical and expandable folder structure. What you really do not want to do is put every image you shoot into one huge folder. That really is asking for trouble.

A simple folder structure would start with a master folder. This would then be divided into sub-folders for specific image categories. These sub-folders could then be divided into even more specific sub-categories and so on.

Notes
- Putting the year first makes it easier to sort files chronologically in a folder.

- If you use Adobe Lightroom (as recommended by Leica), you would rename your images and create folders within Lightroom. This means that Lightroom is able to keep track of where images are and what they are called.

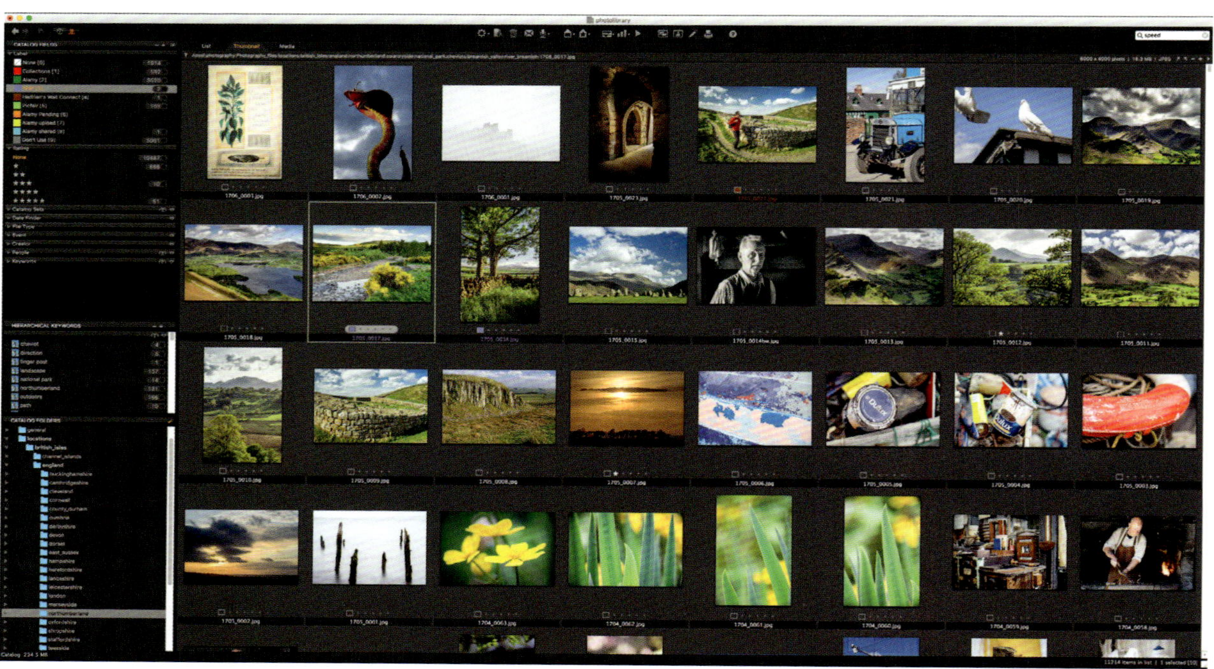

› Backup

All hard drives fail eventually, so it is highly recommended that you *regularly* backup the main hard drive of your computer. External hard drives are now relatively cheap and many come with software to help establish a painless backup routine. For added piece of mind you can maintain several hard drive backups, keeping at least one drive off-site and swapping the drives roughly once a week.

Note
- If you are using macOS you can set Time Machine to backup a hard drive at regular intervals. File History is the Windows 10 equivalent.

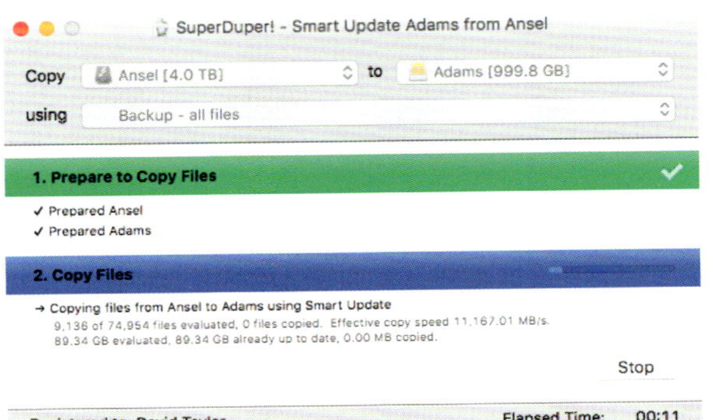

› Keywords

If you use digital asset management (DAM) software or intend to supply stock photography libraries with your images you will benefit from adding keywords to your photographs. Keywords are stored by default in the IPTC area of an image's metadata. Development software such as Adobe Lightroom typically have facilities that let you add keywords to both individual and multiple images.

The most important keywords are those that describe the subject of the photo itself. If you want to keyword a landscape photograph, location details would be important. This would include the specific place name, as well as finer details of the image content. Important portrait keywords would include the name of the subject, sex, facial expression, and (possibly) ethnic background.

Keywords that describe the emotional or conceptual content of photos are often used by image library clients searching for images. This requires careful thought so that the keywords aren't misleading. Think carefully whether your photo has positive or negative connotations. The subject should give you some guide to this, as will the color palette of your image; cool colors such as blue or green are more readily associated with negative emotions than reds or yellows.

« SCHEDULED
I use SuperDuper! on my Mac to schedule daily backups of my various hard drives.

» ETTR
For this Raw image I "exposed to the right" (see page 53). This enabled me to retain a significant amount of detail in the shadows. When it came to processing the Raw file there was enough headroom in the shadows to make adjustments without too much noise appearing.

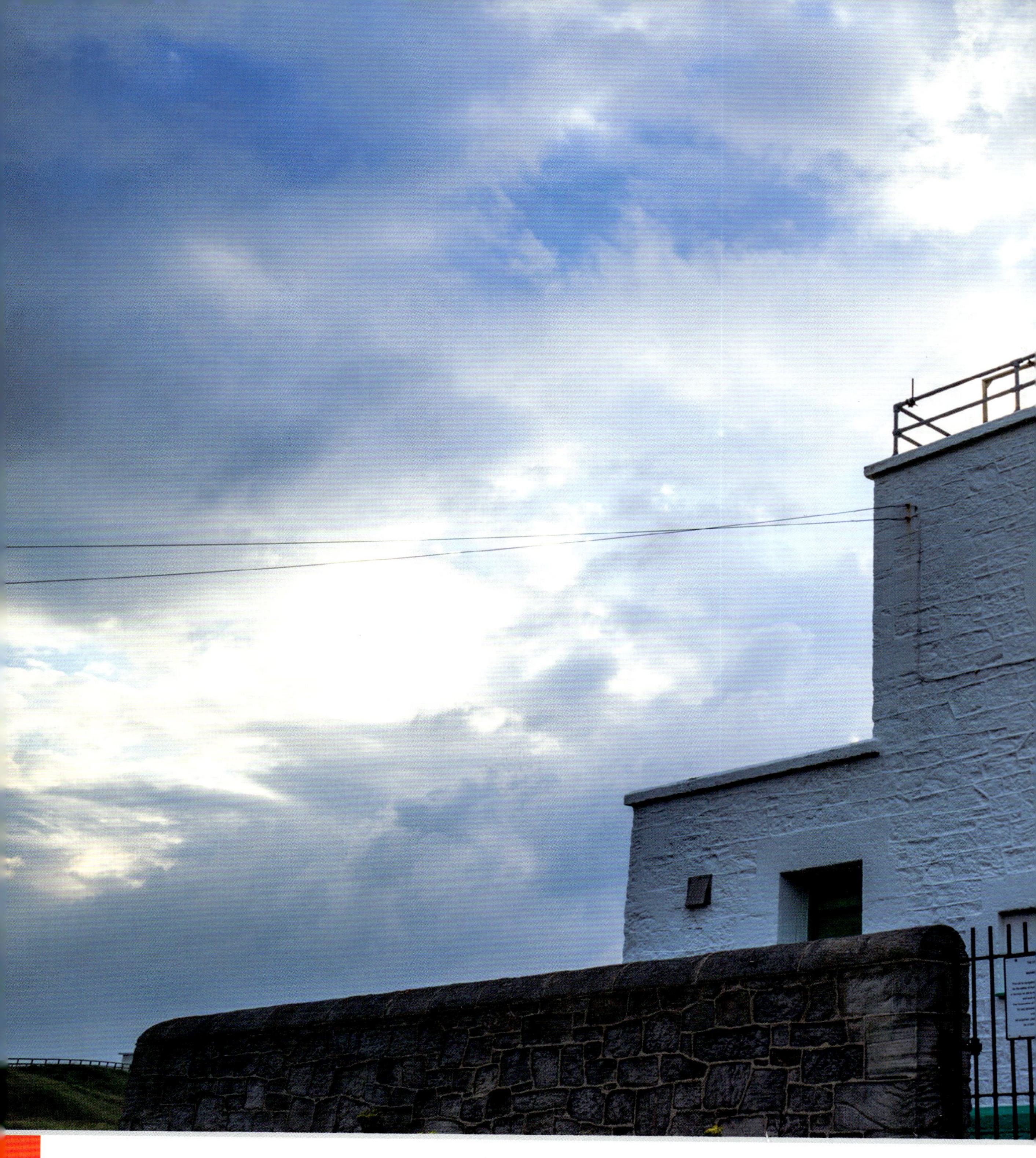

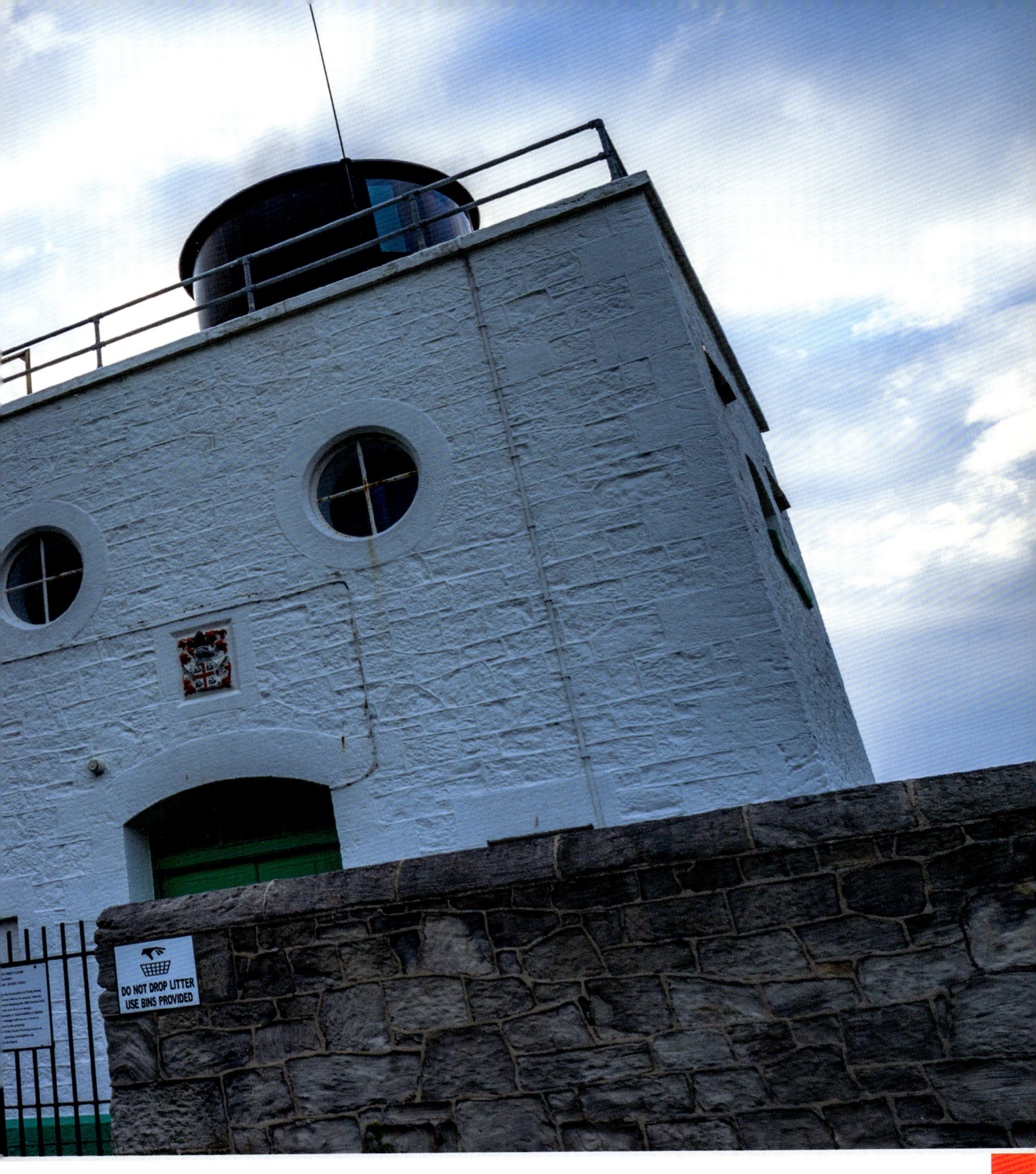
DO NOT DROP LITTER
USE BINS PROVIDED

Aberration An imperfection in a photograph, usually caused by the optics of a lens.

Angle of view The area of a scene that a lens takes in, measured in degrees.

Aperture The opening in a camera lens through which light passes to expose the sensor. The relative size of the aperture is denoted by f-stops.

Bracketing Taking a series of pictures, where one parameter changes between shots. This is often the exposure, although white balance can also be bracketed on some cameras.

Buffer The in-camera memory of a digital camera.

Center-weighted metering A metering pattern that determines the exposure by placing importance on the light reading at the center of the frame.

Chromatic aberration The inability of a lens to bring spectrum colors into focus at a single point.

CMOS (*Complementary Metal Oxide Semiconductor*) A type of imaging sensor, consisting of a grid of light-sensitive cells. The more cells the sensor has, the greater the number of pixels it will produce and the higher the resolution of the final image.

Color temperature The color of a light source expressed in degrees Kelvin (K).

Compression The process by which digital files are reduced in size. Compression can retain all the information in the file, or "lose" data usually in the form of fine detail for greater levels of file-size reduction.

Contrast The range between the highlight and shadow areas of a photo, or a marked difference in illumination between colors or adjacent areas.

Depth of field (DOF) This is controlled primarily by the aperture: the smaller the aperture, the greater the depth of field.

Diopter Unit expressing the power of a lens.

DPI (*dots per inch*) Measure of the resolution of a printer or scanner. The more dots per inch, the higher the resolution.

Dynamic range The ability of the camera's sensor to capture a full range of shadows and highlights.

Exposure The amount of light allowed to reach a sensor (or film), as controlled by the aperture, shutter speed, and ISO. Also, the act of taking a photograph, as in "making an exposure."

Exposure compensation A control that allows intentional over- or underexposure.

Fill-in flash Flash combined with daylight in an exposure. Used with naturally backlit or harshly side-lit or top-lit subjects to prevent silhouettes forming, or to add extra light to the shadow areas of a well-lit scene.

Filter A piece of colored or coated glass, or plastic, placed in front of the lens.

Focal length The distance, usually in millimeters, from the optical center point of a lens to its focal point.

fps *(frames per second)* A measure of the time needed for a digital camera to process one photograph and be ready to shoot the next.

f-stop Number assigned to a particular lens aperture. Wide apertures are denoted by small numbers (such as f/1.8 and f/2.8), while small apertures are denoted by large numbers (such as f/16 and f/22).

HDR *(High Dynamic Range)* A technique that increases the dynamic range of a photograph by merging multiple shots taken at different exposure settings.

Histogram A graph representing the distribution of tones in a photograph.

Hotshoe An accessory shoe with electrical contacts that allows synchronization between a camera and a flash.

Incident-light reading Meter reading based on the amount of light falling onto the subject.

ISO The sensitivity of the digital sensor measured in terms equivalent to the ISO rating of a film.

JPEG *(Joint Photographic Experts Group)* JPEG compression can reduce file sizes to about 5% of their original size, but uses a lossy compression system that degrades image quality.

LCD *(Liquid crystal display)* The flat screen on a digital camera that allows the user to preview digital photographs.

Macro A term used to describe close focusing and the close-focusing ability of a lens.

Megapixel One million pixels is equal to one megapixel.

Memory card A removable storage device for digital cameras.

Multi-field A metering system whereby the required exposure is determined by measuring the light intensity falling on a large number of independent metering zones arrayed across the image space .

Noise Interference visible in a digital image caused by stray electrical signals during exposure.

Pixel Short for "picture element"—the smallest bit of information in a digital photograph.

Raw The file format in which the raw data from the sensor is stored without permanent alteration being made.

Remote switch A device used to trigger the shutter of the camera from a distance, to help minimize camera shake. Also known as a "cable release" or "remote release."

Resolution The number of pixels used to capture or display a photo.

RGB *(red, green, blue)* Computers and other digital devices understand color information as combinations of red, green, and blue.

Rule of thirds A rule of composition that places the key elements of a picture at points along imagined lines that divide the frame into thirds, both vertically and horizontally.

Shutter The mechanism that controls the amount of
light reaching the sensor, by opening and closing.

Spot metering A metering pattern that places
importance on the intensity of light reflected by a very
small portion of the scene, either at the center of the
frame or linked to a focus point.

Telephoto A lens with a large focal length and a narrow
angle of view.

TIFF *(Tagged Image File Format)*
A universal file format supported by virtually all
relevant software applications. TIFFs are uncompressed
digital files.

TTL *(through the lens)* **metering**
A metering system built into the camera that measures
light passing through the lens at the time of shooting.

Viewfinder An optical system used for composing and
sometimes for focusing the subject.

White balance A function that allows the correct color
balance to be recorded for any given lighting situation.

Wide-angle lens A lens with a short focal length and,
consequently, a wide angle of view.

›› USEFUL WEB SITES

LEICA

Leica USA
us.leica-camera.com

Leica UK
uk.leica-camera.com

Leica Germany
de.leica-camera.com

Leica France
fr.leica-camera.com

Novoflex
Lens adaptors
novoflex.com

Phase One
Editing and cataloging software
phaseone.com

Voigtländer
M-mount lenses
voigtlaender.com

OTHER MANUFACTURERS

Adobe
Editing software
adobe.com

Carl Zeiss
M-mount lenses
zeiss.de

Fotodiox
Lens adaptors
fotodioxpro.com

Match Technical
Accessories
matchtechnical.com

Metabones
Lens adaptors
metabones.com

GENERAL

David Taylor
Landscape and travel photography
davidtaylorphotography.co.uk

Digital Photography Review
Camera and lens review site
dpreview.com

Leica forum
International Leica forum
l-camera-forum.com

PHOTOGRAPHY PUBLICATIONS

Photography books & Expanded Camera Guides
ammonitepress.com

Black and White Photography magazine
blackandwhitephotographymag.co.uk

Outdoor Photography magazine
outdoorphotographymagazine.co.uk

» INDEX

» ACKNOWLEDGMENTS

Staring at a keyboard waiting for inspiration doesn't get a book written. You do need to type the odd word or two occasionally, particularly when a deadline is looming. Less tangibly, but no less importantly, you also need help and support from other people. I'd therefore like to thank everyone at Ammonite Press, Chris Gatcum and Jason Hook in particular, for their hard work in helping this book get published. I'd also like to thank Clare Lingfield and Jenny Hodge at Leica UK for their invaluable patience, help and advice. And, last but not least, I'd like to thank my wife Tania, to whom this book is dedicated.

A handy 'camera bag' guide to the Leica M10 can be downloaded as a printable PDF at:
www.ammonitepress.com/books/leica-m10

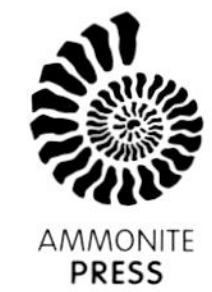

AMMONITE
PRESS

www.ammonitepress.com